The ONE TRUE ADVENTURE

Theosophy and the Quest for Meaning

The ONE TRUE ADVENTURE

Theosophy and the Quest for Meaning

JOY MILLS

COMPILED BY
DAVID P. BRUCE AND ANTON LYSY

QUEST
BOOKS

THEOSOPHICAL PUBLISHING HOUSE
Wheaton, Illinois * Chennai, India

>   Quest Books
>   Theosophical Publishing House
>   P.O. Box 270
>   Wheaton, IL 60189-0270
>
>   www.questbooks.net

Cover illustration by Nicholas Roerich, detail from *Chandra-Bhaga*, 1932.
Tempera on canvas, 79 x 46 cm. Courtesy the Nicholas Roerich Museum, New York.
Cover design, book design, and typesetting by Kirsten Hansen Pott

LIBRARY OF CONGRESS CATALOGING-IN-PUBLICATION DATA

Mills, Joy.
The one true adventure: theosophy and the quest for meaning / Joy Mills;
compiled by David P. Bruce and Anton Lysy.—1st Quest ed.
   p.   cm.
Includes index.
ISBN 978-0-8356-0868-8
1. Theosophy.   2. Spiritual life.   I. Bruce, David P.   II. Lysy, Anton.
III. Title.
BP567.M69 2008
299'.934—dc22   2007050586

5   4   3   2   1   *   08   09   10   11   12

Printed in the United States of America

TABLE OF CONTENTS

TABLE OF CONTENTS

FOREWORD

Human beings have been defined in many ways. The customary biological designation for our species is *Homo sapiens*, that is, "the knowing human." Other terms have also been suggested, such as *Homo faber*, "the skillful human," or *Homo ludens*, "the playful human." Yet our species might quite reasonably be called something like *Homo quaerens sententiam*, "the human questing for meaning." To live at all, humans need air, water, and food. But to live fully, we need also to know the meaning of life. Perhaps that is what *Homo sapiens* ultimately refers to: one who knows what is necessary in order to live fully, that is, one who knows the meaning of life.

We—or at least most of us—are, however, not yet fully human. We do not actually know the meaning of life. We are only on the path to the knowledge that produces full humanity. We are really on a quest to discover that meaning and thus to become complete human beings. To achieve our quest for the meaning of life, we have to pass through four stages:

- First, we need to know where we are starting from. We need to have a grasp on the human condition in which we find ourselves here and now.

- Second, we need to discover, not just where and what we are, but also where and what we might be. We need to have an understanding of our hidden potential.

- Third, we need to acquire inner instruction about how to get from where we are to where we want to be, from what we are to what we have the potential to become. We need to master the esoteric teachings that can activate our potential.

- Fourth, we need to apply those teachings to achieve a change in our natures. We must undergo self-transformation. Only by transforming our concept of ourselves can we discover the meaning of all life.

The Buddha talked about Four Noble Truths: that life is frustrating, that frustration has a cause, that frustration has an end, and that there is a way to the ending of frustration. The stages above are, in a sense, the Four Noble Truths of Theosophy: (1) Our lives are full of frustrating limitations. (2) We have the potential to become unlimited. (3) Teachings are hidden within ourselves that can activate our potential. (4) By discovering and applying those teachings we can limitlessly transform ourselves.

This book is a collection of essays written over many years by one of America's premier Theosophical essayists: Joy Mills. These essays have been sorted into four groups: "The Human Condition," "Our Hidden Potential," "Esoteric Teachings," and "Self-Transformation." Those groups correspond with the four stages in our quest for meaning, although many of the essays within them naturally treat the process as a whole. Written over a long lifetime of highly productive work for Theosophy and the Theosophical Society, these essays represent a summary of the wisdom of a wise woman. Taken in toto, they are also a guidebook to the acquisition of wisdom by anyone who follows their guidance in pursuing the quest for meaning.

The *Book of Common Prayer* instructs us to "read, mark, learn, and inwardly digest" the texts of scripture. If we apply that instruction to these essays, they will become a roadmap on the quest for meaning. This quest for meaning is really a quest for self-transformation. Those who read, mark, learn, and inwardly digest the content of these essays will be well on their way to that transformation, and thus to the achievement of the quest for meaning, which is the ultimate reason for our existence. Godspeed to the reader of these essays who pursues the quest to which they point!

—John Algeo
Athens, Georgia
November 2007

Acknowledgments

Many good friends have contributed, in one way or another, to the creation of this book. I am indebted to all of them, but I would like to express heartfelt gratitude especially to the following:

First, to Dr. Anton "Tony" Lysy, Dean of Studies of the Olcott Institute at the Headquarters of the Theosophical Society in America. The whole enterprise was Tony's idea in the first place, and when he first suggested such an anthology to me many years ago, I was rather stunned by the proposal. But Tony was persistent and followed it up by spending countless hours in the Henry S. Olcott Memorial Library searching through old journals to locate my writings and then making a selection of the most suitable ones for inclusion in this compilation. I must admit it is a delight to see articles I myself had nearly forgotten now resurrected from almost certain obscurity (as few people, if any, ever reread old magazines).

Then, to David Bruce, Director of the Department of Education at Olcott, who revived the project after it had languished for some years in the pralaya of the almost forgotten. His role was to review all the material, to encourage me to reread each article and suggest any possible changes or alterations (particularly updating the language), and then to propose some sort of organization for the pile of documents. First, David sorted the material chronologically by journal, and then he came up with the very happy idea of dividing the articles/talks into four topical areas: The Human

Condition, Our Hidden Potential, Esoteric Teachings, and Self-Transformation. Within each of those topics, the material is arranged chronologically. It took an eye other than mine to see this most logical and helpful arrangement for the work.

And a special word of appreciation to Diane Eisenberg who did all the nitty-gritty work of scanning the articles, incorporating all my revisions, and then turning them into electronic Word documents. I cannot imagine the hours Diane must have spent in such a necessary, yet undoubtedly somewhat boring, task!

To Dr. John Algeo, former National President of the American Section and now International Vice-President of the Theosophical Society, for his willingness to give the anthology a foreword, thus lending the work a flair and vitality it might otherwise have lacked.

And to Mrs. Betty Bland, National President of the Theosophical Society in America, who has taken a special interest in the entire project, giving it her blessing and encouraging the Theosophical Publishing House to undertake its publication.

Finally, to so many other good friends who, through the years, have given their encouragement to my writing and speaking on behalf of the Society and, more recently, as they came to know of this project, expressing their enthusiasm for such an anthology that would give some lasting recognition to my literary efforts. For any flaws in my interpretation or understanding of the great universal principles of the Theosophical philosophy, I alone am responsible.

—Joy Mills
Ojai, California
February 2007

COMPILERS' COMMENT

The articles in this anthology, which span a period of sixty years, have been divided into four general categories: "The Human Condition," "Our Hidden Potential," "Esoteric Teachings," and "Self-Transformation." Within each of these categories the articles are placed chronologically. Admittedly, there is some overlap in the articles and a few of them could fit into more than one category. That being said, a decision had to be made as to placement of the articles. The present arrangement of articles was reviewed and approved by the author.

Copies of the original articles were sent to Joy in the fall of 2005 so that she could review them and make any revisions that were deemed necessary. The reader of this anthology may be interested to know what types of changes were made. Primarily, the changes fall into the following categories:

1. In keeping with modern practices, the language was made gender-neutral with the exception of quotes embodied within the articles.

2. When many of these articles were written, it was customary for writers to employ longer sentences. Many of these have been broken down into shorter sentences to accommodate current writing styles.

3. Diacritical marks over Sanskrit words have been removed in the transliteration, as is recommended in the *Chicago Manual of Style*.

4. References to the 3rd edition of *The Mahatma Letters to A. P. Sinnett* have been transposed to the numbering system used in the newer chronological edition of the *Letters*.

5. Several of the original titles were changed by the author for purposes of this publication. These changes are indicated in the subheadings to the titles where they occur.

6. British spellings were changed to the American version except for quotes. The capitalization of special terms and other grammatical idiosyncrasies found in quotes from Blavatsky's writings have not been altered.

7. When the word "Ego" appears in the upper case, it refers to the immortal higher Self, as was the common in earlier Theosophical writing. When "ego" appears in the lower case, it assumes the more familiar meaning as used by modern schools of psychology.

8. Other minor stylistic changes were made when it was felt that greater clarity was needed.

In no instance has the essential meaning of the articles been changed in any way.

The
HUMAN
CONDITION

OUR FAITH
IN OURSELVES

Published in *The Theosophist*, Volume 77, April 1956 under the title "Man's Faith in Man"

It has been said that the tragedy of the twentieth-century was man's inability to believe in man. This is a tragedy that seems to continue to haunt us. Certainly it is true that while the ideal of brotherhood has been advanced significantly on many fronts, and numerous examples could be cited in support of its widespread acceptance as an article of faith, we still live in a time of distrust and fear, even, in fact, of suspicion, one person of another.

Our inability to believe in either God or our fellow man, the fruit of scientific materialism, was met in the nineteenth-century by the clear and precise restatement of the ancient wisdom by Madame H. P. Blavatsky in *The Secret Doctrine* and the exposition of Theosophy by the many students who have succeeded her. Today, science is no longer defending an absolutism that would deny reality to an Inner Architect, perceivable in the heart of the atom as in the distant galaxies. Nor is religion, at least as interpreted by its greatest leaders, creating an artificial dichotomy between faith and reason. The position of Theosophy in meeting and continuing to meet the challenges in these fields has often been discussed.

But let us consider briefly the challenge stated to be for this time: <u>our inability to believe in our fellow human beings</u>. What does this involve and how may Theosophy cast light on this problem? For we live today not only in a world of atoms and electrons, of electromagnetic waves, of wandering comets and slow-wheeling galaxies, but also, and perhaps at times more importantly, in a world of human beings, of people whose hopes and dreams, aspirations, ideas, joys, and sorrows impinge upon every single one of us. The peoples of the world are no longer remote from one another; barriers of distance, culture, ideologies, language, etc., are being daily resolved by the interchange of ideas through mass communication and vast programs of technical and educational import. Not that cultures or ideologies are becoming similar in aim or outlook, but that the barriers separating them are becoming less opaque and divisive.

Let me cite but one example. Not too many years ago a remarkable conference was held at Bandung, in Indonesia, the Asia-Africa Conference. The late General Carlos P. Romulo of the Philippines keynoted the spirit of the meeting when he said:

> Fellow-delegates, our strength flows not out of our numbers, though the numbers we represent are great. It flows out of our perception of history and out of the vital purpose we put into the making of tomorrow . . . The success of this Conference will be measured not by what we do for ourselves but by what we do for the entire human community. Large as is the cause of Asia and Africa, there is a cause even larger. It is the cause of the human community in a world struggling to liberate itself from the chaos of international anarchy. In short, our cause is the cause of man.

What then is Theosophy's position in this world of ideological conflict, of socio-economic change, in which the main current of human hope over much of the world's surface is directed towards the realization of freedom, as that freedom is reflected in the desire for political autonomy? Writing on "The Case for Hope," the distinguished Nobel Prize winner in Physics, and Professor of Natural Philosophy at Washington University, Dr. Arthur Compton, after surveying the advances of science and technology within the last two generations, states in part:

> What the scientist finds gives us reason to suppose that man in his physical structure is in no essential way different from the rest of the world of Nature: he is composed of the same atoms, obeys the same laws of conservation of energy, of thermodynamics, and so on . . . Nevertheless, men and women have this remarkable characteristic: we are aware of what happens to us . . . There is also another significant realm in which man's actions go beyond the province of science. This is our experience of freedom. With the advent of quantum mechanics, modern scientific theory does not dispute the possibility of the type of human freedom that implies human responsibility.

It is precisely here, perhaps, in this vast area of social, economic, and political science that Theosophy may contribute new understandings, and in which we may bring to bear certain universal principles that can be applied in utter simplicity to assist in the solution of our fundamental human problem, the search for freedom. This search is allied both to our needs as individuals and to our needs as social beings. That is, we seek individual freedom at the same time that we realize our greatest fulfillment, in terms of general welfare and permanent happiness, in our relationships with other human beings.

However, by suggesting that these are areas in which Theosophy's position may be explored and expanded, I am by no means suggesting alliance with particular political or economic creeds. I am rather suggesting that in a world in which political ideologies are in such conflict that the lives and potential freedoms of millions of human beings are at stake, in a world in which automation is vitally affecting the industrial and economic structures of Western society, in a world in which sociological patterns are being changed by the advocacy of bills of human rights and by the introduction of technological changes into primitive cultures—in such a world it is imperative that we bring to bear upon the thought of the world's people the principles, the moral and ethical standards derived from the principles of an underlying reality and order in Nature. To quote again from Dr. Compton:

> This brings us to the question as to what are the goals towards which man should aspire. When one raises this question, he thinks at once of the old Greek ideals of the understanding of truth, the appreciation of beauty, the striving for perfection. These goals are as significant today as they were 2,500 years ago. What is new is that in our effort to attain the true, the beautiful, and the good, we find that now to a greater degree this can best be done when we endeavor to attain these same objectives for others as well as for ourselves. Is not this, then, the distinctive feature of man's aspiration that is characteristic of the age of science? His approach to the great values of life shall be a co-operative effort, an effort in which every man and every woman may do their share toward enabling all to live more fully, an effort in which every person will be respected for the way in which he plays his part. We see ourselves living increasingly in the lives of each other.

These are the words of a scientist of eminent stature; they were not spoken by a philosopher or religious visionary. It is not possible here to discuss all the implications of this remarkable statement, so clearly implying a brotherhood that is indeed not a sentimental emotion, but a fact inherent in the very structure of universal things.

This linking of the concept of a cooperative effort—brotherhood as part of the natural order—to freedom brings us close to the heart of Theosophy in terms of its application to the moral basis for a political and economic philosophy. Dr. Krishna P. Mukerji, Professor of Civics and Politics at the University of Bombay, in a series of lectures to the School of the Wisdom at the Theosophical Society's world headquarters, speaking on "The Basis of Political Philosophy," said:

> It has been well said that the message of Political Philosophy is a plea for freedom. Indeed that one concept—of freedom—when properly understood, can supply the most rational and legitimate foundation of our philosophy . . . *To be free is to live according to the later [sic] of our being . . . To be free is to live according to this Master Plan or Evolution.* How to make the Good available to society is the task of the social philosopher. This obviously can be done by fitting our social, economic, and political schemes of reform to the universal scheme of evolution, which is guided by the same law of or urge towards goodness as the law of our being. We have, in other words, to re-discover our Maker's plan in the context of our social life. This voyage of re-discovering Goodness or Justice or Freedom or Dharma is the lifelong adventure of the political philosopher. He is the Rishi of dharma, the prophet of freedom and justice.

Dr. Mukerji's book *The State* is a magnificent contribution to the position of Theosophy in this aspect of our modern world, and supplements well the earlier statements and research of Dr. Bhagavan Das in his studies on the social order. These are areas in which we of the Western world must come to make our contributions. The key, I believe, is in the concept of *dharma,* as yet so little understood and explored in its context of social and political implications. It was Dr. Radhakrishnan, eminent philosopher and vice-president of India, who said that next to the category of Reality the most important idea of Eastern philosophy is the idea of dharma. We have yet to envisage what it could mean to unite the concept of dharma, as the great idea of the East, with the concept of freedom, the great idea of the West. This is a special task for us in these days, and one which, when accomplished, will restore our faith in our fellow human beings and ourselves.

From an historical perspective, it may be argued that these two ideas of dharma and freedom may be the most significant contributions of their respective cultures in relation to man's individual achievement and to his achievements in the group. So dharma, or the law of one's best being, as it has been defined, can best be expressed in our relation to others, and freedom, though initially achieved as an individual, attains its full meaning only in a context in which others also enjoy freedom. The dharma of freedom, then—to link these two concepts—implies the responsibility which arises from an inner moral conviction, conscience, or sense of rightness; the flowering of freedom arises in the recognition of a brotherhood based upon the perception of the unity of life and sustained by the principle of the harmonic orderliness of the universe.

A Chinese proverb says that there are five points to the compass: North, East, South, West, and the point where you are; unless you know the point where you are, you will not know the direction in which to go. It is necessary always to determine that fifth point, and so determine the direction in which we may move in a united effort on all fronts to meet the challenge of the "cause of man." For this, we may draw out the best in ourselves and in others, making it a cooperative effort, in which we experiment with brotherhood in very practical ways. No longer is this an age of singular leaders of great stature, but an age of group awareness, group development, that *all* may move forward. We discover, not so much excellent persons, but excellence in all persons. For that, we need to have faith in the extraordinary powers of ordinary people. In this way, our ability to believe in ourselves and all people may be restored and a new meaning be given to freedom, as each individual finds in the relationship of brotherhood the completion of their own individual unique self.

New Frontiers for
an Ageless Wisdom

Published in *The Theosophist*, Volume 87, September 1966

The concept of a "frontier" has long influenced the thought of the Western world, and in the United States particularly this concept has always had a rich meaning as a part of our historical heritage. In fact, the word itself was given a new and unique meaning by the experience of the American people in exploring a continent composed largely of wilderness areas. As one raised in the tradition of that experience, and committed to the Theosophical Society as a unique pioneer movement given physical birth in a land whose peoples, drawn together from every world culture, have focused their vision less on the achievements of yesterday than on the promises of tomorrow, I should like to attempt here a leap of the imagination. Such a leap has its physical counterpart in the historical tradition of which I speak, when entire families set forth in covered wagons and other primitive conveyances to traverse the Great Plains and noble upthrusts of mountains to reach a land of promise. In the history of the Theosophical Society, there is a similar counterpart in the journey undertaken by those intrepid pioneers of our movement, the cofounders of the Society, Helena Petrovna Blavatsky and Henry Steel Olcott, when they set forth from the known beginnings of the organization in New York City to establish a home in the land where its spiritual heritage had its roots. The leap represented by those physical journeys was not without risk or hazard, but thought was given less to the numerous obstacles on the way than to the goal that might be achieved.

So we, here in this time and in this place, attempting a new leap of the imagination, may be less concerned with the difficulties that confront us, and more with the course we may chart by the stars whose light leads ever towards a distant horizon. For we stand today, I believe, on the threshold of new frontiers whose exploration demands the same courage and fortitude, the same patience and forbearance, called for by the founders of this movement.

What is demanded in our time is a certain willingness of heart, a readiness to risk all for the sake of the journey. If we expect others to carry us over the rugged terrain of the present, if we look to the Theosophical Society as an organization external to ourselves—with which we have some tenuous kind of affiliation but no identification—and expect the Society to construct for us a comfortable home into which we can move the antique furniture of our prejudices, the bric-a-brac of our personal desires, we shall be doomed to disappointment, and the Society will lack that vigor and strength with which its founders infused it. We have been given a vision not of a predestined end but of the greatness of a journey. We shall be untrue to that vision if we do not accept the individual responsibility for our commitment to investigate the frontiers of truth that lie before us.

Let us move forward, then, across whatever boundaries separate yesterday from tomorrow, accepting the challenges, opportunities, and responsibilities of today. Let us explore some of the paths into the interior of that new continent of thought, which lies all about us.

In venturing into the unknown, one must begin in the known. To take a step forward, one must move from the point where one is. Even a cursory examination of our present position reveals our desperate need to understand ourselves. It has become fashionable in our modern world to adopt a 3-D vision of Despair, Doubt, and Dissent. Young people in more than one nation have turned from the traditional 3 R's of education to the primitive R's of Rebellion, Riot, and Revolution. The Theosophical Society can and must, I believe, restore to the world a vision of our essential unity, of our immortal destiny, our potential divinity.

The First Object of the Society implies that human need is color-blind and that human aspiration knows neither class nor creed. The despair that results when artificial barriers are erected between individuals, groups, and nations is transformed into hope as individuals learn the meaning of brotherhood.

The Second Object of our Society removes uncertainty by the encouragement to study the universals of knowledge in their philosophical, scientific, and religious permutations. Doubt is thus replaced by confidence.

The Third Object leads us, through investigation of Nature's immutable laws and of human potential, from the dissent of rebellion against all that fragments us in the phenomenal world to that willing assent to the law of our own being which is the affirmation of our divinity. For the Third Object calls us to fall in love with human possibility.

In such a perspective, the Three Objects of the Theosophical Society are not boundaries to limit action or to circumscribe thought; they are directional signs pointing the way into new and unexplored territory, into a future with infinite prolongations.

As we accept the challenge of these directional signs, and as we move to explore the frontiers that they so clearly indicate, we may pause to note that the concept of frontier has a dual meaning. It is, in one of its aspects, a boundary, which divides one known land from another, a demarcation between settled areas. In the other aspect, a frontier marks the edge of the known, the point at which the settlement ends and the wilderness begins. I am less concerned here with the first meaning, which I should like to suggest may be related in a most meaningful manner to the Second Object of the Society, for it invites us to explore religion, philosophy, and science that we may come, as already pointed out, to the universals of knowledge. The frontiers of study are clearly indicated, although distinctions separating one discipline from another—religion from philosophy or philosophy from science—may at times become blurred. However, it is more directly to the second meaning of the concept of frontier that I should like to invite attention, and probe in some measure the wilderness area of human possibility. This is the area hinted at in our Third Object, and a study in depth of that Object may lead us into the new continent of our humanness.

The crisis of alienation, so apparent in our time, is a divorce not only of one individual from another, but of each person from himself. We have classified ourselves, along with all the objects and events in the universe, as something to be observed, tested, measured, and standardized. The fundamental fear that grips us is the fear of being dehumanized, and perhaps to a large extent this is responsible for the explosion of disquietude which we are experiencing. Something in us resists the attempt to view ourselves as a *what*, to be probed in the simple objectivity of external observation. We want to believe we are a *who*, to be realized in all the complex subjectivity of experience. Even as we rocket ourselves to the moon and the stars, we feel we may have misfired somewhere along the line, or that the jet propulsion should have been expended in inner dimensions to discover the orbit of our own natures. In the drama of human life, we seem to be reaching the point of a sell-out performance, with standing room only available on our globe, and we debate the expendability of human units with as little concern as we would decide the number of mosquitoes a swamp might accommodate. In such a plight it is no wonder that we are daring to say "no" to God, for we have already said "no" to ourselves when we identify ourselves solely with our objective and external nature. But there are those who seek to learn and long to know, who need a faith to illuminate the ill-lighted world stage, who demand an authentic identity, not an authoritarian creed, who will be satisfied with nothing less than to walk freely with dignity and hope and honor.

The Theosophical Society has an unparalleled opportunity in these closing years of the twentieth-century to speak to our present human condition, clearly and unequivocally calling us to know ourselves in our true identity and so to say "yes" to all that is possible for and within us. The frontiers of human possibility: these are the frontiers now to be explored, not the external frontiers of outer space, but the inner realms of the spirit. The Theosophical Society may become the conscience of humanity, pricking the minds of peoples everywhere to an awareness of their unitary source in an immortal continuum of Reality, stirring their hearts to a recognition that brotherhood is something more than a fact in nature, for it is a way of life and a way of walking and a way of constant being. And the Theosophical Society may do this by virtue of the sacred trust reposed in it by those Adept Brothers who ever constitute the guardian wall of humanity, holding back the flood tides of divisiveness, fear, and ignorance that would plunge the world into darkness. But the Theosophical Society is you and I; it is all of us together, stewards of that sacred trust who, whether we be few or many, have it in our charge to transmit to the world the knowledge that there is an Ageless Wisdom by which man may truly know himself, transform himself, heal himself, become wholly himself, and therefore more than himself, one with all others, humanly divine and divinely human.

In the early days of the Society, one of its prominent members, Mohini Chatterjee, pointed out that the esoteric doctrine teaches with special emphasis that there must exist at every moment of the history of human evolution a class of men in whom consciousness attains such an expansion in both depth and area as to enable them to solve the problems of being by direct perception and therefore with far more completeness than the rest of mankind.

Such direct perception can be attained only in the immediacy of an encounter with first principles—those immortal principles of the Wisdom upon which all secondary truths must be founded. We have that privilege and responsibility to become in our time, and for the present needs, men and women who, having grappled with truth, have won through to that expansion of consciousness which permits of total vision—an expansion induced not by drugs or any external stimulus, but by our own efforts.

Every great voyager and explorer, winning their way across uncharted seas or pathless lands, has marked out their course by the stars. So in the voyage of discovery to which we have been called— that voyage that leads inward to the expanded consciousness of an Immortal Self—we too may lift our eyes to the stars of wisdom that have ever shone in the firmament of time. And the pole star is the star of unity toward which the compass of our being must ever turn.

Taking our course from the bright star of unity, we may fearlessly set out towards the frontiers of human possibility, the frontiers of consciousness, in an effort to answer the anguished cry of modern man, alienated from his own source, estranged from his brother, fearful of his own inventions, doubtful even of his future.

To know the limits of our humanness, we must define what it is to be human. A popular folk song in the United States today asks:

How many roads must a man walk down before you call him a man?

The Theosophical vision of man encompasses all the roads of experience that have led to this moment and points beyond man's actual self to his possible self. It is a vision that defines the human not in terms of what we have been, not in terms of the animal within us, but always in terms of what we may be. It is a vision that comprehends the wholeness of the human—the human as rooted in the permanence of spirit, in the enduring realm of universal life which is also consciousness permeated through and through with a supreme bliss. Rooted in such a realm, which may be more metaphysically described in terms familiar to the student of Theosophy as *chidakasham*, whose nature is also *ananda*, each individual turns outwards to gain the experiences of self-consciousness, and in that outward-turning we walk down the impermanent roads of existence, anchoring ourselves again and again to the shadowy end of spirit which we call matter. And in the here-and-now of this anchorage is played out the drama of becoming human, with all the tragedy and comedy, all the pains and struggles and joys and triumphs of learning the roles of humanness in all their diversity, that one day there may stand forth a god.

The remarkable Jesuit paleontologist-philosopher (Pierre Teilhard de Chardin) spoke of his own fundamental discovery that "we are carried along by an advancing wave of consciousness." "The study of the past," he wrote, "has revealed to me the structure of the future." For the human, emergent from a universal realm of consciousness, possesses all the potentialities of that consciousness—potentialities that may be succinctly summarized in the well-known triplicity of Omnipotence, Omniscience, and Omnipresence, the powers of the enduring center of our nature as *Atma-Buddhi-Manas*. Our task is to realize those potentialities in the lived-out roles of succeeding existences.

So it was that Teilhard de Chardin wrote of a future peculiar to the human being, the "ultra-human" as he called it. The Scandinavian philosopher (Søren Kierkegaard,) whose influence on modern Western thought has been so significant, once remarked: "He who fights the future has a dangerous enemy." But he had the wisdom to add, "Through the eternal, we conquer the future." There is deep meaningfulness in these words, for the future cannot be fought—at least not successfully; not even tomorrow can be kept at bay for long. But we can meet the future, embrace the future of ourselves and of humanity, only by conceding to the eternal. The Ageless Wisdom, Theosophy, leads us to an encounter with the eternal—with immortal principles that abide through all the changefulness of phenomena. And out of that encounter—the grappling with truth, the search for understanding—we learn to conquer the future by drawing into the present all the possibilities of tomorrow. We can then become that group of men and women who, in our time, have achieved such an expansion of consciousness inward that we may be enabled to solve the problems of being by our own direct perception. The perception will be of universals—the universals of law, the universals of truth—and all problems will be referable to those abiding principles.

It is to such a journey as this that we are called by our commitment to the Theosophical Society: the journey across the frontiers of our own being, frontiers that are ever new because each individual is unique in their expression, even as each is rooted in an immortal unity. It is the beautiful journey described long ago in the Chandogya Upanishad:

> There is a Light that shines beyond all things on earth, beyond us all, beyond the heavens, beyond the highest, the very highest heavens. This is the Light that shines in our hearts. There is a bridge between time and Eternity; and this bridge is the Spirit in man. Neither day nor night crosses that bridge, nor old age, nor death nor sorrow . . . When this bridge has been crossed,

the eyes of the blind can see, the wounds of the wounded are healed, and the sick man becomes whole from his sickness. To one who goes over that bridge, the night becomes like unto day; because in the worlds of the Spirit there is a Light which is everlasting.

Exploring fearlessly the frontiers of our own humanness, sighting the stars of immortal wisdom, making out our course by the immutable laws of nature, we may come to discover the precise latitude and longitude of the place whereon we stand at the edge of the frontiers of our own possibilities. For I suggest that we discover the longitude of our being—our own inner stature—as we learn to know what we truly are: an immortal spirit clothed in the garments of mortality. In discovering our own height of being, we find too the latitude of human existence, the breadth of our relations with others, for we are truly human only in relationship. Only as the heart is wide may we grow tall; only in the recognition of our kinship with all life, most particularly with those who share the human quest, do we really and finally become human.

Again to quote Teilhard de Chardin, "There is only one contact charged with an irresistible centripetal and unifying force, and that is the contact of the whole of man with the whole of man." For even as we explore the frontiers implied in our Third Object—the whole of the human and the potentialities, or powers, of that wholeness of man—we are led directly, in full circle, to the ethical, moral, and humanistic frontiers indicated in our First Object, and so to the very foundation of the Theosophical Movement: the realization of that one true, free, beautiful, and divinely human relationship which is brotherhood.

Our age calls for a new kind of faith and a new kind of courage. At a time when frontiers are all too often defined by walls, barbed wire, and the innumerable intangible barriers of hate, jealousy, and bitterness that separate one person from another; we are called upon for the countless small braveries of human brotherhood and human love in daily acts of heroism. When we live on the frontiers of the humanly possible, where there are no jungles of fear and anxiety for sentries to patrol, aware of the unitary source of our being because we dare to lift our eyes to the enduring stars, we greet each other no longer as abstractions, as things to be used, exploited, and possessed. Then we shall learn to speak to each other in the meaningful syllables of kinship, as authentic persons, unique, important, each one here as divinely as every other. And in our journey across these frontiers, let us not mistake speed for travel; let us not mistake destination for direction and rest in the hostels of comfortable beliefs when we should be out ranging across the mountains of ideas. Above all, let us not mistake numbers, which may be but the signs of settled habitation, for that strength which may be achieved by a few alone testing their spiritual muscles against the toughness of truth itself.

Our age needs the kind of faith that perceives in every individual an undying spirit winning through to its own immortal destiny. We in the Theosophical Society, however few or many we may be, have it in our power to call forth the conscience of every person to a recognition of a concern for all of life. In the days of the American Western frontier, when the American Indian guided the white man across the trackless plains, it is said that the white man often feared lest he lose his way, and that many a day and night of anxiety passed in search of a familiar landmark, a sign of camp or outpost. But when this happened, the Indian guide, standing quite still and looking upward to the stars, would say very simply: "Wigwam lost; Indian, he never lost." So today, we few committed to the noble dream of brotherhood may stand quite sure in a world grown anxious with fear and insecurity, and proclaim that the loss of outer possessions—even the loss of the wigwam comfort of fixed beliefs— are not losses that matter. For each of us—the essential person, immortal, endowed with the potentials of godhood—can never be lost, so long as we look to the stars of truth which are not only above but also within us.

So if I began by speaking as an American, whose historical tradition is set in the rootless movement of a people toward an ever-receding frontier, let me conclude by speaking as one who shares with all students of this Ageless Wisdom a profound conviction of the infinite possibilities of the human spirit. The new frontiers that are before us lie across the trackless plains of our own inner dimensions of being; beyond the mountain up-thrusts of human aspirations; over the winding rivers of compassion that may water the arid soil of human misery—here lies our path. Whether we have the fortitude, the patience, the courage, and the wisdom to chart our way across these frontiers, to establish ourselves on that new continent of thought of which the Elder Brothers of Humanity have spoken—that new continent of thought where all peoples shall one day recognize their essential unity of spirit in a brotherhood of the free—whether we can take this longest of journeys in the service of the world depends upon the individual commitment we bring to the cause of human solidarity. The challenge is there, the privilege of beginning is ours, the responsibility to walk forward has been laid upon us. Truly, there is no other way at all to go.

THINKING ABOUT THE UNTHINKABLE

Published in *The American Theosophist,* Volume 62, January 1974

In an issue of the *New York Times* not too long ago, a daring and ambitious venture undertaken by members of the Hudson Institute in Paris was reported. The preparation of a five-volume work to be called the *Encyclopedia of the Future* had been instigated, with more than one hundred eminent authorities in a variety of disciplines invited to contribute original articles, so that, when completed, the encyclopedia would range across every field of knowledge from science and technology to politics, economics, and the arts.

According to the head of the Hudson Institute, the purpose of the encyclopedia was to "shake up readers, provoke them to think." To think about what? The newspaper report of the project indicated that the future to be visualized by the contributors was not necessarily the entire twenty-first century, but simply the next ten to fifteen years. In fact, stated the work's sponsors, most people, however well informed, are not even abreast of current developments in knowledge: "They're thinking 10 to 15 years in the past, laboring under the weight of outmoded ideas that don't correspond to the real present." Accuracy of prediction seems to be most assured in the fields of science and technology, but social forecasting, even for one or two decades ahead, appears to be most difficult if not impossible.

The Theosophical student exhibits no such caution, but neither does he limit his vision to a single decade or two. Taking his cue from the greatest Theosophist of our age, H. P. Blavatsky, the student grapples with ideas that can never become outmoded because they are eternally applicable to the human condition. We are not confused by the noise and din of excitement as small pieces of knowledge concerning the physical universe are added to the complex map of scientific understanding, nor are we glamorized by the scintillating phenomena of psychic fireworks. Steadily, patiently, we work at the frontiers of that spiritual domain whose exploration alone brings wisdom and true comprehension. Whatever predictions are projected for breakthroughs in technology, economics, or politics, the Theosophical student focuses all energies and attention on the one breakthrough that will mark the triumph of the human spirit—the breakthrough into brotherhood.

This is not to say, of course, that the student of Theosophy lacks interest in, or is unconcerned with, the many developments in modern thought. Certainly we have a responsibility to keep abreast of the numerous advances in every field of knowledge, but we are to view them all from a perspective of wholeness, perceiving the emergence of underlying laws and principles. If we follow the example set by H. P. Blavatsky, we engage ourselves fully in the current of contemporary knowledge. Our minds roam through every field of human endeavor, but facts do not cluster meaninglessly. They are arranged so as to reveal their significance. For the central thrust in all our knowing is aimed at awakening the spirit in the human being.

Since the eminent scholars who have been called upon to contribute to the *Encyclopedia of the Future* are convinced that prognostications in the field of social change touch on the realm of the "unthinkable," someone must accept the challenge to forecast mankind's tomorrow. Who better than the Theosophical student, who has at hand the keys of a wisdom-tradition to aid in the task? No better guideline for this undertaking could be found than an article by HPB, "The Tidal Wave," which appeared in *Lucifer*, November 1889. In her usual forceful style, HPB addressed herself to the urgent need to infuse into the thought-currents of her day a living and practical understanding of the spiritual nature of man. Defining the duty of each who aspires to serve, she wrote:

> In order that one should fully comprehend *individual life* with its physiological, psychic, and spiritual mysteries, he has to devote himself, with all the fervour of unselfish philanthropy and love for his brother man, to studying and knowing *collective* life, or Mankind. Without preconceptions or prejudice, as also without the least fear of possible results in one or another direction, he has to decipher, understand, and *remember* the deep and innermost feelings and aspirations of the people's great and suffering heart. To do this he has first "to attune his soul with that of Humanity" as the old philosophy teaches; to thoroughly master the correct meaning of every line and word in the rapidly turning pages of the Book of Life of MANKIND, and to be thoroughly saturated with the truism that the latter is a whole inseparable from his own SELF. (Blavatsky 1889, 5:173–78)

The advent of a new year may be an appropriate time to remind ourselves of the central task for which the Theosophical Society was founded and for which it continues to exist. The ideal of universal brotherhood, "a real Universal Fraternity," was reiterated again and again in the writings of the founders, both those who labored visibly in the world and those who were acknowledged by them as their Adept Teachers. In a world in which cease-fire agreements are regularly shattered and war is a condition of life for many people, in a world in which exploitation of animals and the rape of natural resources continue at an unprecedented rate, in a world in which people know more about the atmosphere of Jupiter than about the needs of their neighbors, for any group of men and women to speak about brotherhood—and to bulwark that ideal with a knowledge of universal law gained through a study of theosophy—may seem the rashest of foolhardy ventures. We would seem to be thinking about the unthinkable, but any other kind of thinking would be a defeat for the spirit of humankind. Only a radical change instituted from within will free humanity from the outmoded ideas of separateness and non-relatedness. Yet such a reversal in the direction of thought and action is imperative. Whatever scientific and technological developments may be forecast, the only human condition that can accommodate all future possibilities is the condition of brotherhood. HPB concluded her article on "The Tidal Wave": "Theosophy alone can gradually create a mankind as harmonious and as simple-souled as Kosmos itself; but to effect this, Theosophists have to act as such." One of the contributors to the proposed *Encyclopedia of the Future* has commented: "One can't speculate too much because otherwise it would become science fiction." Yet we certainly know that the fiction of yesterday is frequently the science of today. So, if our will is strong enough, our vision wide enough, our understanding deep enough, our compassion great enough, what now seems the "unthinkable" ideal of brotherhood may be tomorrow's realizable, experiencable fact of daily existence. At least, it's worth every ounce of our energy, the complete focus of our attention, as we look toward a new year in our work together.

LISTEN TO THE
MARCH OF THE FUTURE

Published in *The Theosophist*, Volume 97, February 1976

In 1575, the French scholar Louis Le Roy published a book in which he gave voice to his despair over the changes and dislocations caused by the social and industrial innovations of his time, a period we now refer to in the history books as the European Renaissance. "All is Pell-mell, confounded, nothing goes as it should," he wrote. We, in 1975, are inclined to echo those words and indeed to believe that the situation is even far worse than it could have been four hundred years ago.

Our inventory of despair grows longer every day: the earth overpopulated, with its resources depleted; an environment destroyed by pollution, with its inevitable damage to human health; the gap in living standards between the rich and the poor continually widened; the arms race accelerated; etc. The list of our present woes could be continued almost indefinitely.

But is the future ever an extrapolation of the past? Must trend become destiny? Or is it possible for human beings, no longer subject as are animals to the tyranny of biological evolution but blessed with the freedom of social evolution, to chart a new direction, remake the present, and build a future in which the world is a safe place for life's full growth and development?

A mood of gloom pervades the world. Yet it is always true that people who fear the worst usually invite it, and those who walk with heads down cannot scan the horizon for a break in the clouds. If we constantly look to the past, we will be pushed backwards into the future.

Undoubtedly the problems facing humanity today do not have easy answers. I do not propose that a Pollyanna attitude will resolve them. But neither will an attitude of despair nor a sense of the inevitability of final catastrophe remove the causes that have produced the problems. While newspaper headlines, seldom if ever, relate the happy events, the positive achievements, in human existence, it is still possible to discern amid today's gloom the faint rays of tomorrow's light.

About a year ago, Dr. Maurice Strong, Secretary-General of the UN Conference on the Human Environment, suggested that there is a case for hope. He outlined six indicators for the existence of such a case: "There is hope in the dawning realization of our basic interdependence . . . There is hope in the attitudes of young people . . . There is hope in the courageous experimentation of some people with new, simpler, more human life-styles . . . There is hope in the growing number of positive examples of the creative uses of technology . . . There is hope in many parts of the developing world where traditional values and cultures have been harmonized with modern technology . . . There is hope in the nature of man himself." And Dr. Strong concluded his arguments for a case for hope with these words, "It is possible to opt for a future of unparalleled promise and opportunity for the human species." The latest discipline that has emerged in the world of academia is known as futuristics, futurism, or futurology. This discipline proposes a new way of thinking about tomorrow, seeking a holistic view of human evolution. It takes up the case for hope, along lines similar to those suggested by Dr. Strong, and urges that we concern ourselves not so much with predicting the future as with attempting to design alternative futures. In this, all of us can become creators, inventors, and designers of our collective futures. We need not wait on events to overtake us, but we can act with a calm confidence in the full potential of our humanity and with an unswerving determination that the human spirit will ultimately triumph.

I do not propose that we should engage in what has been termed in some circles, "future-games"—that is, games that merely create different models of tomorrow, as one would build fantasies of utopia or dreams of impossible achievements. Rather, I would suggest that we must examine the Theosophical case for hope, design the future in accordance with a philosophy that comprehends the ageless verities of existence, and lend our full and total weight to the realization of the ideal of brotherhood, a world community in which all men and women may live together in harmony and in freedom.

For in this watershed year of 1975, a year that ushers in the last quarter of this twentieth-century, we can either stand in numbed horror before the awesome fact that the two major powers on earth today possess between them enough nuclear explosives to represent the equivalent of 50,000 pounds of destructive force for every human being on the planet, or we can accept the challenge laid down for this Society one hundred years ago—"to form the nucleus of a universal brotherhood" without any distinctions whatsoever. It may not be without significance that this Society was founded by individuals whose homelands were those same two countries which today confront each other and the world with so much destructive force.

Yes, as a great Teacher has said, "It is time for Theosophy to enter the arena." We can neither delay nor postpone the assignment that has come to us, we who are the heirs of those founders and today's stewards of that priceless heritage which is the wisdom of the ages, the Ageless Wisdom. We dare not become merely armchair

Theosophists, speculating about *Parabrahman* and *pralaya*, the nature of *maya* and the composition of the *skandhas*. Speculation must give way to knowledge; knowledge must be transmuted into insight; insight must be transformed into compassion. This is the age-old alchemical process whereby we move from the personal to the transpersonal, merging the little self into the One Self.

The Theosophical case for hope lies in our willingness to undertake this process in full self-consciousness. W. Q. Judge, writing on "The Future and The Theosophical Society" in March 1892, stated: "Our destiny is to continue the wide work of the past in affecting literature and thought throughout the world, while our ranks see many changing quantities but always hold those who remain true to the programme . . ." And in her conclusion to *The Key to Theosophy*, H. P. Blavatsky spoke of the work of this Society as it lives into and through the twentieth-century: "It will gradually leaven and permeate the great mass of thinking and intelligent people with its large-minded and noble ideas of Religion, Duty, and Philanthropy . . . [it] will open the way to the practical realization of the Brotherhood of all men . . . Man's mental and psychic growth will proceed in harmony with his moral improvement" (Blavatsky 1972b, 167).

The task, then, is clear before us. If we would hear the drumbeat of the future taking that sound and shaping it into form, we must accept the task before us and become, not only in name, but in fact, *Theosophists*, knowers of the wisdom, following in the footsteps of those who have gone before us on the ancient way to illumination. The Theosophical case for hope culminates in the knowledge of the human's infinite potential for growth into superhumanhood. And that case rests ultimately on the irresistible fact that there have been, and are, those who have achieved such realization, actualized the potential of our deific powers, and attained the status of perfected individuals, Masters of the Wisdom. The fact of the existence of a Brotherhood of such Adepts and the way to Them are among the priceless jewels in the crown of Theosophical teachings. That there is a Brotherhood of "just men made perfect," that there is a path that leads to Them, that there is a way of life which enables the earnest aspirant to find that way and that enables humanity finally to tread that path: these concepts give purpose and meaning to our future, for they lend to the fact of biological and social evolution the ennobling realization that human beings will not only endure, they will surpass themselves.

The future that calls us, the future to which we must devote ourselves, the future whose possibility we must proclaim to all who are seeking for the faint rays of light in the present gloom, is a future of humanity's own awareness of its potential. In her monumental work, *The Secret Doctrine*, H. P. Blavatsky gave in outline the entire course of human evolution, designating each step in the unfolding of consciousness as a "race" and charting the physical, psychic, and spiritual development of humanity in accordance with universal lawfulness. So she presented the vision of the future: "The Cycles of Matter will be succeeded by Cycles of Spirituality and a fully developed mind. On the law of parallel history and races, the majority of the future mankind will be composed of glorious Adepts. Humanity is the child of cyclic Destiny and not one of its Units can escape its unconscious mission, or get rid of the burden of its co-operative work with Nature. Thus will mankind, race after race, perform its appointed cyclic pilgrimage" (Blavatsky 1979, 2:446).

What, then, is the next step? How may we proceed to move from darkness into light? According to *The Secret Doctrine*, four major stages in the development of consciousness, four "races," lie behind us. We today are in the fifth stage, with the focus on the battleground of the mind itself. Wars today are fought less over territorial claims than over ideologies. As the Charter of UNESCO so aptly states the issue: "Since wars begin in the minds of men, it is in the minds of men that the defenses of peace must be built." Today's *kurukshetra* is man's psychological nature, the *kama-manasic* field of the personal self. Here must be waged the good fight; here the victory must and will be achieved.

If we would "listen to the march of the future," to use the words of one of the Society's founders, William Q. Judge, we must understand what it is to be fully human and then live out our humanity as responsible moral agents in a universe of law. A clue has been given to us in *The Secret Doctrine* where, speaking of the present development, H. P. Blavatsky has stated: "the humanities developed coordinately, and on parallel lines with the four Elements, every new Race being physiologically adapted to meet the additional element. Our Fifth Race is rapidly approaching the Fifth Element—call it Interstellar ether, if you will—which has more to do, however, with psychology than with physics" (1979, 2:135).

And one of the great Adept Teachers who helped to inspire this Movement one hundred years ago wrote on one occasion, in a letter to A. P. Sinnett, "We have offered to exhume the primeval strata of man's nature, his basic nature, and lay bare the wonderful Complications of his inner Self . . ." (Mahatma Letter 18). Surely the next and immediate step, as we look towards that glorious future which is our cyclic destiny, is to undertake, in full self-consciousness, the transformation of ourselves.

The world is desperately in need of spiritual alchemists. A new psychology that recognizes our true source in the realm of the Universal must arise to clear away the mental confusion and emotional fog, which obscure that inner reality. Splendid guideposts exist to mark the way, to aid us in performing the ancient alchemical work of transmuting the lead of personal selfhood into the pure gold of the Transcendent Self. "Three halls, O weary pilgrim, lead to the end of toils." So says *The Voice of the Silence*, the great and final gift to the world of that messenger from the Brotherhood of Adept Teachers to our age and time, H. P. Blavatsky. These halls mark the stages on the upward path of unfolding consciousness.

"The name of the first hall is Ignorance—Avidya. It is the hall in which thou saw'st the light, in which thou livest and shalt die." Here, in the phenomenal world of the senses, the world of terrestrial consciousness, as it has been called, we perceive the first glimmer of light; here we must begin. Behind and beyond all the transient display of existence, we must learn to see, however faintly and far off the light may seem, the rays of that one Reality in which the transient and changing is rooted. We have no other place to begin than here; we have no other time in which to begin but now. "Out of the furnace of man's life and its black smoke, winged flames arise, flames purified, that soaring onward, neath the karmic eye, weave in the end the fabric glorified . . ." So is the promise given, and we can move from *Avidya* towards *Vidya*, from non-seeing towards the full vision of the Light. Never again can we "unsee" the future, never again can we fall back wholly into darkness. "Fix thy Soul's gaze upon the star whose ray thou art."

Having now perceived the possibility of our future attainment, we cannot turn back or turn aside from the task before us. Onward we must travel, performing our appointed cyclic pilgrimage. In the language of *The Voice of the Silence*, we move into "the Hall of Learning. In it thy Soul will find the blossoms of life, but under every flower a serpent coiled." For this is the realm of trickery, the psychic world of super-sensuous perceptions and of deceptive sights. How many today are caught up in this realm of psychism, mistaking the flashing fireworks of psychic powers for the genuine light of the Spirit. How many today long for the awakening of those powers, failing to recognize that our great need and destiny is to unfold the essential powers of love and compassion, those powers that alone make of every person a savior of the world. Yet here, in the "Hall of

31

Learning" we may learn much. Here we may become aware of the great needs of suffering humanity. Here we may be awakened by the cry of those who are caught in the enslavement of the personal self. And in the unreal we begin to see the flickering ray of the Real. "Let thy Soul lend its ear to every cry of pain like as the lotus bares its heart to drink the morning sun. Let not the fierce sun dry one tear of pain before thyself hast wiped it from the sufferer's eye. But let each burning human tear drop on thy heart and there remain; nor ever brush it off until the pain that caused it is removed."

The way through the "Hall of Learning" is not an easy way, but even to be human is a dangerous and risky business. "Chafe not at Karma, nor at nature's changeless laws. But struggle only with the personal, the transitory, the evanescent and the perishable." For the universe is one of lawfulness, and we must learn to work with, and not against, that lawfulness. Then indeed, as again the promise is given, "nature will regard thee as one of her creators and make obeisance. And she will open wide before thee the portals of her secret chamber, lay bare before thy gaze the treasures hidden in the very depths of her pure virgin bosom. Unsullied by the hand of matter, she shows her treasures only to the eye of Spirit."

Learning finally to move from the unreal to the Real, to look with the eye of Spirit upon the things of matter, to hear the cry of humanity's deep sorrow, to work in accordance with nature's laws, the great laws of karma and cyclic necessity, we enter "the third hall . . . Wisdom, beyond which stretch the shoreless waters of Akshara, the indestructible fount of omniscience," the region of full spiritual consciousness. It is that "hall which lies beyond, wherein all shadows are unknown, and where the light of truth shines with unfading glory . . . . And now thy self is lost in Self, thyself unto Thyself, merged in that Self from which thou first did radiate." In that "state of faultless vision," as it has been called, we do not rest inert, inactive. "Shalt thou abstain from action? Not so shall gain thy Soul her freedom. To reach Nirvana one must reach Self-knowledge, and Self-knowledge is of loving deeds the child." So we must go forward "armed with the key of charity, of love and tender mercy." For, "Thou hast to be prepared to answer Dharma, the stern law . . . 'Hast thou attuned thy heart and mind to the great mind and heart of all mankind? . . . Hast thou attuned thy being to Humanity's great pain, O candidate for light?' . . . Now bend thy head and listen well . . . Compassion speaks and saith: 'Can there be bliss when all that lives must suffer? Shalt thou be saved and hear the whole world cry?'"

This then is the pattern of the spiritual psychology, which must be understood and applied today. This is the pattern of the age-old alchemical task, the magnum opus of being human. It is a growth in consciousness, an unfolding of the latent powers hidden in the heart of every member of the human family, and to this joyous labor of self-conscious development we must devote ourselves wholly and unreservedly. It is only thus that Theosophy can enter the arena of human thought and affairs, impress its grand and noble ideas on every aspect of human behavior—politics, economics, technology, science, religion, art, etc. Not by tinkering with effects, but by recognizing causes does the Theosophist aid in world renewal and the bringing to birth of a new consciousness. We must be the knowers of the facts of our being, for Theosophy is itself the gnosis, the wisdom of the fundamental Reality that underlies all existent things.

And what are the facts of our being? What is perceived in that "state of faultless vision" which is the consciousness of the Real? It is, first, quite simply that we are both being and becoming. In our essential nature, we are of the essence of eternal being. We are rooted in and participate in the essence of eternity; but in ourselves we represent the eternal order of becoming, experiencing the flow of reality as the time sequences of existence. In that sense, it is we who particularize the universal in the transient. It is for each of us to recognize through the transient that reality which evermore endures. To be human is to become the burning-glass of the universal; and through the human being are focused all the energies and forces of the creative process, the root cause is transformed into the efficient cause. As Krishna so magnificently reveals to Arjuna, on the kurukshetra of daily existence, the primal reality of being, admonishing him then: "Be thou the outward cause." To be human means to be rooted in the One Reality but also to act in accordance with the dharma, the truthfulness, of our existence.

The first fact of our being, then, is that we are both essence and existence, being and becoming. From that emerges the second fact of our being, the fact of a grand design fulfilling itself through the process of becoming—a purpose inherent in the universe because the universe is through and through intelligent, though only in the human can that intelligence become self-consciousness. Therefore, to be human is to be responsible, responsible for the fulfillment of the grand design of evolution. We must accept this moral responsibility; accept, in other words, the consequences of our choices. To awaken humanity to the awareness of this responsibility, this obligation, is to arouse a conscience of concern for the welfare of all life.

The third fact of our being is the principle of rhythmic growth, dynamic intent in the unfolding of consciousness and the powers which that unfolding confers. So we know the cyclic order of things, and move on our appointed cyclic pilgrimage in accordance with universal law. From this knowledge is born the fourth fact of our being, the principle of harmonization, and we learn the lesson of obedience to nature's changeless laws. No act can be without its reaction. No seeds can be sown without their eventual flowering, though it is for us to act without reacting, to perform the deeds of mercy without anticipating the fruits of such action. So our lives can actualize the great truths of our being, and having trod the ancient way of self-realization, pass from the hall of non-seeing through the hall of learning to the Temple of Wisdom. Having undertaken the great alchemical work of transmuting the consciousness of self to the consciousness of the All-Self, we must share that which we know, infuse into the thought climate of our times those larger ideas which provide the basis for true ethics, a true morality, a genuine brotherhood.

Here and now, we may take up the task in all earnestness of purpose, fully aware of the Theosophical case for hope, active participants in the cyclic destiny of the human race. For the human self is not the actual self. It is always and forever the possible self, what the self ought to become and can become. Along-side the little self with which we greet each day, the petty self which all too often intrudes its needs and desires and concerns on our attention, there is the Self of possibility, the Self which once glimpsed and known reveals itself as the Splendor of the One. Envisioning the actualization of that possibility, H. P. Blavatsky could forecast a new humanity taking birth, a new world of consciousness arising. At the conclusion of the volume on "Anthropogenesis" in *The Secret Doctrine*, she wrote: "Thus is it the mankind of the New world . . . whose mission and Karma it is, to sow the seeds for a forthcoming, grander, and far more glorious Race than any of those we know at present" (1979, 2:446). We can be that humanity of the "New World," learning to heal the world because we are healed, learning to serve humanity's deeper need because we have awakened the latent powers of love and compassionate understanding, learning to guide, as we have been told to do, the "crestwave of intellectual advancement . . . into Spirituality." Psychology today recognizes that whole masses of people can be pulled into the vortex of the inner disorder of a single powerful person. Whatever its origin, it is only in the individual that conflict and violence can be fought out. So also does psychology recognize that an ordered person, the fully integrated, psychologically whole individual, can create a vortex of power. History is full of the records of such individuals, and they constitute finally that grand Brotherhood of Adepts, the path to whom is ever open.

We can look out on our age and time and see only the death-throes of the old. We can inventory our despair in a lengthy recital of the woes of the present, pointing to the breakdown in morals, the increase of violence, and the almost universal reign of terror. Or we can look beyond the darkness of the night, perceive the first faint streaks of dawn, and know that we are witnesses to the birth of a new day. The cry of agony we hear is the birth pang of a new order. And we, heirs and stewards of the Wisdom-Religion of the ages, have both the privilege and responsibility to usher in that new day for humanity. Whatever may be the impulse which comes from beyond the snowy ranges of the Himalayas, the spiritual impetus that sets the keynote for the future, it must come through individuals who are open to it, whose eyes can see beyond the darkness of the present hour to the light that ever shines, the light of the human Spirit. It must be taken hold of, and channeled by, individuals who can hear amid the noisy clangor of conflict the quiet drumbeat of the future. "Listen to the song of life," says *Light on the Path*; "Life itself has speech and is never silent. Its utterance is not, as you that are deaf may suppose, a cry; it is a song. Learn from it that you are part of the harmony; learn from it to obey the laws of that harmony."

So the cycles turn, and a new era lies before us. As HPB puts it in *The Secret Doctrine*: "Such is the course of Nature under the sway of karmic Law; of Ever-present and Ever-becoming Nature." For, in the words of a Sage known only to a few Occultists:

The Present is the Child of the Past: the Future, begotten of the Present. And yet, O present moment! Knowest thou not that thou hast no parent nor canst thou have a child; that thou art ever begetting but thyself? Before thou hast even begun to say "I am the progeny of the departed moment, the child of the past," thou hast become that past itself. Before thou utterest the last syllable, behold! thou art no more the Present but verily that Future. Thus, are the Past, the Present, and the Future the ever-living trinity in one—the Mahamaya of the absolute IS. (Blavatsky 1979, 2:446)

Listen, then, to the march of the future.

All its possibilities are here today, as they were present yesterday. Not in time, but in consciousness must the journey be taken. Not in some distant place, but in the space of the human heart, must come the realization that all life is one. The modern poet T. S. Eliot once suggested that when we part from another, we should not say "Farewell," but rather "Fare forward." So as we part from our own past, embark on the path that will lead us to the heights, our work is to fare *forward*.

Tomorrow need not be simply an extension of today, lengthening the inventory of despair with further prognostications of gloom and defeat. We can, if we will, recognize the eternal truth of spiritual evolution, set our feet on the path that leads to the Himalayan heights of love and wisdom, following in the way taken by all the sages and seers and saviors of humanity. There are Those who have achieved, who stand forever as a "Guardian Wall," that wall which invisibly shields mankind from still worse effects of causes set in motion here. It is for us to determine to lend our hands, our hearts, our talents and capacities, our full strength, and all our energies and resources to the maintenance and strengthening of that "Guardian Wall," to join with Them, the Adept Brothers and Teachers of humankind, who though still human, are yet more than human, in the great work of building here on earth that true Brotherhood of Humanity which must one day be realized by all, that great work to which this Theosophical Society was, has been, and must always be, committed.

A Risky Game

A lecture given at the 102nd Convention of the Theosophical Society, Adyar, December 1977, and published in *The Theosophist,* Volume 99, January 1978

A century has now passed since the first book written by H. P. Blavatsky appeared on the world stage of ideas, confounding both scientists and theologians and challenging all thoughtful people to consider the facts of occultism as well as the existence of its guardianship by those who know and who are the servants of truth. In that work, *Isis Unveiled,* authored by the cofounder of the Theosophical Society two years after the frail ship of the Society itself had been launched on the stormy seas of popular prejudice, HPB wrote:

> Is it enough for man to know that he exists? Is it enough to be formed a human being to enable him to deserve the appellation of MAN? It is our decided impression and conviction, that to become a genuine spiritual entity, which that designation implies, man must first *create* himself anew. (1972a, 1:39)

As the age of scientific certainty of the nineteenth-century has now been fully supplanted by what one writer recently described as the age of enduring uncertainty, the questions asked by HPB are even more pertinent. But the answer, that "man must first *create* himself anew," has unfortunately been misread by those who would bring about, on the one hand, a new creation by genetic engineering and by those who, on the other hand, would produce the new man by psychic and psychological manipulation.

In a book called *The People Shapers* by the social chronicler Vance Packard, the distinguished author describes many of the projects now visualized by geneticists and behavioral psychologists to reshape and control the human being. He tells of such plans as "keeping people under surveillance by locking transmitters to their bodies, creating sub-humans for menial work and as a source of spare parts for human bodies, transplanting heads, creating humans with four or more parents, and pacifying troublesome people . . . by cutting into the brain." Such techniques as "sleep teaching" and the use of psychochemicals to control behavior are already standard practices beyond the experimental stages.

Is there still hope for the human being? Is it yet possible that we can learn to define ourselves not by the genetic code of the body nor the computer programming of the brain, but by the distinguishing marks of a spiritual entity? There are other equally valid questions: Can the Theosophical Society, founded for the dissemination of the Theosophical philosophy, continue to serve a vital role in bringing about a new vision of the human? Does the Theosophical perspective give us both the information and the inspiration that we need to advance the human cause, to encourage the creation of a new humanity by the self-transformation of its individual units?

To all these questions I propose the answer must be—and can be—a resounding YES. To refuse an affirmative reply is to deny our humanity and to draw down the curtain of night on the dawning daylight of our possibilities. The description given by HPB's close colleague and co-worker, H. S. Olcott, concerning the theme of *Isis Unveiled* could serve as well to summarize the argument of all her writings in the presentation, or re-presentation, of that occult tradition whose universal character dwarfs all attempts either to comprehend it wholly or to replace it with the spurious revelations of the innumerable latter-day gurus and psychics who are now parading on the world scene.

Summarizing the thesis of HPB's first major work, Colonel Olcott wrote in his *Old Diary Leaves* that the

> sum and substance of its argument is that man is of a complex nature, animal at one extreme, divine at the other; and that the only real and perfect existence, the only one that is free from illusions, pain and sorrow, because in it, their cause— Ignorance—does not exist, is that of the spirit, the Highest Self. The book incites to pure and high living, to expansion of mind and universality of tenderness and sympathy; it shows there is a Path upwards, and that it is accessible to the wise who are brave; it traces all modern knowledge and speculation to archaic sources, and, affirming the past and present existence of Adepts and of occult science, affords us a stimulus to work and an ideal to work up to. (Olcott 1895, 1:294)

Those words of the president-founder of the Theosophical Society—"there is a Path upwards . . . accessible to the wise who are brave"—must surely stir the aspirations and lift the hearts of all who are in earnest in their search for genuine understanding. Such a vision must serve as a goal to our efforts not only to achieve Self-realization, but to awaken others from the sleep of self-isolation to a knowledge of their divine state.

There are hopeful signs all about us that a "universality of tenderness and sympathy" may be moving mankind to rectify old wrongs, as fundamental human rights are recognized. Not too long ago, the ambassador from India to the United States, presenting his credentials to President Carter, said: "In the human cycle, years—

sometimes centuries—pass like a wayward time, and then comes a moment marked by the growing consciousness that an era is emerging and that man is moving in a new direction toward a new life. Humanity is today in that transforming mood. It is restlessly groping its way to the unity of the human race." Then, recognizing that each decade has seemed to have its epithet, the Indian ambassador concluded: "We may look forward, with justified optimism, to the humanized eighties."

If we are to ensure that the coming years will see humanity truly humanized and if in the years ahead of us we are to find our groping way to the unity of the human race, we must be both wise and brave. Over a century ago, in the course of the most amazing correspondence ever recorded, an Adept Teacher wrote to the ever-questioning A. P. Sinnett: "remember: . . . we are playing a risky game and the stakes are human souls" What was that "risky game"? Quite simply it was the making public of a wisdom heretofore taught only in mystery schools and under oaths of secrecy, but a wisdom which in one sense had always been accessible, under glyph and symbol, in myth and allegory, to those brave enough to seek out the keys that would unlock the treasure-house of Truth.

A new kind of courage is needed today, a bravery of the spirit, to live out that wisdom, to convey it not only in words but in the very fabric of our existence as we weave the threads of our own destiny. For the game we play is still a risky one and the stakes are as high today as ever—the very survival of our humanity. As Christian scripture reminds us: "For what shall it profit a man, if he shall gain the whole world, and lose his own soul?"

The wisdom that has become accessible to our age under the name of Theosophy presents so comprehensive an understanding of our human task that even to touch briefly upon some of its aspects necessarily involves us in a grave danger. This is simply that by narrowing our focus to the few elements that we can treat in a brief space, the larger picture may be missed and a seeming injustice done to the total canvas. But the issue is clear before us: a society established to convey to the world a mystery-tradition whose fundamental propositions have been clearly enunciated must continue to speak clearly and unequivocally to our human condition if we are to preserve our humanity and bring to birth a new consciousness of human unity that alone can usher in an age of peace and brotherhood.

The game, indeed, has but grown riskier, but we cannot withdraw from the playing field of existence on which the game has been cast, for the stakes are too high and the alternatives too appalling for our retreat. Therefore, if now we touch on only a few ideas presented in the wisdom-tradition as they relate to our human state, it is but to illustrate and emphasize the gravity of the task before us in ensuring what may be called the "salvation of souls." Perhaps a better expression to use, and one less fraught with religious connotations, would be the preservation of our human-ness, for it is this that is clearly under attack today, as the record of man's inhumanity to man reveals.

The classical literature of myth and allegory affords several excellent examples of our risky game, but I have chosen one that is both beautiful for its happy ending and meaningful for its occult symbology in illustrating our theme. This is the well-known tale of Amor and Psyche, which forms the central story in the second-century work by Lucius Apuleius known as *The Golden Ass*. Apuleius, it is believed, was an initiate of the Eleusinian mysteries and later was initiated into the mysteries of Isis and Osiris. As these mystery schools were the guardians, in the Western world, of the wisdom-tradition of which Theosophy is the modern representative, it is appropriate to draw on such a source as Apuleius' novel. If space permitted, we could also point out in some detail the significant parallels between the age in which Apuleius lived, an age when the Roman empire had already lost its moral and spiritual impetus, and our own period when there seems so much inner decay of values. However, let us look at some of the basic elements of the story itself, elements which point to the nature of the task each soul must undertake if it would win its immortality.

Quite briefly, the story of Amor or Eros, to use the Greek form of the name, and Psyche concerns the beautiful young daughter of a king and queen and the vicissitudes she suffers. So beautiful was Psyche that she aroused the jealousy of the goddess Venus, who commanded her son Eros to see that she would fall in love with the lowest of all human beings. When Eros sees his victim, he prefers to become that lowest human himself. He then exacts from Psyche a promise that she will not ask to see his face, and as he comes to her only at night, such a promise is possible. Incited by her sisters and plagued by her own curiosity, Psyche disobeys her husband. One night she takes a lamp and a knife, first to throw light on her bride-groom and then, if she should discover he is a dragon as she fears, to murder him. She finds instead that he is exceedingly handsome and that discovery so shakes her that she drops the knife, while from the lamp a drop of hot oil falls onto Eros, awakening him. When he awakes, he gives her the greatest punishment a god can give—he leaves her.

Psyche now is completely lost, and her real work begins with the long and suffering search to find Eros again. The story ends happily when the lovers are reunited, but before that can occur, Psyche must perform four extremely difficult, indeed almost impossible, tasks. It is to these that I would particularly call attention, in the context of our present study, because they point to the riskiness of the game in which we are involved. Psyche, of course, represents the human soul which, in the process of achieving self-consciousness, becomes separated from its own higher elements, personified by the god, Eros, and must undertake certain labors or disciplines that will bring it into a condition where it can recognize its essential divine nature and be reunited in full awareness with its own godhood.

Actually, the whole story of our evolutionary journey is depicted in mythological form in this allegory of Amor and Psyche, and the four tasks set before Psyche constitute, as we shall see, the fundamental theurgical enterprise on which all human beings must embark. In this sense, the risky game is that known in the Western tradition as theurgy, a work to which HPB referred in *The Key to Theosophy* as the "mystic belief—practically proven by initiated adepts and priests—that, by making oneself as pure as the incorporeal beings—i.e., by returning to one's pristine purity of nature—man could move the gods to impart to him Divine mysteries."

A full explication of the occult symbolism in this simple tale of Amor and Psyche would take us far beyond the bounds of our present theme, but the dangerous undertaking in which we are involved is well exemplified by the four labors assigned to Psyche in her quest for that which has been lost due to her own disobedience. One may ask, at the outset, what would have happened if she had not disobeyed the divine injunction? The answer to this is quite simply that mythological laws are always transgressed. Otherwise there would be no evolutionary journey, no winning of the SELF in full self-consciousness.

The first task that Psyche must perform is the sorting out of a hopeless muddle of seeds: a mound of barley, millet, peas, lentils, beans, etc., is placed before her, and she must sort them. Quite obviously, although there are many interpretations of this problem which faces Psyche, we may recognize that this first task involves the discovery of what I would call an ordering principle within ourselves. In the terminology of Theosophical literature, we have to learn discrimination. If there is a hopeless muddle within us—a tangle of ideas or mixed-up emotions—we have to put ourselves in order, sort things out, understand what is important and what is unimportant, what is true and what is false.

This is not at all easy, and we can risk losing ourselves either in the hopelessness of the task (which means we do nothing) or in choosing the wrong values and thereby creating a worse muddle. Happily, in our story, Psyche is able to perform the task because some ants come to her aid, the ants representing a kind of unconscious ordering principle. It is this principle that puts everything into its proper place and makes the various seeds, representing the spiritual germs of the higher qualities potentially present in the lower nature, serviceable to her.

2 . Then she is given a second task: to gather a hank of wool from some sheep whose fleece shines as gold. Those familiar with some of the Egyptian and Greek myths will recall the symbology of the ram and the legends of the Golden Fleece. In this labor, the occult signification becomes a little more complex. However, to put it as simply as possible, we must note that the ram or sheep is associated with the zodiacal sign of Aries and suggests aggressive impulsiveness and rather powerful emotions. In the story, Psyche is aided by a reed that tells her she will have no problem if she waits until the sun has gone down, for then the sheep, who have become quite frenzied in the blazing fury of the noonday sun, will grow quiet and approachable.

Similarly, only when our emotional nature grows a bit calm that we are able to pluck from it the golden fleece, that is, its golden treasure. We cannot live without emotions, but we can take from them their essence, which is really a reflection of Buddhi. For every powerful emotion is not only something hot, as indicated by the frenzy of the sheep in the heat of the midday sun, but it is also a treasure which brings light, as the golden fleece was treasured as the symbol of the Buddhic vesture of Atma.

Naturally, as Psyche proceeds, the tasks become more difficult. This reflects the patterns of our own lives, for as the game is played the stakes do seem to become higher and nothing ever becomes easier for us. Decisions are more difficult; experiences seem to pile up in awkward ways; and when we think we have learned one lesson, we find we are tested almost to the limits of our strength. So the final two tasks given to Psyche reflect this increasing difficulty of treading the evolutionary journey. Indeed, as has been said, "the road winds uphill all the way!"

The third task requires that Psyche fill a crystal bottle with water from the spring that feeds the rivers Styx and Cocytus, the streams of the underworld. Here again, however, she is helped, for the story relates that the eagle of Zeus takes the bottle, fetches the water, and brings it back to her. While we cannot explore the full occult significance of this, it will be apparent that the confluence of the two streams represents the union of the highest and lowest, the stream itself representing that vital energy known in occult literature as *Kundalini*. The eagle of Zeus represents the high-soaring flight of intuitive spiritual perception, the Buddhic principle, and the crystal bottle is the symbol of Manas, into which the creative energy must be poured. All of this, as indicated by the risky nature of the task, is a very tricky business. More than one person, attempting the arousal of Kundalini, has fallen into the river Styx, that is, has been destroyed and lost his soul. For it is psychic suicide to play about with these energies, which are represented as the streams of the underworld.

If only we could show those who are beguiled by the desire for power or glamorized by psychic phenomena the dangers of the path they are pursuing. If only we could spread abroad as widely as possible the *Theosophical* understanding of the nature of the human being and the right means of spiritual achievement, we should indeed be performing the greatest service we could accomplish in today's world!

47

4   Now before Psyche comes to the fourth and final task, there is a very interesting development in the story. She has to walk past an old man called Ocnus, who is making a black and white cord or rope, and she must also pass three old women who are weaving. Ocnus, who represents hesitation (and how often even on the threshold of our achievement we hesitate and even draw back from any further effort), is creating the endless rope of the opposites, while the three old women represent, as we know, the weaving goddesses of Fate in Greek mythology. But Psyche must go beyond both the pairs of opposites and the tangled web of the lower realms of her own nature in order to take up the great and final labor which will reunite her with Amor.

The last task demands that she descend into the underworld and obtain from Proserpina the box with divine beauty in it, which she is to bring to Venus. Again, the story is so rich in symbolism depicting the risky nature of the path to liberation, that one wishes it were possible to explore all the elements fully. However, we should note that in the first three tasks, Psyche was given some assistance (the ants, a reed, and finally the eagle of Zeus), but now to accomplish the fourth task, Psyche is left quite alone. For the first time, she is completely on her own and must undertake the heroic task without any assistance. She must descend into the underworld, that is, into all the levels through which consciousness can express itself, and she must not get caught or stuck in any of them. She must do this herself; no one can make the journey for her. Then at the lowest level, which is the world of dense, physical matter, the realm of incarnation, she must find the box of beauty or the box that contains the ointment which is the symbol of the life-giving Spirit and bring this as a gift to the highest which she knows.

Could there be any more beautiful symbol of the supreme task of uniting, in full self-consciousness, the world of matter with the world of Spirit? To use Theosophical terminology, we may say that

Physical and Atma become one, for unless we find the beauty of the Spirit in the very midst of the most material forms and convey it pure and unsullied as a gift to Divine Love, we shall really not be able to find it anywhere.

So the risky game is played out on the stage of human affairs, the risky game of ensuring that through the wisdom teachings of the ages humanity may yet come to a knowledge of its divine state, the risky game of our own labors in seeking and finding the ancient way to union with the true Self. Here in the arena of daily life we must win our immortality. Here in physical incarnation we must perform the tasks of our humanity. Here we must suffer, learn, and ultimately triumph. The modern American poet Robert Frost perhaps has summarized it best:

> Only where love and need are one,
> And the work is play for mortal stakes,
> Is the deed ever really done
> For Heaven and the future's sake.

OUR HIDDEN POTENTIAL

THE VALUE
OF INERTIA

Published in *The American Theosophist,* Volume 36, August 1948

We normally live in three worlds, all interblended: the physical, the emotional and the mental. The physical and mental are planes of form while the emotional is a life-plane. As the life of the emotions flows upwards, we have the well-known *kama-manas;* as it flows downwards, we have desire-action. By means of appropriate vehicles, we come in contact with each of these levels of experience. Our knowledge is derived from our perceptions through each of the vehicles, and our character and capacities are the summation of this knowledge in expression.

As we become masters of each of the vehicles, we release on each level energy or power appropriate to it. On the physical plane, the energy is action, and in controlling action we develop will power. On the emotional level, the energy released is desire or feeling, and controlling that, we develop love-power. The energy generated on the mental level is thought, and the power of thought is gained in controlling that energy. The power of control is supplied by the Ego or Soul. The analogy to a great dam with its adjacent power station is obvious. Until humans learn to control the forces at their command, the power can be and often is destructive.

In the human constitution, there is a perfect correspondence. The physical is representative of the Atmic, or level of divine will. The emotional is linked with the Buddhic, or divine love. The mental has its correspondence in the realm of abstract ideation, the divine mind, Plato's world of the archetypes. The bridge or balance wheel is the *Antahkarana*. That is the suspension point in the timeless-spaceless universe from which incarnation in a time-space universe may take place. When there is not the correspondence between the planes and control from the higher is lacking, there is willfulness or stubbornness rather than will, sentimentality or desire instead of love, and the sharp cut of intellect and wit rather than wisdom.

Matter, it is said, has three principal qualities or attributes. These three conditions reflect the three attributes of Spirit, and they may be seen as analogous to the planes. Matter becomes more spiritual in its ascent, and Spirit becomes more material in its descent. By knowing the characteristics of matter, we may adventure to the discovery of Spirit, for it has been said: "All evolution for us begins from below." The physical plane, where matter is most dense, is the scene of our legend, the romance of our quest. Here must be brought into manifestation and active expression the qualities of the spiritual life; here in the mortal must come the realization of the immortal and eternal.

The aspect of Will as a quality of Spirit imposes upon matter the quality of inertia, the power of resistance. The aspect of Activity in Spirit gives to matter its responsiveness to motion, mobility. The aspect of Wisdom gives to matter its rhythm, the quality of harmony in vibration. So Atma is reflected in the ability to be still; Manas in the ability to move; and Buddhi, the life that unites Atma and Manas, is reflected in the ability to move in rhythm, bringing motion and inertia into harmony. We have here the familiar three *Gunas* of *Rajas*, *Sattva* and *Tamas*.

Always there is a triplicity: duality ever gives rise to the third aspect, which is the relation between the two. Spirit and Matter are linked by Consciousness; Atma and Manas, by Buddhi; Mental and Physical, by Desire. Planes of form are joined by a plane of life—that which flows between them and unites them. Absolute stillness or inertia—rigidity—is brought into harmony with absolute motion—constant change—by rhythm. Through a discovery of these aspects in terms of living, we may develop certain qualifications that build bridges, as it were, from the mortal to the immortal principles—bridges over which the traffic of Spirit may freely flow, and we may come to touch that further shore of understanding.

As we experiment with what it means to "be still," we grow into an attitude of awareness, of receptivity, that makes possible the development of intuition. This is done not so much by making up one's mind to be still, but by an act of will that imposes upon the physical a discipline. Perhaps we might call it the "discipline of inertia," if this is understood as a positive and not a negative inertia. A negative inertia is undirected, uncontrolled—it results often in mediumistic tendencies. In its less extreme form, it would be mere idleness, a tendency to lethargy, and the enjoyment of "doing nothing." As a positive quality, inertia can become very productive as it is directed towards a continual realization *in the midst of action* of that inner center of peace and serenity. It is the characteristic of that individual who maintains in crises, amidst outer disturbances, in the face of calamity and disaster, an even poise, an unruffled calm, an unshaken confidence born of certain knowledge. True inertia is "will"; anything less—idleness—is "won't." The true leader does not need to shout; the silence of his presence commands. The ability to be still permits the flash of Atma.

Similarly may we adventure into the aspect of mobility, the ability to move and discover the quality of initiative. One role of Manas is to initiate new lines of thought and activity, for the mind to take up and act upon, passing them along for the emotional and physical vehicles to translate into their particular modes of expression. Here, once again, perhaps inertia plays its part. Unless the mind that plots and plans and schemes can "be still," Manas cannot initiate the flow of creative thought. Before the bridge between the higher and the lower—the Antahkarana—can be built and opened for traffic, there must be an attitude of constant awareness and the discipline of inertia in the vehicles, which will serve as "expressors" in the time-space universe of the impulses initiated in the timeless-spaceless realm.

There is an adventure, too, into the aspect of rhythm, and it is the discovery of balance in all things. There is a harmony possible between absolute stillness and absolute motion, which is rhythm. This rhythm is characteristic of the emotional level. It is the flow of love (or on its negative side, of hate) that brings ideas that the mind has initiated into expression on the physical plane.

"In the night of Brahma," says an Indian scholar, "nature is inert, and cannot dance till Shiva wills it: He rises from His rapture, and dancing sends through inert matter pulsing waves of awakening sound, and lo! matter also dances, appearing as a glory round about Him." In the dance is rhythm, motion that is harmonious.

As rhythm joins together motion and inertia, as the ability to move gracefully blends the extremes of movement and non-movement, so must there come another quality to harmonize the receptivity of stillness and the initiative of creative thought. That quality might be called adaptability, or steadiness, or dependability. In a sense, these are all one. Initiative can run rampant, can ride roughshod over new needs that arise, unless it be tempered by the capacity to become adaptable. Only when there is this adaptability can there be a dependability, a steadiness always to be relied upon. Perhaps here again there is the discipline of inertia, that the ability to move in rhythm, to be adaptable and dependable, comes from a stilling of the emotions and a consequent willingness to flow with life.

There can be then a discovery of, and adventure into, the aspects of stillness, of motion, and of rhythm. In each there is a discipline of inertia that brings a corresponding receptivity on each level. On the physical level this is expressed in an awareness of will, pure action; on the emotional level, it opens the channel for the steady flow of love, pure desire; mentally, it prepares the way for initiative, pure thought.

Carrying the correspondences a step further, we might postulate perhaps the significance between these aspects and qualities as they are developed and the six primary forces in nature spoken of in H. P. Blavatsky's *The Secret Doctrine* (1979, 1:292–93). Through the discipline of inertia on the physical level, there is awakened *Ichchhashakti*, the power of will, whose "ordinary manifestation is the generation of certain nerve currents, which set in motion muscles." The ability to move in rhythm may have a relation to that force known as *Mantrikashakti*, "the force or power of letters, speech or music." And the motion of the mind may give rise to *Jnanashakti*, the power of intellect that has two aspects: that of interpreting sensations when under the control of material conditions, and when liberated from that control, clairvoyance and psychometry. These latter capacities would be self-initiated, whereas the first aspect of Jnanashakti is initiated from below, as it were, through memory and anticipation.

As the faculties of the mind are turned upwards to pure Manas, there is the beginning of *Kriyashakti*, "the power of thought to produce external results by its own inherent energy." As the power of the emotions is raised toward Buddhi, Kundalini *shakti* is activated, for it is the "universal life-principle" that "includes the two great forces of attraction and repulsion." It is this shakti that "brings about the continuous adjustment of internal relations to external relations" and the "continuous adjustment of external relations to

57

internal relations." In this aspect, it again indicates the nature of a life-plane (the emotional in the personal world and the buddhic in the immortal realm) in relation to the planes of form (mental and physical in the personal, and atmic and manasic in the immortal). There may also be a correspondence between will on the physical level and *Parashakti*, when that will is turned upwards to Atma, "the great or supreme force or power" that "means and includes the powers of light and heat."

These correspondences we can perhaps only hint at, but they open out fascinating fields for investigation and application. In the development at any level and through all the qualities and powers, there seems to emerge a recognition of the value of inertia. It is, as was pointed out previously, not a negative attribute, but a positive characteristic, the imposing of a discipline of will that is calm, serene, full of peace and power. Inertia is the flow with life, never setting up at any time obstacles or dams in that flow that will restrict or hinder. It is the ability to be still, to find the center and identify oneself with that rather than continuing to revolve on the circumference of the wheel of life. It is symbolized in a faith in life, a confidence and trust in the experiences that life may bring. It is that faith which has been defined as "not belief in spite of evidence, but life in scorn of consequence."

So inertia is both a "giving up" and a "giving in," though far from the usual sense of those phrases. It is a giving up to the immortal of all that is good in the mortal, and a giving in to the center of all that is worthwhile on the circumference. Perhaps the greatest adventure of all, then, is the adventure into inertia, the discipline of will.

NOW IS THE TIME
TO BE HUMAN

A lecture given at the 95ᵗʰ International Convention of the Theosophical Soicety, Adyar, 1970 and published in *The Theosophist*,
Volume 92, March 1971

As we have has sought to cope with the various problems confronting humanity, we have become quite expert in defining
the external world in which we live. A very excellent and detailed
technical language has been developed, so that we have convinced
ourselves that we are in control of the external realm of things largely
because we are able to define that realm by means of language. In
fact, it is not unusual today to find even a small child able to describe
in a very knowledgeable manner the intricacies of electronic computers, satellites and supersonic aircraft. We tend to believe that if
we have named a thing, we not only understand that thing, but we
can also manipulate it.

We have also become rather competent in defining our own
problems, the crises which afflict us in modern civilization. This
competency in definition often deludes us into the fancy that we
have thereby solved the problems, so that no further action is necessary. We speak, in this manner, of the major problems of war and
violence, of pollution, of drugs, of racism, etc. We argue about

priorities in facing these problems, believing that when we have established such priorities, we have in some miraculous manner resolved the problems. We derive a certain sense of virtue from speaking about the problems, convinced that in speaking about them we have become involved in them and so have acted to bring about their solution. We voice our concern, calling attention to the fact that we are aware there is a problem, and this exhibition of our concern tends to make us feel we have taken action. In an age of slogans, we retreat behind the well-known statement attributed to some social service workers: "If you are not part of the solution, you are part of the problem." Convinced we are surely not part of any problem, we believe we are contributing towards the solution of all problems simply because we have defined them, identified them, and expressed concern over their eradication.

The time has come, I believe, to face the truly central issue involved in being human: the issue not of defining problems external to ourselves, but of confronting ourselves as the definers of problems. The issue here is not so much with an examination of the nature of human beings, finding a response to the question "Who am I?" but rather with the essence of our humanity. In what does our humanity consist? What does it mean to be human? We must learn to speak the language of our humanity, of our humanness, so that we can speak to each other, not about things, about technical achievements, technological advances but in the truly human language of the heart. Such speech, of course is not alone of words; it is a language of one's intimate being given expression in the total communication of ourselves to others.

The uniqueness of our humanity is basically of a psychological order, defined by reference to feelings and thoughts, to attitudes and to actions prompted by these. We act out in every moment of our lives the vision we hold of ourselves and of life in general. Emerson was correct in his well-known statement: "What you are speaks so loudly I cannot hear the words you say." The manner in which we see ourselves, the value we give to our lives, is constantly given expression in our actions. We cannot, of course, define our humanity without encountering the essential problem of who we are, but for the moment I suggest our focus be on how we reveal ourselves in the mode of behavior we adopt. Most of us play games with each other, even with ourselves. A rather popular book on human psychology is one entitled, *Games People Play*, reporting on the tendency in human nature to assume various roles in an effort to hide ourselves from others. Now when we play games, we do not really communicate; we view the other as the opponent, someone to be defeated or at least tested in some manner. Our moves are not free moves, but are reactions to the moves of the other, so that we develop a kind of strategy or counterstrategy, in which we hope to outwit him without revealing our own hand, so to speak. Watch two people when they meet: there is, as it were, a tentative feeler put out by one, and depending upon the response of the other will be the further extension of that feeler or its prompt withdrawal. We may begin to smile at another, but if the other does not smile in return, we immediately cease to smile. Naturally, we say, we are afraid of being hurt; we cannot reveal our vulnerability, and so we shield ourselves in some way.

There are those who say that man is simply an animal, a little higher animal, of course, but still an animal. Consequently, since congregations of human beings may be called a "human zoo," we can learn about human behavior by observing animal behavior. I would suggest that man is not an animal, even an extension of the animal, with the faculty of reason and the skill of tool making added; nor is man the opposite of the animal. The opposite of the human is the demonic, the realm of supernatural forces unorganized by reason and love; it is these forces, the demonic forces, that we have let loose upon the world today, because we have failed to channel those forces through our own being in a constructive manner. Our special obligation is to seek out our humanity in such a manner that we may channel the universal forces through our own humanness to bring about the transformation of the world.

This is the message, I believe, so many of our young people today are trying to convey to us: to be human, which is to be oneself; be a person, not a thing or an animal, and treat every one else as a person, not as an object to be used or exploited. Act humanely; do not inject into the bloodstream of humanity the poisons of bitterness, resentment, jealousy, and fear—the poisons that produce the real pollution of the spirit. Communicate your humanity by letting your lives speak.

The eminent Jewish philosopher, Dr. Abraham Heschel, has said: "Every generation has a definition of man it deserves." Our actions, our mode of behavior, constitute our definition. Today it seems to be more fashionable to define the human as a machine; the mechanistic description seems widely acceptable. Our technology has taken hold of us to such an extent that we tend to identify ourselves with the machines we have created, endowing those machines with living powers. Not only are there machines which are extensions of ourselves, but many machines seem to exceed us in capacity: there are machines that can think faster, hear more, see further, even compose poetry and music better than we can ourselves. We pride ourselves that we have abandoned the absurd notion that we were made in the image of some God, but we have only displaced that fancy with what we assume to be a more sophisticated one: we are made in the image of the machine, computers with a built-in mechanism for feedback. Someone has said that we are simply machines into which we put what we call food and produce what we call thought. Another writer has described a human being as an "ingenious assembly of portable plumbing." In the Eleventh Edition of *The Encyclopaedia Britannica*, this definition occurs:

"Man is a seeker after the greatest degree of comfort for the least necessary expenditure of energy." Much of our so-called materialistic civilization, with the growing disparity between the very rich and the very poor, is the outcome of such a definition.

In many Eastern psychological texts, the individual is enjoined to contemplate death, particularly one's own death, as a reminder that we cannot postpone our decisions and that any hesitation to fulfill our obligation as a human being is to risk losing our humanity. The contemplation of death is not a morbid preoccupation with the end of things, but rather a spur to the realization that death, far from pointing to the futility of life, directs our attention to the immediate and intrinsic importance and value of achieving our humanity here and now. Something of this same concept is hinted at in the rather somber and sometimes disturbing novels of the Western writer, Franz Kafka, who was certainly a master at the rather ingenious art of depicting people who did not use their potential humanity and therefore suffered the loss of their sense of personhood. In his most famous work, *The Trial*, as well as in *The Castle*, Kafka refrains from giving his chief character any name; in both stories, the identification is by an initial, a mute symbol of a lack of identity. In the very frightful parable, *Metamorphosis*, Kafka illustrates, in a very powerful manner, what happens to a human being when he forfeits his human powers. The hero of the story is a typical middle-class young man, living a quiet routine life as a salesman, going out each day and returning each evening to a typical middle-class home. Kafka implies that the young man's life was so empty that it was inevitable that he should awaken one morning to find himself a cockroach. He had not fulfilled his human-ness and so he forfeited the right to be human, for a cockroach, like rats and other vermin, lives off the leavings of others. It is a parasite and, in the minds of most people, is associated with all that is unclean and repugnant. Surely there could be no more powerful symbol for what may happen when a human being relinquishes his nature as a person, loses his humanness because he has not fulfilled it, and retreated from the human estate altogether.

In some Buddhist texts, our active aspects are summed up in four simple propositions. First, it is necessary for us to decide here and now whether we shall advance our humanity or retreat into the nonhuman. We cannot stand still and the decision cannot be deferred. Second, our humanity is not an accident. It is the outcome of our actions, so that only by acting in a human way do we become fully human. Third, we are therefore under an obligation to act in such a way as to preserve our humanity. Finally, this is possible only as we are reminded of our humanity at every moment. These propositions are not basically dissimilar to the thesis put forward by Dr. Heschel in considering the dilemma of the modern individual: "It is indeed conceivable," wrote Dr. Heschel, "that man may continue to be without being human. Dehumanization is the liquidation of being human." According to the great Christian mystic, Meister Eckhardt, Saint Dionysius said that man, to be man, requires three things: the possession of his mind; a mind that is free; and a mind that can see. The modern novelist, Jerzy Kosinski wrote recently that "we are a culture of the denial of the self." Speaking of the tendency so prevalent among students, particularly to share situations in order to escape direct contact with others, Mr. Kosinski suggests: "In its increasing collectivization, modern society offers every conceivable escape from the realization of self . . . Some of us claim to have the courage to give our lives if the need arises. Few of us have the courage to face it as it comes to us day to day."

It may be suggested that all of these statements—from psychological texts of Buddhism to the statements of the Christian mystic, the Jewish philosopher and the modern novelist—point to the same essential need, the central issue of our time. Now is the time to be human, to accept the monadic mandate of our humanness, and to exhibit in a direct and meaningful manner the fullness of our humanity. We must learn to transmute human pervertibility into human perfectibility; we must harness the demonic forces gripping us and our world, if we are to fashion a truly human environment in which all peoples can achieve their highest potential. The realization and actualization of the powers latent in humanity, the truly human powers, must be our central concern, our primary objective, if evolution itself is not to be defeated.

In *The Secret Doctrine*, H. P. Blavatsky sets forth this obligation, this essential responsibility to achieve our humanness, in discussing the three fundamental propositions upon which the occult wisdom-tradition is based. The third of these fundamentals postulates "the fundamental identity of all Souls with the Universal Over-Soul . . . and the obligatory pilgrimage for every Soul . . . through the Cycle of Incarnation . . . in accordance with Cyclic and Karmic law." In elaborating upon this primary postulate, HPB then states: "The pivotal doctrine of the Esoteric Philosophy admits no privileges or special gifts in man, save those won by his own Ego through personal effort and merit throughout a long series of metempsychoses and reincarnations" (1979, 1:17). In other words, we as human beings have the clear responsibility to take our own evolution in hand and to achieve thereby full self-consciousness. It is only in this manner that we can make conscious the entire universe, revealing in its totality that which has hitherto been concealed in primordial Unconsciousness.

It is said that every organism has one and only one central need in life: to fulfill its own potential. The acorn must become the oak; the puppy must become the dog; the caterpillar becomes the moth or butterfly. The human task is much more difficult, for man's development is never automatic, but must to some extent be chosen. We fulfill our potential humanness, realize our humanity, by self-conscious and self-chosen means and goals. We must make choices as individuals. If we do not take our own evolution in hand, if our choices are abrogated, so that we permit the demonic forces to flow through us to poison the world, it will be of little use for us to attempt the solution of problems of the external world, for the source of the poisoning will have remained untouched and the poisons emitted as a result of our failure to be human will break out in cancerous growths on the collective body of humanity to contaminate the pure stream of life itself.

To be human implies the capacity to make choices. Our continuing to be human, and the development of our full human potential, will depend upon the choices we make. A price is always paid for the birth of self-consciousness; it is the price of our choices, for we alone must pay the consequences of those choices. As St. Dionysius put it: "We must not only learn the truth; we must suffer it." This suffering is the bearing of the fruit of our choices. There is a most mysterious, but very significant, reference to this essential truth in the First Letter of the Initiate Paul to the Corinthians: "For ye are bought with a price: therefore glorify God in your body and in your spirit, which are God's." The implication here, of course, is that both poles of our being, body and spirit, are expressions of or derivations from a single immortal Source, one Divine Essence. The price is the limitation of unconditioned consciousness or unconsciousness in conditioned consciousness. Each human being, as the reflection of the macrocosm, pays a similar price for the achievement of self-consciousness.

The struggle to become a person, to become human, takes place within, for the basic conflict between that part of us which seeks growth and expansion and that part which longs to remain infantile, immature, dependent, permitting others to make our choices for us, is an internal one. Human development always moves from a continuum of differentiation from the "mass" or collective towards freedom of the individual; with every advance towards freedom, however, comes greater responsibility. This process is very much in evidence today both among nations and in individuals; much of the rebellion of youth, as well as much of the striving in many of the new nations for a sense of national identity, is simply part of this basic movement in human development from a state of unconscious dependency to a condition of conscious freedom. We want to make our own choices, although we are not always willing to accept the consequences of those choices.

While the struggle to become human, as an independent, freely choosing individual, is a deeply interior one, it is at the same time a struggle that never takes place in isolation. It is always in relationship that we come to know ourselves. Psychological annals cite many instances of children who, for one reason or another, have been isolated from human contact and who have grown up among animals or at least completely separated from any human beings. The chief characteristic noted about such individuals is their complete lack of personal identity in any human sense. To know what it means to be human, we must know what it means to be related. Unfortunately, while we have developed an excellent vocabulary of technology, we have neglected, and perhaps even lost, any language of meaningful inter-personal relationships. We may only note the degradation of the word "love" as it is used in today's literature, in the cinema and on the stage, to recognize the tragic misunderstanding and abuse of a language of relationship.

The task before us is to relearn the language of our humanity, to learn it now before it is too late. It is not only the big words that must be learned: brotherhood, peace, compassion; we must learn to speak the little words of every day that spell out understanding, concern, awareness of another's needs, and gentleness. In every action, our lives must speak the syllables of our humanity. We must move from the situation in which we are an unthinking, unfeeling, unfree part of a collective mass, through the experience of the birth of self-awareness, with its crises of growth, its struggles and choices, to an ever-widening consciousness of our total human potential, an ever-deepening freedom and responsibility, and a progressive integration of ourselves with others in freely chosen love and creative work. Each step of this journey, during which advances are made as a result of stubbing our toes against the events and experiences of existence, is marked by the realization that we must live less as servants of automatic time. The question is whether we can fulfill our own capacity for self-conscious choice at the moment, whether we assume now the risk of our own decisions and so live by that meaning we freely choose.

To live in such a manner involves the proper use of time in a constructive dealing with the here and now of our situation. If we live in the *then* of the past or the *when* of the future, we live artificially, automatically, without freedom. It takes courage to live in the present, to *be* human now, as well as to *do* the human act. For example, what happens when I meet another person? "To meet" means not only to come upon, to come within the perception of, but also to come into the presence of another. In the most casual of meetings, I am in the presence of the other. Even if I do not say anything, I communicate by my presence, as others communicate by their presence. What I communicate will depend upon the value I place upon the other, a value that may be influenced by my past experiences with the person (in which case I may see them only in the light of what they were or of my past reactions to what I assumed them to be) or by my expectations of what I think they ought to be in the future. Only if I meet each person in the present can I see him or her without distortion.

The value I place upon another is also dependent upon the value I place upon myself as a person. The injunction of the Christian Master to "Love thy neighbor as thyself" was not an idle commandment nor was it a permission to be self-centered in love.

Rather was it a recognition that only if one learns to value the Self sufficiently, as that Self is represented in one's own nature, can one love another truly, realizing the other as but another facet of the Self, another representation of the Self which may have innumerable representations. It is, in other words, to perceive the uniqueness of the Self as revealed in the preciousness of the other. The particular individual whom I meet may not be dear to me at all; in fact, I may not like that person very much, but each individual is dear to someone and even more importantly, every person is dear in their own Self. It is this essence of dearness that we encounter when we meet another, when we enter into the presence of another.

To be human, then, is to know the essential preciousness, the essential dearness, of the other, and to act always out of awareness of the quiet eminence of another's being. Such action must necessarily be harmonious, founded on an inward ethic of self-giving. The key point in the ethics propounded by the Master Jesus was the shift in emphasis from the external rules governing morality—the "Thou shalt not" of action—to an awareness of the inward motive. "Out of the heart are the issues of life." The ethical issues of life were and are the inner attitudes toward other persons. Such inner motive is referred to in one of the most beautiful of the Beatitudes: "Blessed are the pure in heart, for they shall see God." When the heart is pure, one can see naught else but the Divine wherever one looks, for all things, all people, all beings, are representations of the Divine and therefore dear to one. This ethic, founded on an inner harmony of thought and act, gives rise to an infinite patience with ourselves and with others. It is the kind of patience, forbearance, of which Paul spoke in his Letter to the Galatians: "Brethren, if a man be overtaken in a fault, ye which are spiritual, restore such an one in the spirit of meekness; considering thyself, lest thou also be tempted. Bear ye one another's burdens."

In the early seventeenth-century, the Fifth Dalai Lama spoke of virtually this same ethic when he wrote: "The way of thinking which prevails nowadays consists in looking, as it were, at the misery of others from the viewpoint of an extroverted mind and in quoting a few scriptural texts; it is never a load on one's heart." To sustain the pain of another as a "load on one's heart" calls for a certain dauntless energy, born of the true perception of the self as universal and therefore universally present in all. Do we, when we meet another, repeat the technical language, commenting on their sorrow that it is their karma? Or do we rather touch that person's dearness in some direct way, sustaining them inwardly in the ceaseless awareness of that which is immortal within each individual? Such caring, of course, goes beyond words or actions, although both may be utilized in the service of the other.

One of the most beautiful manuals depicting the path to our humanness, which is at the same time the path to divinity, to immortality, and to liberation is *The Voice of the Silence* by H. P. Blavatsky. It describes these inward attitudes of heart as the six-fold *Paramitas*, the transcendental virtues, the perfections of a life lived from an inner wisdom. These ideals of spiritual perfection are called, in that text:

1. *Dana*, "the key of charity and love immortal." This is not the charity of material giving, but the tender mercy, sympathy, and compassion that arise out of a boundless concern with the dearness of others. The word "charity" is derived from the Latin, *caritas*, which connotes the dearness of a thing. When everyone and everything is dear to us, the preciousness of all perceived because all things enshrine divinity, a conscience of concern is born that leads to right action.

2. *Shila*, "the key of harmony in word and act." Recognizing the dearness of each one we meet, we act in harmony with that dearness, out of a boundless morality. So action is ever right, for it is based on an inner self-giving.

3. *Kshanti*, "patience sweet that nought can ruffle." The harmonious act is never the impatient or impetuous one, so one must cultivate endurance, practice forbearance, exercise fortitude. The dearness of another may not be immediately apparent, but we are infinitely patient with the other, for his dearness will flower in its own proper time.

4. *Vairagya*, "indifference to pleasure and to pain, illusion conquered, truth alone perceived." The wayward mind and the unsteady heart are given focus in the perception of the One Reality, a perception that looks upon all things in an uncolored manner. Sight is not distorted by the agitation of the emotions nor the prejudices of a conditioned mind.

5. *Virya*, "the dauntless energy that fights its way to supernal truth." The perfection of strenuousness never lets us go, for there is a perseverance in the vision of Reality, a boundless industry, a glorious and steadfast exertion in the perception of the Self through all its multifarious forms. Our conscience of concern is ever maintained because it is born of the sixth of the virtues.

6. *Dhyana*, "ceaseless contemplation" of the Real. The mind and heart are united in willing the one thing which is the only thing essential, the enlightenment of all. Here is the supernal wisdom: "For this, thou hast

71

to live and breathe in all, as all that thou perceivest breathes in thee; to feel thyself abiding in all things, all things in Self." Inwardly focused in the ceaseless contemplation of the One, we act, simply and beautifully, at every moment in such a manner as calls forth from all the fragmented parts of that One, the multitude of selves, the Divine Image of the Immortal Self. So dear is the Self that the multitude of selves are dear in reflecting, however inadequately, however faintly, the One Universal Self.

But what is necessary is the courage to begin here and now, not to wait for some other time, some other place, nor for some other person to face up to the responsibility of being human. Now is the time to be human, to accept the monadic mandate for humanness; *we* are the ones to become human. As Dr. Heschel has put it so effectively: "It is always one man at a time whom we keep in mind when we pledge: 'with malice toward none, with charity for all.'" Humanity always begins in the individual man, as history takes its rise from a singular event.

Perhaps all that has been said here can be summed up in the little story of the traveler who, climbing a hill, came upon a small child carrying an even smaller child upon his back as he struggled up the incline. The traveler paused to ask the child if the burden were not too heavy for him, to which the child replied: "He's not a burden; he's my brother."

To be human means to live out our humanity every day, every moment; by whatever we do, by every act, every word, every gesture, we either advance or obstruct the possibility of our humanness; we either reduce or enhance the demonic powers let loose in the world. It is for us to either build or destroy the sense of community, which is the realization of brotherhood. To speak of love and then reject another is to diminish our own humanity. For this we need freedom, but we must know in what our freedom consists. For freedom is not escape from external conditions, but release of the Self and the removal of the obstacles to that release. We need courage, which is the affirmation of our choice. And such affirmation is possible only when we accept the consequences of our decisions. We need love, which is the true encounter with each one in whose presence we may stand.

Perhaps the achievement of our humanness is too much to ask of any of us, certainly too difficult to gain in one bound. But one has to make a beginning. When Socrates was describing the ideal way of life and the ideal society, Glaucon countered: "Socrates, I do not believe that there is such a City of God anywhere on earth." Plato records that Socrates answered Glaucon in this manner: "Whether such a city exists in heaven or ever will exist on earth, the wise man will live after the manner of that city, having nothing to do with any other, and in so looking upon it, will set his own house in order." This at least we can do: set our own houses in order by acting now upon the inner imperative of our being, for now is the time to be human.

"O Hidden Life . . ."

Published in *The Theosophist*, Volume 97, June 1976

Sometime in early 1923, Dr. Annie Besant, then president of the Theosophical Society, penned some lines that have since become familiar to members throughout the world. They have been translated into several languages, and have, indeed, become a nearly indispensable part of every Theosophist's vocabulary. The words have been set to music. They have been chanted and sung. Few gatherings of the Society have been held since that year that have not been opened with the recitation of these words. At every International Convention, successive presidents of the Society have inaugurated the proceedings with the antiphonal recitation of what has come to be known as the "Universal Prayer" or "Universal Invocation." Simple in the extreme, the words possess the magical power of a *mantra:*

> O Hidden Life, vibrant in every atom;
> O Hidden Light, shining in every creature;
> O Hidden Love, embracing all in Oneness;
> May each who feels himself as one with Thee,
> Know he is therefore one with every other.

So familiar have these words become that it may be their significance and depth of inner meaningfulness have escaped us. When we become habituated to anything, be it a person, a situation, or an idea clothed in the fabric of language, there is always the danger that we come to take it for granted. In times of stress, we may even mouth words we learned in our childhood, as in the simple prayers of our faith. People have been known to do this automatically at times of crisis. Even avowed atheists have been heard to utter prayers they deny knowing or remembering. But words are precious and often fragile vehicles not only for thought, but also for the aspirations of the heart. They can convey not only mundane meanings that get us about in the world and relate us to each other, but also the hunger of the soul and the beauty of the spirit in their reaching out to that "more-ness" which remains forever indefinable and therefore unspeakable.

Can we pause, then, to examine the lines which Dr. Besant gave the Society and the world? What inner meanings, what deeper realities lay behind the words themselves? To what new insights may we be led, even as we pronounce the words and speak the separate phrases? Have we become attached to these words simply because they came from that heroic soul, Annie Besant? Would it matter if some other individual had served as a channel for their impartation to the world? Undoubtedly, constant repetition has endowed the verse with a certain inner significance, a sacredness if we may call it that, but repetition can also dull the spirit and memorized phrases can be mouthed with little attention of either mind or heart.

Before we examine some, at least, of the inner meaning of the verse, it may be of interest to note its specific origin. In her Watch-Tower notes from *The Theosophist* of June 1923, Dr. Besant wrote that the lines were prompted by a request from a number of members who were helping to organize a "Brotherhood Campaign" in South India. This "campaign" had been inaugurated some time earlier in Great Britain and was just then being taken up in India. Her comment continues:

> I wrote . . . a few lines for daily repetition, morning and evening, as I did not feel that I could write a meditation, as they had asked me to do. Meditation seems to me to be a very individual thing, the working of one's own mind on some special theme; the most I could do was suggest a theme. Here it is, as it chanted itself. (Besant 1923, 243)

Then follows the verse already given above. Further, she adds,

> It sends forth successive waves of color, pulsing outwards from the speaker, if rhythmically intoned or chanted, whether by the outer or the inner voice, and if some thousands would send these out over successive areas, we might create a very powerful atmosphere . . . (ibid.)

The fact that Dr. Besant tells us that the verse "chanted itself" to her may indeed indicate that its true source lay in a deeper or higher realm beyond her own conscious mind, perhaps even from that Source to which she herself always gave the deepest and most profound reverence and obeisance. Surely, we must concur that the words, as she gave them, are of such beauty and majestic sweep that any alteration or modification would be improper. The effect on the surrounding environment or community, and on the individual who may be reciting the words as the verse is spoken, can only be guessed at, although many testify to its efficacy in producing an inner peace and even actual healing.

Turning now to the verse itself, we may consider it phrase by phrase, suggesting some of the meanings latent within it. First, "O Hidden Life, vibrant in every atom." The immediate question that arises is: Why hidden? Is not life in evidence all about us? Life surely is not hidden! But what is referred to here, what is invoked, must be beyond or above the obvious. Dr. I. K. Taimni, in his work, *Glimpses into the Psychology of Yoga*, reminds us that: "The Ultimate Reality exists only in the Ever-Unmanifest and is the source of all relative realities which can be within the realm of human experience." The highest principle, then, is present everywhere, and yet, is beyond all existence. It is truly the "hidden life" that underlies all of manifestation.

Inherent within that Reality is its own dynamism, as it were, making possible the production of all things, all existence, for there, at the heart of Reality, is the throbbing pulse of creation. Without that pulse, nothing can exist. It is ubiquitous, and contains within itself the power of resonating throughout all that ever was or will be. That potency is locked up in every atom and every element of the manifested universe. Truly, it is "vibrant in every atom." So all of nature pulsates with the rhythm of the Eternal One, hidden forever, but known by its countless manifestations, as the One becomes the many, and yet remains forever One. This initial phrase is a call to that eternal, Unmanifest Principle: the Supreme Reality which is beyond the cycles of manifestation and yet forever vibrating through the manifested universe. In terms of human consciousness, it is an invocation to that Atman which is hidden in our very nature, as present here in the physical as at its own level because its resonance vibrates through all the atoms of all our vehicles—carriers of that Atman—from Buddhi to the physical.

"O Hidden Light, shining in every creature . . ." Again, we may ask: Why hidden? If there were a light shining in every creature, surely that light would be observable. The very nature of light is that it glows and therefore it can be seen. Light radiates outwards, but we are called on to invoke a *hidden* light, a light that shines within but is not radiating outwards in a visible manner. So, a deeper meaning must be implicit in the words.

The One Reality, when it manifests, may be said to become Light. It is this interior light of the Supreme Reality, of *Ishvara*, the manifest Deity that is present in every creature. Life has now become light; its very vibrancy is now shining with an inner dynamism. In humanity, Buddhi—the "light of the soul"—is now united with Atma, ready to turn outwards into activity. It is this light which must illumine our entire nature. This light makes consciousness possible, and it is "hidden" because it is not objective to consciousness but is of the very nature of pure consciousness itself. And that light is present, shining through every atom in space.

"O Hidden Love, embracing all in Oneness . . ." From the polarity of Life and Light there now springs creative activity, Love. Wherever there is polarity, relationship between the poles comes into existence. The purest of all relationships, the one relationship that is not sullied in any manner by any object of either attachment or repulsion, is the relationship of Love. This we may call the underlying "glue" which holds together all manifested things, all parts of the universe, all elements that appear with manifestation. Therefore it is Love that "embraces all in Oneness." The One has become the many; out of unity has come multiplicity. Yet however great the multiplicity, all is held in the one embrace of that pure relationship which arises when Life and Light come into existence, that relationship of Love.

Love lies at the very heart of the creative process. It is therefore the principle of universal lawfulness, which underlies evolution. Hidden, then, at the heart of the manifold is Love, which binds the many into the unity of the One. This is the law and the fulfillment of the law, bringing everything into perfect equilibrium, for whatever happens anywhere in the universe has its repercussions everywhere. There is no external authority, no extra-cosmic deity, weighing the scales of justice. Love is at the heart of the universe and brings about balance because all that is in the universe is held in its embrace.

Here, too, is the creative principle: Atma-Buddhi joined with Manas, turned outwards now on the great involutionary-evolutionary journey. Manas, or creative activity, is truly love in action. The mind, when infused with intuition, embraces the universe, perceiving all things as they truly are. The mind that can fragment the Real in order to grasp or realize its manifold nature can also be brought into a condition of stillness, in which the modifications of the thinking principle have ceased. In that condition, perception, or awareness, is undivided. The undivided state of consciousness embraces "all in oneness."

The first three phrases of the mantram remind us of the great triplicity of the Supreme Reality—Life, Light and Love. But this triplicity is "hidden," because it is not known objectively, but rather underlies the entire process of manifestation. It is "hidden" because the mind alone cannot grasp its essentialness, nor can it be experienced through the instrumentality of the senses. As Dr. Taimni points out, in the above quoted work, "According to the Occult philosophy there is a method of knowing the Reality . . . and this method consists in suppressing the modifications of the mind completely." That method, of course, is yoga. "Then," continues Dr. Taimni, "the individual consciousness becomes freed from the veil which separates the individual consciousness from the universal consciousness and knows this Reality directly by becoming one with it."

In the first three lines of our verse, we invoke the triple nature of the One Reality. In that invocation, we may perform a supreme yoga of Self-Realization. Our attention is drawn to the sublime fact that underlying each individual and the universe is the One Reality in its triple aspect of Life, Light, and Love. Its realization lies in a realm beyond the mind, but by invoking it, we bring that Reality into direct awareness, into our consciousness attuned and harmonized with the One. The final two lines of the verse affirm this realization, "May each who feels himself as one with Thee". Here the use of the word *Thee* indicates that the triplicity of Life, Light, and Love is indeed One—the One Supreme Reality. Note, however, that the emphasis first is on the word *feels*. What is it to feel oneself as one with the Supreme? Feeling is acute awareness—awareness without any distracting thought, without any disturbing influence. It is an awareness that is total, which overwhelms us and takes hold of us wholly and utterly. Perhaps it may be compared to the moment of pain when one stubs one's toe against a stone abutment. At such a moment, there is no other awareness than the awareness of pain. No thought even intrudes at the sharp moment of impact. Only later may we say, "I stubbed my toe" or "I felt pain in my toe."

The feeling that must come, and must be affirmed in the realization of oneness, is such a feeling: total, entire, complete, without analysis or reason or logical deduction. Only in such a condition can true *knowing* arise. In one sense, this ability to "feel . . . as one with Thee" may be described as the pain of oneness, the burden of oneness, that we all must bear, if we would know the reality of life itself. It is not, in other words, a selective feeling: "I will feel one with you, but not with that person; I will feel one with a tree, but not with a snake." When we say, "May each" or "May all," we are invoking in ourselves a consciousness that has no divisions, no barriers. It is a consciousness infused only with Life, Light and Love, and therefore it is pure and whole.

Out of that acute awareness of feeling must follow a knowing: "Know he is therefore one with every other." So the mantram concludes with an affirmation of the certainty of knowledge. Humanity is not only meant to *feel*; it must *know*. This is the full burden of *self*-consciousness. It is a knowing that is not simply a surmise, an opinion, an idea, or a belief that may be altered when some other notion comes along. It is rather a conscious act that arises because we have been immersed in a consciousness that was uncompounded, undivided, whole, and pristine in its nature. As a result of the contact with that consciousness, of that non-verbal awareness that we are one with the Universal Reality, that we are truly Atma-Buddhi-Manas, we have to know, to be fully conscious of our oneness with all other units of Life who are equally infused with that Reality, vibrating with it, shining with it, embraced by it.

In some versions of the mantram, the word *also* has been substituted for the word *therefore*, but it may be noted that in Dr. Besant's original version, the latter word is used. There is a subtle, but very definite, difference between the two words. "Also" is an additive word; it means "in addition to," "this plus that". "Therefore" has the connotation of "subsequent upon," or "as a result of"; it is not augmentative. What is intended in the mantram is the realization that when the feeling of unity is present, there is recognition of the oneness with the Supreme Reality that is Light, Life, and Love. There follows upon that recognition the realization that one is inevitably united with all other creatures. For how can we be one with the Supreme and remain separate from, distinct from, all others who are equally rooted in the One Reality?

Many more meanings may be discovered in this magnificent verse that Dr. Besant bequeathed to us. It is truly a reaffirmation of the entire creative process in which we—and all life—are immersed; a reaffirmation that we hold within our power, as self-conscious units of life, the ability to perceive life, whole and splendid. This is the vision we can send shining out over the entire world, the vision to which we can give wings and voice and form. This is the vision that can recreate ourselves every time we chant the mantram, and so recreate and transform our world. Such a vision alone can bring about a new consciousness in the world, a consciousness of unity, of brotherhood, of peace and harmony, of wholeness and holiness.

When we repeat these few simple lines, either alone or in a group, we invoke the One Reality to manifest itself anew, and this is to make whole and make holy all that is in the universe about us. A more wonderful act we could not perform.

THE DECLARATION OF
INDEPENDENCE AND
INDIVIDUAL FREEDOM

Published in *The Theosophist,* Volume 97, September 1976

In July 1776, a group of fifty-six men, of whom at least fifty were members of the Masonic fraternity, signed a document that has come to be considered one of the great landmarks in human history. Largely authored by one of the most illumined and literate men of the eighteenth-century, Thomas Jefferson, that document—the Declaration of Independence—established the separation of the American colonies from England on the basis of certain philosophical premises current in the Age of Enlightenment. The significance of the Declaration has been said to lie in the fact that it translated concepts concerning the inherent rights of man, rights that every human being was presumed to possess simply by virtue of being human, from the philosophical sphere to the political arena.

The basis of American independence has focused the attention of nations throughout the world on the radical concept on which a democratic nation was first established. For the Theosophical student, this singular event may provide a useful occasion to examine certain correspondences between what may be called a collective intent to achieve national freedom and the stages required for the individual achievement of personal freedom. Students of the esoteric philosophy are inevitably concerned with the question of freedom, a term which may be taken as synonymous with liberation and even with Self-realization. The question of what constitutes true freedom has always engaged the philosophical mind. Philosophers both Eastern and Western have attempted to resolve the question of whether or not man is essentially free. The men who signed the Declaration of Independence, however, did not debate the philosophical issue. They stated, rather, that all people have an inherent right to enjoy liberty and towards that end may establish their own government, which derives its powers from the governed.

An exploration of what may be termed the "American experience," based on the Declaration of Independence, may be helpful in understanding our own situation. Often ideas that first emerge in the collective consciousness of a group or institution must ultimately be brought into full realization by each individual, for only thus is their validity proved and the evolutionary progress of the whole assured. For example, we may suggest that the world today is experiencing a kind of "Roman moment" of history, a time when the forces of materialism are set in direct opposition to all that would uplift and advance the human spirit. In a parallel manner, every individual comes to the point in their life, a "Roman moment," when the forces that would hold the person in bondage to material interests, selfish concerns, personal desires are sharply opposed by their spiritual aspirations, their concern for the welfare of others and a recognition of the brotherhood of humanity. Similarly, the American experience founded on a declaration of the equality of all men and women, and the consequent right of all to enjoy certain freedoms must become the experience of every individual seeking to free oneself from bondage to the past and to all that would enslave them.

In tracing the correspondences between the collective and individual experience of freedom, there are three aspects, especially, which deserve our attention. A study of the state of affairs in the American colonies in 1776 reveals, first, that the Declaration of Independence was drawn up and signed in the very midst of the struggle to achieve that independence and not after the war for independence had been won. In fact, in July 1776, the outcome of the conflict was even in some doubt, as the men who signed the Declaration knew full well when they mutually pledged "to each other our lives, our fortunes, and our sacred honor." Second, it must be noted that the Declaration marked not so much the achievement of freedom as the *intent* to establish that freedom by the enunciation of principles on which an independent state could be founded. The third aspect that deserves consideration is the fact that the union, which was visualized by the Declaration, was not achieved all at once, even when the conflict then raging was ended. The goal of union of the separate colonies was realized in a series of stages and after several failures (e.g., the Articles of Confederation were replaced by the U. S. Constitution, but even then the issue of federalism versus states' rights was resolved only after a bitter Civil War nearly a century after the Declaration of Independence was adopted).

Now what is the significance of those three factors revealed by a study of the collective experience in achieving national independence when we consider the individual or personal experience in the attainment of freedom or liberation? There are, I suggest, certain valid parallels between the group experience and individual realization. At the outset, we may note that just as the colonies were subject to a foreign power which many began to feel was an unjust relationship, so in our individual lives we may come to recognize that we are in bondage to desires, illusions, and prejudices that actually constitute a "foreign power" within us and from which we must free ourselves or continue to pay tribute to that power. So the idea of freedom must first arise within us. We must know it is possible to break the bonds that have held us subject to the past or enslaved us in the present. There must be born in our consciousness an awareness of the inalienable right of the Self to be free, free from the illusions of the personal self, the desires and passions that bind us and shadow our lives. And then, in the very midst of the struggle to be free, we must declare our intention to liberate ourselves. There can be nothing vague about this, nothing equivocating: we must commit ourselves fully, pledging our total resources to the task of winning through to Self-realization, which is true freedom.

The first step, then, is a declaration of the way we intend to travel, a statement of the goal we intend to achieve. We must define the nature of the freedom we expect to gain. We must know in what liberation consists. It may not be possible to know in detail how we shall achieve our aim. Just so, the men meeting in Philadelphia to draw up a Declaration of Independence did not at the same time devise plans of military action or accompany the Declaration with schemes of military strategy. They set the goal toward which all subsequent actions would be directed. In a similar manner, we must clearly perceive the end we would achieve and recognize that all of our energies must be applied towards that end.

This first stage may be analogous to the prerequisite for reaching Bodhisattvahood, the state of compassionate enlightenment, as outlined in Mahayana Buddhism. In many Buddhist texts, the aspirant is told that at the outset there must arise in the mind, and be held steadily present in consciousness throughout all the struggles that follow, the thought of ultimate enlightenment, *bodhicitta*. The men of the colonies in 1776 had one thought clearly before them, the thought of independence as a free and self-governed nation. We too, if we would achieve self-realization, must have a clear vision of our goal and set forth fearlessly and unhesitatingly our aim.

We cannot wait until the inner struggle is won before we announce our intention. Indeed, the very declaration we make may serve to intensify the conflict between the powers that would deny us our freedom and that Immortal Self which must disentangle itself from the bonds of personal enslavement. Not every aspect of ourselves will join in the struggle nor even consent to engage in the revolution that must take place. It would be a mistake, for example, to believe that every one in the American colonies supported the cause of independence or even favored separation from England. Many wanted to continue the ties at any price. The Loyalist sympathizers were legion. So in our own nature, there will be many elements that militate against our achievement of spiritual freedom. Many aspects of our personal selves will resist any breaking of ties with the animal instincts, with our normal desires and customary ways of thinking and reacting. Some parts of us may even prove traitors to the goal we seek, and we may find ourselves seeking compromise with our own shadow, hoping to have the best of both worlds as it were. To effect a revolution in ourselves is no easier than to establish a nation's independence.

Finally, out of the group experience exemplified in the Declaration of Independence, we may learn that freedom is sometimes achieved by stages and that ultimately true freedom is best guaranteed when there is a centrality of government which will uphold the rights and exact the obligations of each constituent part. In full self-realization, the federal authority of the Atman has been established, but there cannot be violated the natural rights of the mind now freed from prejudice, of the emotions now purified of unwholesome desire, and of the physical vehicle through which action that is selfless may flow unimpeded by reaction. But in the achievement of that self-realization, we may need to proceed by stages, establishing first a kind of loose confederation among the vehicles, each demanding its own "rights" until each has learned that true freedom may require the surrender of some portion of those rights in order that the whole may prosper. If the mind, for example, claims complete independence, but the emotions are bound by desires for self-aggrandizement, for self-gratification, how can the mind be truly free? It is weighted by the pull of emotion and cannot be free to receive spiritual insight and respond to intuitive understanding. Only when the governance of the self is vested in the Self, the Atman, can there be true freedom for all aspects of the self.

The path to such freedom, to true liberation, has been given many names. In the East, it is called Yoga. Dr. I. K. Taimni has pointed out, in *Glimpses into the Psychology of Yoga*, that "the whole philosophy and science of Yoga is based upon the assumption that man is completely free to free himself from the illusions and limitations in which he is involved and to become established in the world of Reality to which he really belongs." Here essentially is the final freedom. It was exemplified by the action taken by fifty-six men in July 1776 and it is reconfirmed every time an individual determines to follow the path to self-realization. The ultimate freedom is our freedom to free ourselves. We are similarly free to bind ourselves, to clasp about us the chains that spell enslavement, that hold us in bondage to the personal self and its desires and passions. The choice is always ours: "none else compels," as *The Light of Asia* so beautifully phrases the primary fact of our humanity. To be human means to have the inalienable right to a choice of ways.

WHO IS THE TEACHER?

Published in *The Theosophist,* Volume 99, June 1978

In *The Golden Stairs,* the beautiful and concise statement given to her students by H. P. Blavatsky, two of the steps contain reference to the Teacher:

> a loyal sense of duty to the Teacher, a willing obedience to the behests of Truth, once we have placed our confidence in and believe that Teacher to be in possession of it. (1980, 12:503)

For sincere students who are endeavoring to guide their life by the precepts given by HPB, the question inevitably arises: Who is the Teacher? It is a question particularly relevant in these days when the so-called guru-industry produces a new model almost every year. Before one can feel a loyal sense of duty towards another, and certainly before one can willingly obey the behests of Truth which come from another, one needs to have some assurance that the other is the possessor of Truth.

Among the basic concepts presented to the student of the Theosophical philosophy is the idea that there exists and has existed at all times throughout human history a hierarchy of adepts. Many who read the history of the Theosophical Society recognize that those who were responsible for its establishment in the world attributed its ideals and the message it was meant to convey to certain spiritual Teachers or Mahatmas, Masters of the Wisdom. Consequently, the Theosophical student repeating the steps of *The Golden Stairs* may automatically identify the Teacher with one or another of the Mahatmas spoken of by H. P. Blavatsky. But such unthinking identification does not necessarily answer our question. Even if one accepts that the reference in *The Golden Stairs* is to HPB's own Teacher, how can we come into contact with that Teacher (or our own Master) in such a way as to have absolute confidence that he or she is in possession of some truth that we are to obey?

The entire matter is further complicated by a factor which is emphasized again and again not only in Theosophical literature but in all literature dealing with genuine occultism. That factor is the need for every student to engage in independent thought, to come to their own realizations, to develop self-reliance instead of following blindly the dictates of another. So the question becomes an extremely subtle one. How can we be loyal to a Teacher we do not know and at the same time accept the need to think out things for ourselves? To whom are we loyal, and in what does loyalty or willing obedience consist?

QUESTION OF AUTHORITY

We may be loyal to a good friend, willing to defend that friend under all circumstances, because we believe that person to be basically honest, moral, and ethically upright. We value the judgment of such a friend and often accept their advice. We say that we know our friend and can trust them implicitly. But we do not know the Teacher and, because we do not know such a person for ourselves, often tend to accept, without much thought, that whatever others *say* has come from that Teacher. This inevitably leads us to a consideration of what constitutes authority for us. We all accept various authorities for different aspects of our existence and, in many cases, we submit willingly and unthinkingly. For example, if we are in a strange city and need directions, we assume that a person in a police uniform will give us correct directions. If we consult a doctor, we assume we will receive a correct diagnosis, so that even were we to ask for a second opinion regarding the diagnosis, we seek out another doctor. We invest different individuals with authority because of what we believe to be their qualifications in particular professional areas, often accepting what we are told by such individuals without any question.

In matters that have to do with our own spiritual growth, however, we must exercise a certain care and understand precisely what it is we are doing when we accept some authority or other. There are those, as we well know, who will accept only the words of H. P. Blavatsky as authority. While for others, the statements made by Annie Besant, C. Jinarajadasa, G. de Purucker, or W. Q. Judge constitute the ultimate authority in occult matters. In such cases, there comes about an unquestioning acceptance of everything that individual has said or written. One tends to quote such people almost constantly, arguing not from one's own independent judgment and knowledge but from the presumed authority one has unthinkingly accepted. If we are in an occult or esoteric school, we may come to feel a certain security in simply following whatever the head of that school has told us to do. However, in such a case, we have failed to recognize the principal hallmark of the genuine schools of occultism: that the Teacher never absolves the disciple from responsibility for their own decisions. In all authentic occult traditions, whatever pledge is taken is a vow to one's own Higher Self. In the Buddhist tradition, for example, it is said that there is no one to whom an aspirant can take the Bodhisattva vow. Such a pledge can only be taken to oneself! We must invoke only the authority of that Self, knowing that the breaking of a pledge so solemnly taken severs one not from some external authority or Teacher but from the Higher Self, the center of one's own being.

So the question resolves itself into one concerning how we may come into contact with that Higher Self, that Self which is invoked as surety to whatever pledge we may take to follow the spiritual path. If this is the final authority, the true Teacher, then we need guidelines for coming into touch with that Higher Self. Occult schools have always been in existence for providing such criteria in the world, but the hints given are often difficult to discern and nearly always paradoxical in nature. For they require both a willing obedience to the dictates of Truth and the development of a self-reliant spirit in the quest so that one neither accepts nor rejects without careful consideration and reference to one's own interior perception. While it takes courage for the sincere student to become the independent thinker, there is no substitute for that bravery of the spirit, which is willing to examine every idea that is presented. Unless we are able to accept responsibility for our thoughts, our decisions, our beliefs, we are not likely to become genuine *knowers* of Truth.

QUESTION OF RESPONSIBILITY

What, then, are the criteria to be followed? Perhaps the first and simplest, although often difficult in its demands upon us, is that we must start where we are. That means we have to learn to accept our present condition and operate within the orbit of whatever it is we know or do not know. One may be able to fool others into thinking one knows more than is the case but one can never fool oneself! Acceptance of our "unknowing" does not mean the adoption of an open-mouthed gullibility. It is, rather, an honest admission that, while we may not know much, we can only increase our knowledge or understanding by being certain of what it is we *do* know. Inevitably, at this initial stage, we may turn to others outside us who appear to be in a position to teach us. We may turn to books which we intuitively feel carry an aura of authenticity about them, not so much because they contain what we may assume to be final truths but because they seem to point us in the direction in which Truth may lie.

However, in turning to any outside authority, we must know what we are doing and be willing to assume responsibility for our choice and acceptance of that outside Teacher. In other words, if something goes wrong (as well it may) and we find ourselves in deep water, we have to be willing to admit that we made the choice that led us into the morass of our difficulties. How much easier it is, on such occasions, to blame the Teacher! We would like to say, "But the Teacher told me to do that," or "I was only following what the book said." But who chose the Teacher? Who selected the book? Of course, it may also be true that we heard only half of what the Teacher said, or read only part of the book! The point is simply that if we quote someone else whom we consider to be more knowledgeable than we are ourselves, we should do so out of our own deep conviction that what has been said has in it the ring of truth. We do not use our "authorities" to silence the "authorities" of others, but we begin to trust the inner quiet authority of our own perception, humbly aware that we may not yet perceive the fullness of Truth. As we proceed, through study and meditation, testing out ideas by considering them in the light of our own intuitive understanding as well as in the arena of daily existence, we will naturally gain more confidence, more assurance, and with that confidence, new knowledge is born. Paradoxical as it may seem, knowing increases only by knowing.

QUESTION OF AUTHORSHIP

We may examine the question from another point of view in our effort to arrive at an understanding of who is the Teacher. One of the difficulties confronting the earnest student of Theosophy, especially when reading the early literature of the Society, revolves around the question of who wrote what. This may seem a strange statement, but even a cursory examination of the facts surrounding the production of such works as *The Secret Doctrine* and *The Mahatma Letters to A. P. Sinnett* (to take only two examples of often-quoted texts) highlights the problem.

Consider the matter for a moment: the name of H. P. Blavatsky appears as the author of *The Secret Doctrine*, but who was HPB? There was, first of all, a woman who had certain peculiar characteristics and personality traits—an incarnation that confounded the experts, we might say. Then there was a highly advanced occultist who served consciously as a mediator between those she considered her Adept Teachers and the world about her. Further, if we are to accept the testimony of those about her, she relinquished on occasion her vehicles to her Teachers for their direct use.

Without pursuing a detailed study of the mystery of who was HPB, we are directly confronted with the question as to which aspect of this multiple complex using the name of H. P. Blavatsky wrote which sentences or statements in *The Secret Doctrine*. Can we, by our own thinking, by our own intuitive perception, by our own understanding, consider each statement in those volumes *on its own merits*?

Even more puzzling may be the question of who wrote, and who were the real authors, of the famous letters, attributed to two Adept Teachers and even bearing their signatures, addressed to A. P. Sinnett, A. O. Hume, and others. Statements within the letters themselves indicate that in many instances these were transcribed by *chelas*, but chelas, we are told, are at several different levels of occult achievement. Other statements in the letters suggest that several means were used in their composition, including "precipitation." In some cases, the letters were written *in propria persona* by the Teacher whose name was duly signed at the end of the communication. It is not our intention here to examine this question in detail, but rather to point out the simple fact that whatever may be the source for any of the teachings to which we may turn for instruction and inspiration, we are not absolved from the necessity for independent thinking if we are to discover Truth for ourselves.

Consider again the question of the authorship of *The Mahatma Letters*. Some, it is said, were the product of chelas who were later termed "failures." Does this invalidate the contents of those letters? We may well ask what it is to be a failure, for in one sense the failure is simply the individual who has attempted more than can be achieved. But all honor to the one who attempts the heights, even if there is a failure to reach them! The occult tradition would indicate that the failures of one cycle might be the *Dhyan Chohans* of the next. Surely in the spiritual life it is better to have set our vision beyond our reach than to have rested content within the smaller orbits of our views. So, whether the letters were penned by the Teachers themselves or communicated through chelas, there still remains something in them that inspires the mind and stirs the heart. We sense an inherent validity in the teaching that points to the existence of a Teacher. The question of authorship becomes secondary when we are concerned, not with using the letters to invoke an external authority, but as a challenge to live the life and discover our own pathway to Truth. When seen in that light, the teaching that points to the presence of a Teacher points beyond to the Master within—our own Higher Self.

Recognizing, then, the Teacher in the teachings outside ourselves, we turn within to test the teaching by our obedience to the commands of Truth. Loyal to the inner vision, we find the horizons of our knowing forever expanding, discovering that what appeared to be a Teacher without is actually the true Teacher within, for there is but one Teacher—the supreme Atman in which abides all Truth.

It is to that Teacher we pledge our duty, as it is to that Truth we give our willing assent. Lead the life and you will come to the wisdom has ever been the dictum of all genuine schools of occultism. Perhaps a clue has been given to us in a simple statement found in *The Mahatma Letters*. It matters little who wrote the words—Master or chela—for they carry the authentic ring of truth: "I can come nearer to you, but you must draw me by a purified heart and a gradually developing will. Like the needle the adept follows his attractions" (Mahatma Letter 47). Whether the "I" of that statement is an external *Mahatma* or the Higher Self of each genuine aspirant, the Atman-Teacher abiding in the heart, is less important than the simple requirements for coming to the Truth. These have been the requirements given in all ages for the one who would know who is the Teacher: a pure heart, a heart aflame with love and compassion, and a will that is born of a steadiness of purpose and a faithfulness to duty, the will that is never daunted by either failure or success, serene amid all circumstances, carrying us ultimately to the realization of the Supreme Truth, where teaching, Teacher, and taught are one.

THE MYSTERY OF HUMAN IDENTITY

Published in *The Theosophist,* Volume 112, November 1990

The age-old question, "Who am I?" continues to haunt and perplex the minds of today's men and women. Is it really possible to know who we are? Where do we turn for a clue to self-knowledge? Are we simply bodies, with appendages called minds? Or are we something more? Religion speaks of spirit and soul; psychology of emotions and drives; science of physical mechanisms such as glands, brain, and so on. Where, in all of this, is that which we call the human, the person, the individual?

As we survey the many conflicting views on what it is to be human, there does indeed appear to be a "mystery," the mystery of our human identity. The very use of that term implies that there are aspects of experience, the human experience, which defy complete and final definition or description, aspects that cannot be limited by the mental processes by which we seek to define ourselves. The Theosophical worldview seeks to unravel that mystery by pointing to the multidimensionality of the human and suggesting that within those many dimensions of our being there lie capacities and powers yet to be explored and developed. We are already familiar with some of the dimensions, but even within those there are capacities still to be unfolded.

The search for human identity has been the subject of literature, art, and music throughout the ages. It has been central to every religious tradition and the foundation of all great mythologies. The question, "Who am I?" has been asked in every age and in all cultures. Only we, only the human in us, can give an answer, for only we can look within to discover our own humanness. We are both the mystery and the clue to understanding the mystery! Only we possess the answer to our own questioning. If the reply seems to come from without, from religion, philosophy, psychology, mythology, from scripture or science, from faith or philosophy, it is simply because all of nature and all of our studies of nature provide only the sounding board for our own projected voice. One day we must learn that the voice we think is outside ourselves is actually only an echo of our own interior speaking.

The Theosophical worldview concerning the human constitution posits, first of all, a grounding in a universal field of consciousness which may be called Atman or "spirit." We may be said to be focal points, individual centers, in that universal field, but because it is a universal field, it is universally present in all. This spiritual component, or dimension, of our being is recognized in all the great religious systems. In moments of deep reflection, during times when we feel at one with Nature, or in moments of pure love, we sense this inner reality of our being and acknowledge spirit as the core of our existence.

H. P. Blavatsky, one of the founders of the Theosophical Society, set forth in her major work, *The Secret Doctrine*, the fundamental proposition that supports the view that we are rooted in one universal field or ultimate reality. There is only one life, however diverse may be its expressions. This is the basis of the Upanishadic statement that "Brahman is Atman; Atman is Brahman." The same concept was expressed by the Christian Master, when he said, "I and my Father are one." Blavatsky phrased it thus:

> The Secret Doctrine teaches . . . the fundamental identity of all Souls with the Universal Over-Soul, the latter being itself an aspect of the Unknown Root. (1979, 1:17)

At that lofty level, there is no other, for differentiation occurs only as that One expresses itself through the many dimensions or garments of existence. The eminent Jungian psychologist, Dr. Erich Neumann, once defined the human as *Homo mysticus*, mystical man, because that center of our being can never be objective. It is always ultimately the eternally subjective and so cannot be an object for or of itself.

The Self, or Atman, as a focal point within the universal field of consciousness or Spirit, is clothed first in what we may call, metaphorically, the finest raiment of light to which the name Buddhi has been given. This is also a universal field, whose chief characteristic is intuitive knowing. The resultant combination, Atma-Buddhi, is referred to in Theosophical literature as the Monad, or more properly the Spiritual Monad. It is the Pilgrim, which sets forth on the evolutionary journey through all the other fields or dimensions of existence. We may call the field of Atma-Buddhi, the realm of the Monad, that dimension in which we are truly "at home."

H. P. Blavatsky refers again and again to the septenary nature of the human, but this sevenfold system can be correlated with the well-known Pauline triplicity of body, soul, and spirit so familiar to the Christian adherent. Spirit, in that system, is the Atma-Buddhi, or Spiritual Monad, of Theosophical literature. Similar correlations can be found in other systems, such as the Vedanta and the Buddhist. The important point to note is that here is the essentially and uniquely human, or *Homo mysticus*. We are, at the very center of our beings, the immortal pilgrim, Atma-Buddhi, the Monad. For our journey into and through existence, more is needed. There are other fields in which we must and do function, awakening potential after potential, capacity after capacity, power after power. All are fields of consciousness, simultaneously present.

As we are all aware, we have physical bodies, emotions, and a mind that thinks and reasons. We have spiritual aspirations and even on occasion experiences that we may define as mystical, experiences that convince us of an underlying unity of existence. Where is the link between the personality, consisting of our psychological nature and the mask we show to the world, and that inner realm of spirit? H. P. Blavatsky said that "to complete the septenary man, to add to his three lower Principles and cement them with the Spiritual Monad . . . two connecting principles are needed: *manas* and *kama*." This may seem very technical, so let us examine what she meant. Very simply, of course, the Theosophical perspective shows us that there is a continuum at one end of which is Spirit, or the Spiritual Monad, to which we have just referred, and at the other end, our psychophysical existence.

We may look at this a little more closely, recognizing that just as the universe is sevenfold in its constitution, so every aspect of the universe, the macrocosm, is reflected in and made conscious through the human, the microcosm. The key to the process, and so the key to the mystery of our own identity lies in the central connecting principles: manas, the mind, the cognizing principle, and kama, the motive or driving energy usually translated as desire. The Monad alone, or Spirit, does not constitute the human, just as the body alone, the physical form, cannot be said to be all there is to us. What defines us, what defines the human, lies in this middle realm, the field of manas, for our uniqueness lies in our capacity for self-reflective thought. For example, as you are reading this, you are probably thinking about the meaning of the words and whether the ideas make sense to you. So you are reflecting upon the subject. You are responding, we can say, to the field of manas or the mind. Let us say, however, that in the midst of your reflection on these ideas, you become aware you are hungry and there arises in you a great desire for food, perhaps even for some particular kind of food. When the mind is driven outward by desire or passion, it is called Kama-Manas, because the energy of kama—desire, longing, or passion—is moving the mind to seek some outward satisfaction. On the other hand, you may pause in your reflection on these ideas, and turn inwards in meditation or contemplation. You may become aware of spiritual values you wish to incorporate into your life or you may feel a creative inspiration or gain an intuitive glimpse of a deeper reality. When the mind is turned inward in this way, it is called Bud-dhi-Manas, for now the mind has been energized by and united to the realm of Buddhi or intuitive knowing.

As said previously, we have access to all these fields, but the central focus of being human is in manas, the mind. Today that is the battleground, as we see the efforts to win over the minds of peoples, through propaganda, advertising, and all the forms of manipulation that would influence our thinking. The preamble to the charter of the United Nations Educational, Scientific, and Cultural Organization stated it most clearly: "Since wars begin in the minds of men, it is in the minds of men that the defenses of peace must be built." As humanity is becoming aware of the dangers of pollution, of environmental contamination, and all the other problems that are afflicting us and our planet, we begin to give thought to corrective measures. The very need to become aware is one aspect of the awakening of manas, or the mind. And, as just indicated, the mind can be driven outward by kama, or desire, or it can be pulled inward by buddhi, creative love and intuition. Within the mind are both destructive and constructive powers, and so in many myths (such as the legends of the Holy Grail) the mind is symbolized by a sword, which has the power to cut but also to discriminate. In some of the Grail legends, the sword had both the power to wound and the power to heal. Today, very clearly, the emphasis is on the transformation of the mind, a transformation that has been defined as a shift from the kama-tending mind, the mind which is separative, subject to conflict, possessive, dominated by desire and passion, to the buddhi-tending mind, the mind that is peaceful, intuitive, compassionate, aflame with love for all beings, a mind which is capable of true creativity.

However, we still must complete the sevenfold pattern of our being. We have identified the center of the human mystery as spirit, or Atma-Buddhi, the Spiritual Pilgrim or Monad. In essence, these are the first two dimensions of our septenary nature. Next, we have identified the mind, or manas, the thinking and cognizing principle within us, and noted its link with that aspect of the Monad known as buddhi. Here, in Christian terms, is the soul, sometimes called the causal vehicle in Theosophical literature. We have noted that the mind can be moved outward through emotion, kama, which is desire, or passion, and become enmeshed in that realm of our being. Some Theosophical books speak of that dimension or realm as the astral, although Blavatsky reserves the term "astral" for a dimension of our nature which provides the pattern or mould for the physical.

When we speak of the physical body, we must take note of two other aspects or dimensions of our being. There is not only the solid physical, but also a pattern "body" or etheric, as it is sometimes called (it is this which Blavatsky called the "astral"). This subtler dimension may be likened to a mold which provides the pattern on which the dense vehicle is fashioned. The contemporary biologist Rupert Sheldrake has proposed the existence of a "morphogenetic field" which provides the pattern for all forms and to which all forms resonate in terms of structure. This postulate of Sheldrake provides us with a useful analogy to understand the etheric or pattern field. In technical terms, this has been called the *linga* (or subtle) *sarira* (or vehicle), while the dense physical is known as the *sthula* (or gross) sarira. Both these fields are interpenetrated by a third principle, which is called *prana* or the life-energy and which is closely associated with the breath. As we know well, when the breath ceases in a physical form, we say that death has taken place.

Here, then, is the multi-dimensionality of our being, from Spirit to body, from Atman to physical. Consciousness exists at each level or within each of the fields, in accordance with the nature of the field. We can say, then, that in essence we are a continuum of consciousness, from highest spirit to densest matter. Yet that which says "I" in each of us is still a mystery, for that "I" can never be an object of its own subject. When the physical body is hungry, we say "I am hungry," identifying ourselves with the body. When we aspire to the loftiest ideals of spiritual awareness, we say "I long to know the One, the All, the Godhead, the Source of all existence." We say, "I desire, I want, I think, I breathe," and in that "I" lies the ultimate mystery of our human identity. Within each of the fields, the dimensions of our nature, the focus of consciousness takes on a structure that has sometimes been called a "body." Through such bodies, or vehicles, the energy of the field is experienced, and we discover the potential capacities and powers of the field.

The mystery of human identity finally lies not only in the many dimensions of our being, the fields of consciousness in which we can and do operate, but also in the powers and capacities of those fields. These are the great potentialities of the human spirit that we seek to actualize through the long evolutionary journey of the Monad. Because we do not know the full potential of which we are capable, we can never fully define and certainly can never limit the boundaries of the self. Such is the Theosophical vision: the spirit and the soul as its reflection, acting through the body, is a center of consciousness whose growth and splendor have no limit!

"A Direct Beholding"

Published in *The Theosophist*, Volume 112, May 1991

The greatest incitement to courage is to have the highest of all aims: to save and free the mind from the powerful bonds and fetters which constrain it from infancy. Without this no one can learn anything sound or true.

—*HPB*

Steps of the path!
Steps of the path!
They all come down to three short words:
Look far ahead,
Think very big,
Keep a pace.

—*Geshe Dolpa*

The Goal in sight! Look up and sing.
Set faces full against the light,
Welcome with rapturous welcoming
The Goal in sight.

—*Christina Rossetti*

"Theosophy," wrote H. P. Blavatsky in the first issue of her journal, *The Theosophist* (October 1879), "is the exact science of psychology . . . It develops in [us] a direct beholding." In the course of her teachings and writings, HPB left us many definitions of Theosophy as well as explanations and expositions of its fundamental principles. Yet, perhaps, none pointed as clearly to the importance of this world-view for the individual as the statement just quoted. For psychology, however it may be defined and with whatever school of thought it may be identified, is concerned above all with the human psyche, with the nature and development of consciousness in the individual human unit. To what extent, then, do those universal principles that comprise the Theosophical worldview provide us with "the exact science of psychology," and how do they awaken and develop within us a "direct beholding"?

The third fundamental proposition set forth in the Proem of *The Secret Doctrine* establishes "the fundamental identity of all Souls with the Universal Over-Soul . . . and the obligatory pilgrimage for every Soul . . . through the Cycle of Incarnation (or 'Necessity') in accordance with Cyclic and Karmic law" (Blavatsky 1979, 1:17). This provides us with the central thesis of a Theosophical psychology, a starting point to understand our own nature and the means to develop a "direct beholding," which is to view all things as they really are, to use HPB's words by way of clarification.

Metaphysically, there is an Ultimate Reality, one without a second; non-dual in its nature; beyond both consciousness and unconsciousness; beyond darkness and light and all the dualities or polarizations we can think of. It may be said to reflect itself as the creative potency by which universes and all they contain come into manifestation and from which everything in a manifested system emanates. We in our inmost nature are one with that universal root of existence. We are not different from it and we are not even similar to it. We are, as the proposition states, "identical" with it. Yet our knowing of that fact, our full realization of the tremendous implications of such a statement, is far from complete. Our vision is veiled, obscured, and in our blindness we have lost touch with the essential truth of our being.

The recovery of sight involves us in a long journey, an "obligatory pilgrimage," in accordance with the inherent lawfulness of the system of which we are so intimate a part. To see the reality underlying or within the *mayavic* veils which shroud all that exists, to develop a "direct beholding," calls for an inner stamina of the spirit, a courage of the heart, a bravery of soul. Yet to be a Theosophist means to undertake the journey in earnest. At the same time, the journey is not for ourselves; the pilgrimage is not that we may attain some exalted height from which vision is clear and whole. As HPB and her Teachers constantly reminded us, the journey is taken so that we may be of service to others, that seeing we may aid others to see, that knowing we may aid others to know. Truly, as *The Voice of the Silence* tells us: "To live to benefit mankind is the first step."

What is the way then to that direct beholding, to that uncovering of the true sight within us by which we may perceive the reality underlying all existence, discern the true from the false and recognize even in the transient that which is eternal? As the "exact science of psychology," Theosophy focuses our attention on the true nature of the psyche by clarifying the distinction between that which is spiritual, and therefore enduring within us, and that which is psychophysical, and therefore subject to mortality. Expanding this fundamental dyad of our nature into a septenate, HPB clearly differentiated between the spiritual soul or buddhi and the human soul, centered at manas. Writing of the seat of animal desires and passions (kama), she said: "This is the center of the animal man, where lies the line of demarcation which separates the mortal man from the immortal entity." Manas she called "a dual principle in its functions," and defined it as "mind, intelligence, which is the higher human mind, whose light or radiation links the Monad for the life-time to the mortal man," adding

> The future state and the Karmic destiny of man depend on whether Manas gravitates more downward to Kamarupa, the seat of the animal passions, or upwards to *Buddhi*, the Spiritual *Ego*. In the latter case, the higher consciousness of the individual Spiritual aspirations of *mind* (Manas), assimilating *Buddhi*, are absorbed by it and form the Ego. (Blavatsky 1972b, 56)

It is at this crucial midpoint of manas that the transformative journey must take place. Our task is to reverse the normal gravitational pull which links manas and kama, shifting the center of gravity upwards to bring the light of buddhi into manas.

HPB adds by way of explanation: "Since Manas, in its lower aspects, is the seat of the terrestrial mind, it can, therefore, give only that perception of the Universe which is based on the evidence of that mind; it cannot give spiritual vision" (ibid., 100). When our vision is limited by manas in its union with kama, we can scarcely see clearly. For a direct beholding, we must awaken the sight of the divine soul, and this calls, as just suggested, for a serious transformative effort. No easy task lies before us, but such is the work we are embarked upon as our human responsibility.

No gift of HPB to the world speaks more clearly of the trans-formative journey than *The Voice of the Silence*. In her presentation of passages from the *Book of the Golden Precepts*, which she told us was derived from the same source as the Stanzas from the *Book of Dzyan* on which *The Secret Doctrine* was based, we have invaluable keys to the way by which we may ultimately attain a direct behold-ing. Our present obscured vision is described in that exchange between teacher and pupil, which HPB gives us in Fragment 3:

Look on. What seest thou before thine eye,
O aspirant to God-like wisdom?
The cloak of darkness is upon the deep of matter; within its
folds I struggle.
Beneath my gaze it deepens.

Then comes the dramatic moment of awakening, when the aspirant can say:

I see the Path . . . And now I see the ever narrowing Portals on the hard and thorny way to Jnana.

And the reassuring words of the teacher:

Thou seest well, Lanoo. These portals lead the aspirant across the waters . . . Each Portal hath a golden key that openeth its gates.

We come to a direct beholding as we learn to turn the keys that open the portals on to a new vision or a recovered vision as veil after veil is removed by our own efforts from our sight. The "golden keys," as HPB terms them, are known in the Buddhist tradition as the paramitas, the excellent or exemplary virtues. Usually listed as either six or ten in number, HPB gives them as seven-fold, though perhaps we should view them as six modes of being in the world which culminate in the state of consciousness indicated by the seventh, *prajna*, which as HPB explains, "makes of a man a God, creating him a Bodhisattva." It is prajna, then, which provides the liberated soul with that direct beholding characteristic of a god-like consciousness, the consciousness of the Bodhisattva whose very nature is wisdom and compassion. However, as prajna may be thought of as the culmination of the work to be undertaken by the pilgrim soul, it may also be said to be the first requirement. Some of the Buddhist *sutras* regard prajna as the directing principle, as without prajna the other paramitas are unable to know by themselves where they are bound or for what they are intended. Paradoxically, that which we realize at the end of the journey is essential to begin the journey: right vision or right perception leads to the direct beholding.

Thus considering the seventh "key" of prajna as both the beginning and the climax of our journey, the preceding six stages enumerated by HPB mark out the way of transformation leading to that "unveiled spiritual perception" which is truly a direct beholding of Reality even in the midst of phenomenal existence. In HPB's terms, the six "keys"—*dana, shila, kshanti, vairagya, virya,* and *dhyana* provide us with the means whereby we act in the world from a mind and heart cleared of all obscurations. Manas illumined by the light of Buddhi, which is prajna, directs our conduct from a clear perception of the spiritual basis out of which all material existence arises. Here indeed is the "exact science of psychology," for the keys given us in *The Voice of the Silence* provide us with the means to clear the field of vision.

There are various ways in which we can understand these keys as psychological tools to awaken our direct beholding of the reality in all existent things. Quite simply, the first three—dana, shila and kshanti—form a triad of ethical behavior flowing naturally from a consciousness established in the fourth, vairagya. For dana is not only charity, as HPB translates the term, but it is a liberality, a generosity of one's total being, a complete caring in which there is a constant radiation of one's very being for the welfare of others. Shila enables one to act at all times in a harmonious manner. Kshanti provides us with patience, never expecting anything and never fearing anything. Out of such ethical behavior, there arises within consciousness a sublime non-concern for the petty self, vairagya, which is not so much indifference as an attitude of interior acceptance. The final two keys, as HPB gives them, virya and dhyana, provide us with an understanding that there is a deep center of energy which is joy ever active within us, not the kind of energy that thrusts itself forward, that produces outer exertion, but an energy born of dhyana, the "ceaseless contemplation" of the Real, the ultimate, which is supreme happiness. That interior bliss, that knowing, which is beyond words and yet expresses itself in a realization that all life is one, the Self in each is one with the Self in all, produces within us a direct beholding and we are at peace. Wherever we look, we see but the One Self. Being at peace, neither anxious nor fearful, seeing clearly and truly beyond the manynesses of existence the true light of the One, Self-Existent, we can glimpse beyond the confusion and chaos of today's world the shaping of a new world order and aid in bringing about the transformation of human consciousness, the spiritual regeneration of humankind, so necessary to ensure that such a new world—a world in which brotherhood and understanding among people everywhere prevail—will become reality in our time.

THE EXTRAORDINARY NATURE OF THE ORDINARY MIND

Published in *The American Theosophist*, Volume 81, November 1993 and also in *Theosophy in Australia*, Volume 58, March 1994

Eleven centuries ago, the Chinese sage Huang-Po was asked about the nature of the Buddha. He replied, "Buddha is the ordinary mind." In the second chapter of the Bhagavad Gita, Arjuna questions Sri Krishna: "What is the mark of him who is stable of mind?" Arjuna, as the ordinary individual faced with a serious problem, is eager to learn how such a one, the yogi or the sage, talks and sits, walks and eats, and carries on all the normal activities of everyday life. Sri Krishna's response is a little more detailed than was Huang-Po's: "When a man abandoneth . . . all the desires of the heart, and is satisfied in the SELF by the SELF, then is he called stable in mind. He whose mind is free from anxiety amid pains, indifferent amid pleasures, loosed from passion, fear and anger, he is called a sage of stable mind." Surely such a one, the "sage of stable mind," may be said to have the nature of a Buddha.

While many students have denigrated the mind, quoting the well-known passage in *The Voice of the Silence*: "The mind is the great slayer of the Real," few have taken note of the many aspects of the mind referred to in that beautiful Theosophical classic. True, early on in HPB's text, we are advised to "seek out the Raja of the senses, the Thought-Producer, he who awakes illusion." Later, however, in the Third Fragment of *The Voice of the Silence*, we read: "Thou hast to reach that fixity of mind in which no breeze, however strong, can waft an earthly thought within." And of the one who walks the Bodhisattva Path, as it is defined in *The Voice of the Silence*, we are told: "He standeth now like a white pillar to the west, upon whose face the rising sun of thought eternal poureth forth its first most glorious waves. His mind, like a becalmed and boundless ocean, spreadeth out in shoreless space. He holdeth life and death in his strong hand."

The Buddha . . . the ordinary mind . . . the sage of stable mind . . . the "Thought-Producer" . . . "Slayer of the Real" . . . a fixity of mind. What, indeed, is the mind? Where in all these descriptions is the mind itself? And what of the ordinary mind? Whence does it derive, and what is its essential nature? Can we live without the mind? Are mind and heart such opposites that one must choose either to be mindless or to be heartless? Shall we cease thinking because thought itself can entrap us in illusion? Such are only some of the questions that must be raised as we seek to understand the nature of the wise mind, the illumined mind, the mind that is Buddha, the mind of the true yogi, the sage, the Master of Wisdom.

THE ORDINARY MIND

The ordinary mind must be the mind in its original condition. Perhaps it is the original mind itself. Surely it is the mind that is established in order, which arises out of that essential order which is basic to all universal processes, for the Theosophical view proposes that consciousness is primary. It is the mind, then, whose very nature is beauty and harmony. It is the mind cleared of all impediments, all obstructions, all that would obscure clear vision, what HPB called "a direct beholding" of the noumenon underlying all phenomena. If "Buddha is the ordinary mind," as the Chinese sage informed his questioner, then the ordinary mind must be the mind that is awake, that is wise, that is established in true knowing.

Because for so long, particularly in the Western world, we have identified the ordinary mind with the analytical, the scientific, and the logical aspect of thinking, we have failed to recognize the full potential of the mind and its amazingly extraordinary nature. Dividing the mind into two parts, we have scorned what has been termed the *lower*, according value only to that aspect we have called the *higher*. Yet lower and higher are not spatial locations. Rather they describe functions of a single principle, manas, the mind, the cognitive principle, and neither term—lower or higher—should be used in any pejorative sense.

In his book, *Life's Deeper Aspects*, N. Sri Ram, late president of the Theosophical Society, made some very helpful comments that are directly relevant to our present inquiry. Asking the question, "Is man then his mind, and if so, of what nature is that mind?" Sri Ram suggests:

> Obviously the mind is an energy which at every point of its action exhibits consciousness with all its implied capacities in some degree or other. In the process of thinking, this energy moves so quickly, changing direction very readily, is so sensitive and influenced by every circumstance and factor, that it develops an extraordinary complexity in the way it operates.

Proposing that "consciousness, in its essential nature, is sensitiveness itself," he adds that: "The modified consciousness as we find it in ourselves can have varying degrees of sensitivity." Further, as Sri Ram states, "there is no distinction to be made" between being sensitive to one thing or another. In other words, when we are sensitive to the objective world—to that world which lies outside us and all about us, the world that we can examine and measure according to some external standard—we may be said to be using that aspect of the mind, which has been called *lower*. It is the mind outward-turned to the world of matter, of things and objects that appear to be distinct from us, the world in which we live our everyday lives.

There is truly an extraordinary quality to the mind when it is turned outward to seek knowledge of the world of existent things. For such a mind can become extraordinarily sensitive to beauty, whether that beauty be perceived in the face of another, in the form of a great work of art, or in the exquisite harmony of a mathematical equation. The sensitivity of the mind of a great scientist exploring the wonders of the cosmos finds its counterpart in the sensitivity of the great artist perceiving in the world about him the wonders of form and color. True, such a mind, absorbed in the world of things, can become obscured by what Patañjali, the great expounder of yoga, called the *kleshas*, the psychological afflictions which cast shadows on the mind, distorting vision and thereby reducing sensitivity. Most dangerous of these afflictions producing the greatest distortions of true vision are egoism and desire for the personal self, leading to attachment and all its attendant problems. Hence, the aim of yoga: to bring the mind to its original nature by the cessation of the modifications of the thinking principle. For this, one must, as *The Voice of the Silence* advises, "seek out the Raja of the senses, the thought producer, he who awakes illusion." To quote *The Voice* further: "Thou shalt not let thy senses make a playground of thy mind."

THE SUBJECTIVE MIND

So when the outward-turned aspect of the mind is cleared of all personal attachments and repulsions, free of desire for the personal self, when it can see the world about it without distortion, perceive its exquisite beauty and wonder, the mind displays an extraordinary quality. Equally extraordinary is the quality of the mind that may be called subjective, the mind turned inward toward the realm of the noumenal, which underlies the phenomenal, the realm of the archetypes, of spiritual reality. In such a movement within there is, as Sri Ram has said, "the possibility of knowing all that exists, responding to it and experiencing it." And he has added: "Although we do not know this possibility as a fact, yet it is an illuminative idea, logical and satisfying to one's sense of fitness and completeness." In even approaching that possibility, via the inward-turned mind, we begin to recognize the great creative powers of the mind, the image-making faculty we call imagination and the faculties of inspiration and discriminative wisdom. Here too we touch on the awesome quality of love or compassion, which is a direct reflection of the One Supreme Spirit, the One Creative Energy in the universe. And that primal energy is not only love; it is thought, ideation, the outpouring of the Universal Mind.

HPB referred to the two aspects of the mind's function in many of her writings. Discussing the "Nature of the Thinking Principle" in *The Key to Theosophy*, she wrote:

> The clue lies in the double consciousness of our mind, and also, in the dual nature of the mental "principle." There is a spiritual consciousness, the Manasic mind illumined by the light of Buddhi, that which subjectively perceives abstractions; and the sentient consciousness (the lower "Manasic" light), inseparable from our physical brain and senses. (Blavatsky 1972b, 110)

That the mind is essential to our human state is made very clear in *The Secret Doctrine*:

The two higher principles *can have no individuality on Earth,* cannot be *man,* unless there is . . . the Mind, the *Manas-Ego,* to cognize itself. (1979, 2:241)

In addition, there must be what HPB called "the body of egotistical desires and personal Will," even though it is from or within that "body" that arise the psychological afflictions that obscure or contaminate the mind. To complete the picture, HPB indicated that it is these two principles, the fifth (manas) and the fourth (kama) which "cement the whole, as round a pivot . . . to the physical form of man."

MANASAPUTRAS

Considering further the fifth principle, manas, we must give attention to its uniqueness, for it is the very uniqueness of its origin that gives to the mind its truly extraordinary nature. Two quotations from HPB will help us understand this subject. First, from *The Key to Theosophy,* again from the section on the "Nature of the Thinking Principle":

Manas is a principle, and yet it is an Entity and individuality or Ego. (Blavatsky 1972b, 113)

Elaborating on this point, she indicated that this entity incarnated in nascent humanity at a certain stage of development to awaken manas into full activity. This "entity is called in its plurality Manasaputras, 'the Sons of the (Universal) Mind . . .'" Then follows a most significant statement:

Once imprisoned, or incarnate, their essence becomes dual: that is to say, the "rays" of the eternal divine Mind, considered as individual entities, assume a twofold attribute which is (a) their "essential" inherent characteristic, heaven-aspiring mind . . . and (b) the human quality of thinking, or animal cogitation . . . the "Kama"-tending or lower Manas. (ibid., 113)

When HPB wrote the *Key*, this description of manas as an entity had already been explained in some detail in *The Secret Doctrine*. The entire subject of the descent of the Manasaputras deserves close study if one would understand fully the implications of the teaching given to us in regard to the fifth principle or manas. Suffice it for our present purposes to quote just one passage from *The Secret Doctrine*:

Between man and the animal—whose Monads (or Jivas) are fundamentally identical—there is the impassable abyss of Mentality and Self-consciousness. What is human mind in its higher aspect, whence comes it, if it is not a portion of the essence—and, in some rare cases of incarnation, the *very essence*—of a higher Being: one from a higher and divine plane? . . . man is an animal *plus* a *living god* within his physical shell. (Blavatsky 1979, 2:81)

The relationship between those whom HPB termed the Manasaputras, those great intelligences who awakened the spark of manas within the gradually developing human forms at an earlier stage of evolution, and ourselves, is a fascinating study, however difficult and abstruse. Even the few references cited above should indicate to us the extraordinary nature of the mind, the mind in its ordinary or original condition. Manas is truly "embodied spirit," to use one of HPB's designations for it; it is a god within the outer form of our existence, and it provides us with access to the Supreme Reality which is Universal Consciousness. For we are rooted in consciousness, *Mahat,* the Universal Mind, as indeed is all existence. In us, in the human, that consciousness is flowering into full Self-consciousness. In us, therefore, are all the powers, all the beauty, wisdom and splendor of self-reflective consciousness.

THE MIND AS MANTRA

In that profound and beautiful text of Kashmir Shaivism, the *Siva Sutras,* which Dr. Jaideva Singh called the *Yoga of Supreme Identity,* there is a simple but highly significant aphorism, "*Cittam mantrah.*" Dr. Singh has translated this as "The mind is mantra," commenting that "By intensive awareness of one's identity with the Highest Reality enshrined in a "mantra" and thus becoming identical with that Reality the mind itself becomes mantra." This mind that is or becomes mantra must be the inward-turned, the heaven-aspiring aspect of the mind, or the mind that is, as one commentary has it, "a throb or pulsation of pure Consciousness" (see *Looking In, Seeing Out* by Menas Kafatos and Thalia Kafatou). According to Dr. Singh, the term mantra in the context of the aphorism in the *Siva Sutras* is more than a particular combination of letters or a sacred formula. It is, he suggests, "the heart-seed of *Siva,*" or the Supreme, adding, "He who can enter into the spirit of this mantra will be identified with the Supreme I-consciousness and will be liberated." At the same time, as Dr. I. K. Taimni points out in his commentary on the aphorism (see *The Ultimate Reality and Realization*), the word mantra basically means *sound,* but in its widest sense "any vibration or motion." Elaborating on the idea that the "differentiated states of mind are nothing but mantras" because they are composed of different "vibrations," Dr. Taimni proposes that since thoughts and ideas are essentially motions in consciousness, we can consider "the manifested universe from a deeper point of view . . .

as an ocean of thoughts and ideas on the subjective side and a flux of motions and vibrations on the objective side."

Now bringing these concepts together—that manas or mind is truly a "living god," an "embodied spirit," and is also mantra or vibration—we can begin to explore further something of the extraordinary nature of the mind. Even the ordinary mind, which as we have suggested is the original mind, the mind or consciousness in its original state, possesses extraordinary capacities. Preeminent among those capacities must be the power to create, to produce images that embody the great archetypal patterns in Universal Mind. As we are rooted in the Universal Mind or Mahat, we must possess or at least reflect those faculties inherent in that Source which HPB called the *Great Architect*. We, in our turn, can become creators of forms from patterns in Universal Mind. This inherent, yet extraordinary, power we may call the spiritual imagination. It is the power that makes us cocreators with the Universal, for truly we live in a participatory universe as many prominent scientists today are suggesting.

While science has to a large extent made the logical, analytical, and mathematical functions of the ordinary mind the basis for all knowledge, we may now recognize the necessity to couple those functions with the deeper, more all-embracing, creative aspects of consciousness which arise in and flow from the mind, inwardly illumined by the energy of wisdom, compassionate understanding. Only through an awakening of a genuine spiritual imagination can we discover that the liberation of the human spirit may be achieved. This is not anti-science, for the function of science, in terms of its essential methodology, is to test the imagination, as every genuine scientist knows. The liberation of the human spirit is possible, as much through that science which is open to intuitive perception or imagination as through the leap from the analytical and logical mode of thought into the creative and symbolic mode. The flow of energy may be, and must be, as much from below upwards as from above downwards.

What may be proposed, then, is that there needs to be, first, the recognition that manas, the cognitive mind or consciousness, is a god within us, and, second, that it therefore has god-like capacities of imagination and creativity. These are indeed extraordinary capacities, but ever present in and available to the ordinary mind, the orderly and original mind. These are the capacities, which not only give meaning and purpose to existence, but also draw us into the future. Over a century ago, the American philosopher, Ralph Waldo Emerson, said: "What lies before us and what lies behind us is a small matter compared to what lies within us." To which his colleague, Henry David Thoreau, added: "And when we bring what lies within us out into the world, miracles happen." When we tap the extraordinary powers of the ordinary mind, that mind which is a "living god" and which is mantra, we do indeed perform miracles, for we remake both ourselves and the world. This is the genuine reformation which is necessary today.

We may well ask: What is the nature of the act of thought when, in one brilliant moment, there is a sudden veering of attention, a consequent grasp of new understandings, and a new idea is born? What is the nature of that act by which we suddenly see a new aspect of life, perceive a meaning that is so much more complete and whole than any perception we have had before? The sudden, accurate leaping of mind across all barriers and into new fields of knowledge and understanding is perhaps best described as a "flash of insight." It is the moment of coming fully awake, the moment so beautifully described by Arjuna when he said, "Destroyed is my delusion, I have gained knowledge . . . I am firm, my doubts have fled away." At such a time, insight must be translated into *outsight*, to coin a word, which means into action in the world.

When the Third Object of our Society directs our attention to an investigation of still unexplained laws of nature and their corresponding powers latent in every individual, I would suggest that one aspect of that exploration must be into those capacities of manas, of mind and consciousness, which lead to an awakening of a new mode of perception and consequently a new mode of action in the world. What we are talking about is not psychic perception as it is usually understood, although from a psychological point of view it may be the total perception of the psyche when it is illumined by the light of buddhi, moved by that energy which is compassionate wisdom. It is the perception of the spiritually illumined consciousness to which HPB gave the designation *manas-taijasa*, the radiant or resplendent mind.

AWAKENING THE IMAGINATIVE MODE OF THOUGHT

The question now arises as to how to awaken that imaginative mode of thought, a mode all too often neglected and even excluded from any consideration of the mind. Yet it is only as we nurture the imaginative mode, the intuitive, the symbolic, the mode of conceptual synthesis, that we come to realize the full potential of the mind and its extraordinary nature. It is the imaginative mode of thought which helps to awaken true insight and understanding. While it is the outward-turned aspect of the mind that may all too easily become ensnared by the energies of desire and passion and may even create devices for destruction as well as forms of great beauty, it is the deeper aspect of the mind, the mind illumined from within and responsive to the light of buddhi, that gives rise to ethical action. For the ethos that will characterize our total behavior will arise naturally and spontaneously from the vision we embrace.

When that vision is one of wholeness, of oneness, of unity, we will act accordingly for the benefit of all humanity.

There seems to be general agreement in the spiritual traditions regarding the two essentials required for awakening the intuitive or imaginative mode of consciousness: conscious effort and intense concentration or one-pointedness. When the mind is held steady, focused, then the sudden and unexpected flash of illumination marked by a feeling of certitude may occur. This is the leap into a new state of consciousness, in which the personal self and its attachments disappear. But the mind needs to be equipped with materials with which to make the leap, for imagination cannot flower in a vacuum. The flash of inner illumination is favored by a disciplined grasp of, and an intense concern for, the fundamental principles that provide the stimulus needed to precipitate the new vision.

Actually, imagination—the spiritual imagination—is the universal and indispensable instrument of all levels of living in our world. Our daily lives are dependent on it, for all day long we imagine our way from one activity to the next, from one location to another, visualizing alternate courses of action as well as alternative consequences. It may be suggested, in fact, that the principal function of the imagination is to enable the human being constantly to build thought models of the real world. By thought, we create the virtual reality in which we live and when thought is uncluttered, free, unfettered by desire and egoism, the virtual reality we create is closer to the one true reality out of which all existence emerged.

M. C. Richards in her work, *Toward Wholeness*, has expressed the implications of a truly spiritual and creative imagination. She has written:

> The renewal of society will come when we can imagine it differently and when we are ready, like artists, to take on the actual work of creating new forms. (1980, 191)

But we are called not simply to creativity, but to a creativity which is in the service of compassion, for compassion is the goal of the spiritual journey.

When we promote imagination to the rank of the primary creative agency of the human mind in its highest functioning, we can, to coin a word, "nirvanise" the world. As William Blake, the great English poet and mystic, once wrote: "If the doors of perception were cleansed, everything would appear to man as it is, infinite." It is for us to "cleanse the doors of perception," through meditation, concentration and one-pointed attention to the highest we know. This is the supremely human task, to see things as they really are, to rid ourselves of the illusions brought on by selfish motives, to lift ourselves out of the sham world of hypocrisy and cant, to straighten out our values, and through the awakening of the creative potential within us, to bring about a new vision of a world in which peace and brotherhood are the norms of existence.

It has been suggested that imagination can tidy up the chaos of sense experience, for it can perceive a deeper significance to daily events and can awaken us to the need for a genuine morality, an ecological morality, which is the ethic of the spirit. It is the stable mind, the mind, crystal clear, reflecting the light of wisdom, the mind that through the exercise of its extraordinary nature can visualize and therefore bring into existence the noble society of which we dream.

When we recognize the role of the mind and its vast possibilities—the mind as Buddha, the mind as mantra, the mind as that principle in us which is a "living god" and which at the same time defines our human state, we begin to realize that the function of imagination is to make palpable the fact that matter in its subjective aspect is spirit, while spirit, regarded objectively, is the material world. This is to say that the world of things (samsara) is nirvana, and nirvana is samsara. All depends on our point of view. The realization of this changes our total vision and with a change of perception, our behavior, our modes of action in the world, completely change.

According to Dr. Carl Jung, images are the basic givens of all psychic life and the privileged mode of access to the knowledge of the Self within. Imagination, then, underlies all perceptual and cognitive processes. Indeed, from an epistemological point of view, images are the only reality we apprehend directly: everything we know is transmitted by images, for images are the fundamental facts of human existence. It is from the stuff of images that we create our world, just as we ourselves were "imaged forth" into time and space from the "stuff" of Universal Mind. Nurturing our spiritual imagination, calling on our own deific powers of creativity, we may image forth into manifest existence a nobler and more beautiful society.

So the ordinary mind reveals its extraordinary nature. It is the mind illumined from within, the mind awake to the direct perception of the One Reality abiding in all things. It is the mind alight with the refulgence of the Spiritual Self. It is the mind, therefore, that is one with the heart in seeking to serve all beings. Our task, it may be said, is to transform kama-manas into buddhi-manas, the mind driven by desire to the mind illumined by love. In that transformation we release all the potentials of the "living god" within us: compassion and caring, humility and gentleness, patience and an infinite concern for the welfare of all. And in that transformation, we will have obeyed the injunction of the Buddha, "to produce love in one's mind," a love that *knows* there is no other. For there is only the One ever remembering Itself as It reveals Itself in countless forms.

DHARMA:
THE LAW OF OUR BEST BEING

Published in *The Theosophist,* Volume 127, January 2006

Some years ago, at a convention of the Theosophical Society in America, Dr. Ravi Ravindra gave an address using as his title the simple question, "Pilgrim, What Calls You?" The talk itself opened with the suggestion that Dr. Ravindra "wished to engage in what may be called an inter-pilgrim dialogue." Now, as a fellow pilgrim (and I really think all true Theosophists are fellow pilgrims), I have been pondering how to answer that question, "Pilgrim, What Calls You?"

Perhaps what really calls each of us may be the fulfillment of our individual unique vocation, whether we are able to express that calling clearly and succinctly or only intuitively feel that there is a goal towards which we are moving, but which we cannot define in words. Let me suggest, however, that there is one concept that may prove to be a useful answer to the query before us. That concept is best comprehended in the one word dharma. That word itself is one of many meanings, while at the same time pointing beyond any of the meanings that may be assigned to it.

As we know, the word appears in the original Sanskrit version of the motto of the Theosophical Society, a phrase taken from the

great Indian epic, the Mahabharata: "*Satyat paro nasti dharmah.*"
H. P. Blavatsky translated the word as "religion," so we have the
English version of our motto, "There is no religion higher than
Truth." In the Bhagavad Gita, the word appears about twenty times
throughout the course of the eighteen chapters of that work. While
Annie Besant in her translation of the *Gita* most often translated
dharma as "duty," she also translated it as "family traditions," "caste
. . . and family customs," "knowledge," "righteousness," "law," "life-
giving wisdom," or "right." In her little book entitled *Dharma*, Dr.
Besant referred to it as the law of our best being, the law that pulls
us to the future (in contradistinction to karma, which pushes us
from the past). Dharma, she said further, is "the law of the unfolding life . . . the law of growth" and is intimately connected with
morality or how one conducts one's life.

As I was contemplating all the meanings inherent in and surrounding the word *dharma,* I had occasion to visit my tax consul-
tant, who is a Jain, an émigré from north India. As he is familiar
with the Theosophical Society, we often speak of India and our
respective experiences in that country, he as a native-born Indian,
and I as a one-time resident at, and frequent visitor to, our world
headquarters, Adyar. So on one occasion, I asked him if the concept
of dharma was part of the Jain religion, to which he responded in
the affirmative, although, he said, it is more a part of Buddhism
than of Jainism. Then as I explained my feeling for the word, saying
that it pointed to the idea of lawfulness and order in the universe
and in one's life, he said: "Yes, it is really the idea of the way things
should be." That, I thought, is really a very good definition: the way
things should be. And the way things should be represents what
calls us, as pilgrims, on the journey towards truth or understanding.

Now I realize that Theosophists are often criticized for using
too many Sanskrit terms, and I, myself, have often been asked why
we must employ a language so unfamiliar to the general public in

order to explain many of the principles and concepts of Theosophy.
Of course, the word *karma* has entered into the English lexicon and
even the term Atman is not unknown to the non-Sanskrit student.
But dharma? Interestingly enough, as I was considering this topic as
the basis for an article, I received an announcement from the C. G.
Jung Foundation of New York, listing their continuing education
classes. Among the offerings listed was one entitled "Turning Karma
to Dharma," the presenter being an American Jungian. So I decided
to consult my dictionary—*Webster's Third International*—and, lo
and behold, there was the word, with quite a lengthy definition—in
fact multiple definitions—including "that which is established . . .
duty . . . custom . . . body of cosmic principles by which all things
exist . . . essential function . . . moral law . . . justice . . . conduct
appropriate to one's essential nature . . . establishing the morally
sound life." Now if the word has found its way into an American
dictionary, then surely the concept or concepts it conveys cannot be
alien to us.

So I propose that it is not inappropriate to use this beautiful
word, dharma, and to spend a little time exploring, in our inter-
pilgrim dialogue, this multi-meaning concept of dharma, for if this
is what really calls us—or at least calls me—then it is necessary to
understand the idea as comprehensively as possible. Dr. S. Radhakrishnan, one-time president of India, has written in his work,
Indian Philosophy (1951, 1:52), that next to the category of Reality,
that of dharma is the most important concept in Indian thought. It
is, as Prof. Radhakrishnan goes on to point out, a necessary sequence
of the basic postulate of the One Reality, for as "the law of morality"
dharma is "an invitation to perform a task—the greatest task—
which is realizing" Brahman or the One Reality in ourselves. In a
relatively little-known book, *The State*, by Dr. Krishna P. Mukerji,
published by the Theosophical Publishing House, Adyar (1952,
321–46), a lengthy appendix explores in some depth the "Hindu

Conception of Dharma." Dr. Mukerji writes that the one factor in common among all the definitions of dharma is "the assumption of a *law of our being* inspired by the One Reality pervading and penetrating the entire universe, to act according to which is *desirable, moral,* and conducive to fulfilment . . . The moral or dharmic life is an imperative necessity for an awakened soul or one who is alive to his relation with the universe, for dharma or natural law is the law of the universal order . . . The discovery of one's dharma in a particular situation (on which one's ability to lead a moral life entirely depends) would mean the discovery of a way of life or mode of conduct which would be in consonance with the law of one's being."

The Theosophical writer, Dr. J. J. van der Leeuw, in his beautiful book, *The Conquest of Illusion,* speaks of dharma as "that which is lawful, right and fitting," going on to explain that this rightness would be law in social procedure, duty in the life of the individual, and truth in religious and philosophical matters. Dharma, in other words, applies universally, in all areas and circumstances, in all fields of existence as well as in our individual lives.

In an article which appeared in *The American Theosophist* in 1982, the art historian and critic, Dr. Jose Arguelles, wrote of "Dharma Art: Universal Law and Human Order." Arguelles proposes that "there is no separation between art, politics, or religion," adding: "What this assumption implies is a universal principle which, while imbuing humanity with its purpose, also extends to a definition of the purposefulness, orderliness, and beauty of the universe itself." The very idea of a "universal purposefulness" suggests Arguelles, is "a common ground of goodness which extends equally to every living being." To describe that universal principle, as well as the idea of a common ground of goodness, Arguelles focuses on two terms: first, to express an idea "common to the heritage of the East," he has chosen dharma, joining with that a concept "common to the heritage of the West," defined by the Greek word *aristos.*

Both terms, he suggests, refer to the "basic goodness" (which for the Greek world was the natural basis for aristocracy) and the "all-embracing law or principle" implied by dharma. The two terms are complementary, each supporting the other, one giving validity or meaning to the other. As Arguelles explains:

> If we look back to the earlier stages of our common development to that age when reflection and contemplation first began to embellish the leisure time of our forebears . . . some such notion as dharma presented itself. Indeed, it is impossible to consider everything that dharma means and implies without some recourse to the very same act of contemplation by which the concept revealed itself and the word was uttered in the first place. In fact from the perspective of natural aristocracy . . . one cannot fully appreciate the meaning of *aristos* apart from the act of contemplation by which dharma is experienced. (Arguelles 1982, 70, no. 8)

Then he goes on to suggest, "From this we draw the common inference that our basic goodness and our dignity . . . are inextricably interwoven with dharma, just as dharma is imprinted upon all that is." In other words, when that which is the best in us (which from the Platonic point of view would be the good, the true, and the beautiful inherent in our essential being) is in concord with the lawfulness, the purposefulness, the order of the universe, then we will act or do what is right and appropriate in every situation. Or, to put it in another way, as Arguelles states: "When society develops in disregard of the . . . process by which insight into dharma is joined with aristos, conflict, war, and degradation arise. In fact, no intelligent action is conceivable without the union of dharma and aristos." This, we might say, is very clearly the lesson that Krishna imparts to Arjuna in the Bhagavad Gita. What is required, Arguelles argues, "if the present dark age is to be illumined at all," is "skilful behavior, based on the contemplation of the universal law, dharma." Such a statement could well have been taken directly from the Gita.

It may be useful to pause here to consider at least briefly the concept of aristos, a term from which we derive the word "aristocracy." In what we conceive to be a free and democratic society, there seems a natural distaste for, a deep-seated suspicion of, that word. But as with so many words, the accretions of human prejudice, often born of ignorance, have caused the original meaning of aristos and its derivatives, "aristocracy" and "aristocrat," to be enshrouded to such an extent that we are no longer comfortable in using them. To quote Arguelles on this matter, "Human institutions, and indeed the very order of society, reflect the inescapable reality of aristos as an enduring human value. Aristos, in fact, is the primary creative, shaping force of human society, for inherent in the basic goodness of human nature is the invisible structure of natural hierarchy." We naturally turn to those we regard as embodying more of that basic goodness than we do ourselves and whose lives, therefore, reveal in their conduct what we may call an "aristos of the spirit." In the context of Theosophical thought as expressed through the structure of the Theosophical Society, many members acknowledge the existence of Mahatmas, or Masters, and their role as Inner Founders of the Society. This is not a dogma, not a required belief, but for many, the natural consequence of their studies into what HPB called "the triple evolutionary scheme": spiritual, intellectual, as well as physical or biological. That is to say, in spiritual and intellectual evolution, there must be those who are superior to us in knowledge, wisdom, and the great spiritual qualities of compassion and understanding.

At the risk of over-quoting Arguelles, let me refer once more to his perceptive analysis of the unique concord between aristos and dharma:

> There is no human society based on recognition of inherent goodness and natural hierarchy that does not also possess that insight into the nature of reality summed up by the word dharma: all-embracing law, that which supports and permeates all different views, elements and experiences of reality.

This, of course, is the ideal, but in our pilgrimage do we not always strive towards the ideal, or at least towards that which we conceive at the moment to be the ideal? And in so striving, do we not attempt to bring forward the best in us, our own "aristos of the spirit"? Was this not indeed the call of Krishna to Arjuna, to remember your "aristos," your natural dignity as a human being, and so fulfill your dharma? Karma may have placed you in difficult circumstances, or at least in circumstances where to know what is right to do demands a difficult decision, but the other side of the law, if we may refer to the ultimate law of the universe as double-sided, demands that you act in accordance with your dharma, that which seeks the fulfillment of the divine purpose to which you have been called. When Arjuna falls down in despair, Krishna reminds him not of the past which brought him to the battlefield, his karma, but calls him to his present obligation, ". . . looking to thine own dharma, thou shouldst not tremble . . . He who doeth the dharma laid down by his own nature incurreth not sin" (Bhagavad Gita, 2.31 and 18.47).

In considering the many definitions of the term dharma, we begin to realize that no single English word conveys all its richness of meaning. So we may say that while in so many instances the word *duty* is used, there is always the overtone of that lawfulness and purposefulness which derive from the realization that there is but One Reality in which all life and all existence is rooted. We need to keep this in mind, I suggest, when we read certain statements concerning duty in those letters written by HPB's Adept Teachers to some of the early members of the Society, most notably to A. P. Sinnett. For example, while the word *dharma* is not used, surely it is implicit in such statements as those made by the Mahatma Morya, in Letter 29 of *The Mahatma Letters to A. P. Sinnett*: "law is LAW with us, and no power can make us abate one jot or tittle of our duty." In that same letter, there is the beautiful expression of what has been called throughout the letters an "unconditional absolute principle of morality"; as the Mahatma tells Sinnett: "I am as I was; and as I was and am, so am I likely always to be—the slave of my duty to the Lodge and mankind; not only taught but desirous to subordinate every preference for individuals to a love for the human race." Pilgrim, what calls you? In the life of the Mahatma, what calls is his compassion for all humanity; in our lives, what calls us must surely be our growing awareness of the One Life in which all existence is rooted.

In Letter 126, the Mahatma K. H. echoes his Brother, indicating a wider meaning to the word *duty* that can only be understood by recognizing its spiritual as well as ethical connotations. K. H. tells Sinnett, "duty . . . is for us stronger than any friendship or even love; as without this abiding principle which is the indestructible cement that has held together for so many milleniums, the scattered custodians of Nature's grand secrets—our Brotherhood, nay our doctrine itself—would have crumbled long ago into unrecognizable atoms." Note the words, "abiding principle"; these must surely apply to the larger context in which the word "duty" is normally used, to the fullness of all that dharma means and implies.

So when HPB, in writing of "What is Practical Theosophy?" in *The Key to Theosophy*, states, "Theosophy is the quintessence of *duty*," she also must have had in mind that larger meaning of the word "duty" which derives from the whole idea of "dharma." Remember that in adopting the Sanskrit statement from the Mahabharata, borrowing the family motto of the Maharaja of Banaras, she translated the term "dharma" as "religion." Therefore, one could say that HPB might just as well have written that the "quintessence of Theosophy is religion" or equally that "Theosophy is the quintessence of Law." In fact, as she discusses the subject of practical Theosophy further, writing that "Duty is that which *is due* to Humanity, to our fellow men, neighbors, family, and especially that which we owe to all those who are poorer and more helpless than we are ourselves," she adds, "This is a debt which, if left unpaid during life, leaves us spiritually insolvent and moral bankrupts in our next incarnation," thus linking the two great aspects of Universal Law, karma and dharma; and, if we need but one word for the Law itself, a word that truly unites karma and dharma, we find it in *The Voice of the Silence*: compassion. Recall the words: "Compassion is no attribute. It is the Law of LAWS . . . the light of everlasting Right, and fitness of all things, the law of love eternal. The more thou dost become at one with it, thy being melted in its BEING, the more thy Soul unites with that which Is, the more thou wilt become COMPASSION ABSOLUTE" (Fragment 3. 300–1).

Now in all of this exploration of the multi-meaningfulness of as simple a term as dharma, and even staying with its interpretation as *duty*, where are we—you and I—answering its call on our inter-pilgrim journey? To what task does dharma call us? In one of the early letters to Sinnett, the Mahatma K.H. puts the matter very directly: "it is the duty of every [individual] who is capable of an unselfish impulse to do something, however little, for [humanity's] welfare" (Mahatma Letter 15). Yet even this could make it seem too large a work for us, if our every action or thought must be directed to the greater cause of human welfare, while we are all the time absorbed in daily affairs that have little if any relevance to the world at large. The immediate question really is: how can we, as one writer has put it, "give [our] religious and spiritual ideas the incarnation of daily activity?" (A quote from an interview with Dr. Robert Coles, child psychiatrist, who teaches at Harvard University, as published in *Parabola*, Spring 1994.)

There is a brief letter from the Mahatma K. H. to Mr. Sinnett that, to some extent, addresses this issue of incarnating dharma in our normal round of activities. Although undated, this letter has been placed as number 123 in the chronological edition of the *Letters*, which seems quite appropriate considering the circumstances of Sinnett's life at about that time, early 1884. Those familiar with both the *Letters* and the events surrounding Sinnett at that period will remember that Sinnett, having lost his post as editor of the Allahabad *Pioneer*, returned to England with his wife and son in 1883. Within a few months after his return, there was to be an election of officers in the London Lodge, of which Anna Kingsford was then president and therefore a candidate for re-election. Sinnett assumed that because of his correspondence with the Mahatmas, as well as his exposition of the Theosophical philosophy based on that correspondence published in his two books, *The Occult World* and *Esoteric Buddhism*, he would naturally be elected to the presidency of the Lodge. However, without going into further detail concerning the election itself and the several Mahatmic letters about it, we may just complete the story of that event by noting that neither Mrs. Kingsford nor Mr. Sinnett was elected, but a compromise candidate, G. B. Finch, became the London Lodge president.

So to return to Letter 123, we do know that Sinnett's departure from India, following the loss of employment, the entire episode at the London Lodge, the concern over financial matters in resettling in England which entailed finding a suitable house for the family— his wife, Patience, and his ailing son, Denny—as well as locating a journalistic position that would provide a steady income, all conspired to leave him rather discouraged and despairing of the future. After the publication of *Esoteric Buddhism*, much of which had been written on board ship during their long journey homewards, Sinnett was now having less and less time for the study of occultism and therefore less time to address questions to his two Adept correspondents. We can well imagine his mood of despondency, perhaps even a feeling of failure, causing him, we may assume, to write to the Mahatma K. H. that he had been so caught up in family duties that he had had no time for more serious and, as he thought, more important matters. It is to this whole complex of emotional and mental turmoil on the part of Sinnett that K. H. addresses his brief note, saying to Sinnett:

> Does it seem to you a small thing that the past year has been spent only in your 'family duties?' Nay, but what better cause for reward, what better discipline, than the daily and hourly performance of duty? Believe me, my 'pupil,' the man or woman who is placed by Karma in the midst of small plain duties and sacrifices and loving-kindness, will through these faithfully ful filled rise to the larger measure of Duty, Sacrifice and Charity to all Humanity—what better path towards the enlightenment you are striving after than the daily conquest of Self, the perseverance in spite of want of visible psychic progress, the bearing of ill-fortune with that serene fortitude which turns it to spiritual advantage. . . . Be not discouraged that your practice falls below your aspirations, yet be not content with *admitting* this, since you clearly recognize that your tendency is too often towards mental and moral indolence, rather inclining to drift with the currents of life, than to steer a direct course of your own . . . this is but a line of sympathetic recognition of your efforts, and of earnest encouragement to hold a calm and brave spirit towards outward events in the present, and a hopeful spirit for the future. (1993, Letter 123)

This was certainly a beautiful and heartwarming response to Sinnett's downcast mood. And a reminder that dharma does not always call us to the great and noble acts of charity and compassion nor always to heroic action on the vast battlefield of the world's Kurukshetra. It may well be that in the performance of the "small plain duties" of daily existence we are heeding the call of dharma. In fact, it may be suggested that those very "plain duties," when perceived as the fulfillment of our immediate responsibility, our dharma, that which we are called to do at the moment, may be invested with an aura of sacredness. In other words, by considering the everyday tasks to which we are called as our present dharma, the dharma of the moment, so to say, we bring to bear on their performance the richer meaning inherent in the very word dharma.

As we consider the full range of meaning implicit in the concept of dharma, then, we may recognize that we must also consider the extent to which that concept frees us to act in accordance with our best being and so to move us forward or onward or upward, whichever term seems to describe the direction of our movement, towards the fulfillment of our essential purpose. How we choose to act at every moment, to engage ourselves in the necessary tasks of daily life, determines the extent to which we feel free or bound. Always there is the freedom of choice, and that too is part of our dharma. The normal course of living demands that certain things be accomplished, but it is I alone who will determine how those things will be done. If I choose to feel constricted and entangled by the "small plain duties" that characterize my day—preparing meals, sweeping the floor, washing the dishes—then I am indeed bound and may even begin to resent what seems to be my karma in binding me within the confines of circumstances that appear to hold no possibility for the growth of spirit. But if, on the other hand, I choose to see in each of the necessary tasks of the day an opportunity to be more efficient in their performance, to learn whatever lesson each task may hold, to do my very best, then to some extent at least I have begun to turn karma into dharma, to loosen the bonds that have held me captive to the past in order to move freely into the future.

Numerous examples come to mind, but perhaps one out of my own experience will suffice. I recall so vividly one of the first tasks I was given when I joined the American Section headquarters' staff in 1942. It was to collate the pages of a study course which had just been produced on a very old mimeograph machine, so what was entailed was walking around a long table on which the pages had been stacked, picking up the pages one by one and ultimately stapling each set. A boring task, if ever there were one, and tiring as well; my mind, of course, was taunting me with rather devilish statements: "So this is what you went to graduate school to do!" and "So much for your noble motive to serve the Society." Then, after a while, I began to sense there could be a kind of rhythm to the work and that it was even possible to find different ways to organize the process. Finally, by realizing the simple fact that someone had to do this, and so it might as well be me, the youngest member of the staff, I consciously decided to "will" that each set, as I completed assembling it, would go to someone who would join the Society as a result of studying the papers I was putting together as neatly as I could. I even developed a little mantra: "Join, join, you will like it!" And I visualized 500 new members joining the Society, and of course somewhere in the ledger book of karma, I would receive the credit!

Freedom? At least I began to have a little fun in performing a task that, at first, I had found boring, and I certainly realized that I was free to choose my reaction to the assignment I had been given. My karma or my dharma? Perhaps a bit of both: ready-money karma, as we used to label it, for the pride I felt in bringing my graduate-school (superior) mind to the service of the Society; and at-the-moment, or perhaps it should be called in-the-now dharma, in performing a task that could or might ultimately bring

Theosophy to an unknown number of students who would be taking the study course. There indeed lies freedom: in the choice we make of our reactions to, our attitudes towards, our behavior in, any situation or circumstance in which we find ourselves. Fulfilling the responsibility of the moment, seeing it as a step towards what the Mahatma called "the larger measure of Duty, Sacrifice and Charity to all Humanity," we follow that inner lawfulness of our "best being," the highest we know in ourselves. We respond to the call of dharma and move confidently towards the ever-expanding frontiers of our own nature. There, or rather, here, is the adventure!

"Pilgrim, what calls you?" If I have responded with that single and, to me, singularly beautiful, word dharma, it is because within that word or surrounding it is all that draws me onwards and forwards: love and compassion and understanding and truth itself, as well as duty and responsibility, and the task immediately before me. All that has ever been, all my past, has brought me to this moment, to these circumstances, to this present unique occasion, as the Buddhist teacher, Tsong Khapa, spoke of the place where one is at any given time. But as a pilgrim, on a long and frontierless, even pathless, pilgrimage, I am called to bring to this here-now, this only time-place, the full aristos of spirit, and so to act in obedience to the one universal Law which is both wisdom and compassion, both truth and love, both beauty and goodness.

I can do no better in concluding these remarks, as my contribution to our inter-pilgrim dialogue, than by quoting Dr. Ravi Ravindra, whose question, "Pilgrim, what calls you?" has been my own inquiry. Concluding his talk on that question, Dr. Ravindra quoted the *Theologia Germanica*: "As God is simple goodness, inner knowledge and light, he is at the same time also our will, love, righteousness and truth, the innermost of all virtues." "The realization of this truth," Dr. Ravindra went on to say, "vouchsafed to the most insightful sages in all lands and cultures . . . needs to be continually regained, lived and celebrated." Thus it is that the adventure continues as that which calls us, lures us, ever onwards.

ESOTERIC
TEACHINGS

WHAT IS IT TO LIVE THEOSOPHY?

Published in *The American Theosophist*, Volume 32, December 1944

A professor of education, with whom I once studied, facetiously described the learning process as the "transfer of ideas from the teacher's notebook to the student's notebook without passing through the heads of either." This is all too often the case, for it has become an accepted educational axiom that it is more important for the student to know where and how to find a piece of knowledge than to know that knowledge itself. Indeed this is in large measure true, for the "walking encyclopedia" may be intellectual, but he is by no means the complete person.

However, the value of an axiom lies in the exceptions that prove its effectiveness. The transfer of ideas from notebook to notebook leaves the mind sterile, and often it is of more importance to know than to know how to know. It may be more expeditious to know that in chapter 12 of *The Ancient Wisdom*, Dr. Besant gives a concise summary of rounds and chains than to carry constantly in mind exact and complete information on this very erudite subject. Yet it is far more eminently practical to realize the value of such knowledge for daily living. This must ultimately mean that if study is to be practical in its applications, it must not merely pass from mind to mind, but in that passage must flow through the vital channel of the heart, which alone can synthesize and transmute knowledge into living reality.

In the five-fold system in which we are at present evolving, Atma, Manas, and Physical represent the planes of form, and Buddhi and Astral, life. When *Adi* and *Anupadaka*, which at present we do not consciously contact since they are still "in silence and darkness, and are not actually part of our system," are added to complete the seven, we have the familiar three planes of life and four of form. [Here Annie Besant by including Adi and Anupadaka in the sevenfold system departs from Blavatsky's terminology.] Picturing the planes in the usual ladder-like formation, we sometimes fail to appreciate the interleaving that actually exists. A life plane is fluidic and therefore overlaps and actually enlivens the form planes, rather than separating them one from another, it is the life that links and unites them. Thus the alternative heart or mind standard of evaluation is eliminated by the realization that only by the combination of the two is knowledge made complete in life.

The mind and the emotions are then inseparable, for they stand in the complementary relation of form to life. In the Fifth Root Race, the task is to bridge Lower and Higher Mind, while in the Sixth Root Race, Astral and Buddhi are to be united. When these unions begin in consciousness, it will depend on the line of the individual, occult or mystic, whether Understanding or Intuition will first make its appearance and become dominant, although ultimately, of course, these will be blended. The average man of today is self-conscious as a personality, of which the life is mainly or principally in the astral. Because of this, the comment is frequent that we are too emotional without rationality. The criticism is not valid when we realize that the life or astral unites the form planes of physical and mental, and does not supplant or divide them. It is for each individual to discover that they are an Ego, of which the life is

Buddhi, for the astral is only, so to speak, a projection of Buddhi on a lower plane. Buddhi is the center of our octave of planes from Adi to Physical, and will be realized as such when we become truly human, linking the highest spirit with the lowest matter self-consciously, for Buddhi is the true seat of consciousness of every human being.

It is usual to conceive of Buddhi and Higher Manas, its vehicle, as associated together, but it is only by realizing that Buddhi and Astral are of the same essential quality that we may understand them. The mind must interpret the intuition and express it through the physical in order to be of service to the world, since the physical is the personal synthesis for other planes. Buddhi, then, is the seed, while the physical is the flower and between them are the connecting links: Higher Manas, Lower Manas, and Astral, all needed in this flow of the life principle. If the mind dominates, it is a cold, clear and not a particularly attractive presentation of the intuition that results. If the emotions dominate, a considerable waste of force results. We must seek to govern our lives from the Egoic level, aiming at equilibrium, balance, poise, and impersonal activity. As we utilize this knowledge in directing our own lives, we raise our information from the diagram stage to the practical application of living Theosophically. No one can do this for us. New concepts may be built, new interpretations given, but the actual work of living remains for us to do alone.

In the "Notes on Some Oral Teachings" of H. P. Blavatsky, appended to the third volume of *The Secret Doctrine*, 1897 Adyar Edition, there appears this statement:

The consciousness which is merely the animal consciousness is made up of the consciousness of all the cells in the body except those of the heart. The heart is the king, the most important organ in the body of man. Even if the head be severed from the body, the heart will continue to beat for thirty minutes. It will beat for some hours if wrapped in cotton wool and put in a warm place. The spot in the heart which is the last of all to die is the seat of life, the center of all, Brahma, the first spot that lives in the fetus and the last that dies. When a Yogi is buried in a trance it is this spot that lives, though the rest of the body be dead, and as long as this is alive the Yogi can be resurrected. This spot contains potentially mind, life, energy, and will . . . The heart is the center of spiritual consciousness, as the brain is the center of intellectual. But this consciousness cannot be guided by a person, nor its energy directed by him until he is one with Buddhi-Manas; until then it guides him—if it can. Hence the pangs of remorse, the prickings of conscience; they come from the heart, not the head. In the heart is the only manifested God, the other two are invisible, and it is this which represents the Triad, Atma-Buddhi-Manas. (Blavatsky 1897, 5:555)

It is, consequently, by making the potential center of the heart active that the life flows through the forms which are its expressions. Remaining as potentialities, life, mind, energy, and will are of as little value as a beating heart stored in a chemical solution. It is the complete infusion of the potentiality of life in the actuality of living that produces the whole person, self-conscious on the Egoic level. The discovery of this interleaving process, in all its aspects, is the fascinating study to which we are led when considering the ramifications of Theosophy in the field of human or social relationships. When viewed as a creative endeavor, the dynamics of emotions are no longer conceived of in patterns of sloppy sentimentality or gushing romanticism, but rather appear as the laborious result of hard thinking. By that we mean that effort, exertion, courage, patience, and inspiration are needed to force knowledge through the straight and narrow channel of the heart, which is the only path that leads to the practical application of wisdom to the service of humanity.

To live Theosophy, then, is to release it from the notebooks, textbooks, diagrams, lectures, and pictures that would retain its heartbeat in an intellectual mold. The mind is needed, but only when it has been infused with the living spirit, derived from the astral, and through the astral from the buddhic. Then it will bring to the world the vital message of a living truth. What is it to live Theosophy? It is to sing with joy, to walk with the rhythm of the universe, to speak in tones of beauty, to work with love, to believe with the confidence and faith of the pure in heart, and to know with an assurance and certainty beyond doubt. To live Theosophy is to live completely. To live completely is to have synthesized the mind and the heart in the interests of the One Self which is in all, and which is All.

THE SECRET DOCTRINE AND ITS STUDY

Published in *The American Theosophist*, Volume 49, May 1961

From time to time, members, individually or in groups, feel that a study of *The Secret Doctrine* is imperative to the deeper pursuit of Theosophical understanding. Such a feeling is both legitimate and justifiable, for until we have come to a contemplation of those universals of the wisdom upon which *The Secret Doctrine* is based, we are as children playing with the mosaics of experience, unperceiving of the magnificent pattern out of which they have emerged. Only as these mosaics are referable to immortal principles can they find their usefulness in applications that are life-releasing.

As search for the jewels of wisdom is undertaken, certain questions arise quite naturally concerning the study of *The Secret Doctrine*. Where do we begin, and how do we proceed? There are as many approaches to the wisdom as there are students, but it may not be amiss to suggest a path whose traversing has proved exciting to one student. It was Plato who said that he was not wise, *sophos*, but a lover of wisdom, *philo Sophia*. Here, too, there is no claim to wisdom but only the love of the chase in pursuit of wisdom. *The Secret Doctrine* is a lifetime study; its pages are not the end of understanding, but channel markers leading to the oceans of universal

148

truth whose reaches stretch to the distant horizons of wisdom. Before we become master mariners, however, we must learn some principles of navigation.

How do we study, then? The reading of any book does not constitute its study. One may read through a great many books, Theosophical and otherwise, and still know very little. To study is to come to grips with the author's thought, with the ideas, the understanding, the illumination that the author has expressed. It is to permit the ideas to permeate without prejudice, without any obstruction, into one's own mind, heart and intuition, so that truth meets truth, the truth in the book studied meeting the truth of one's own inner being. Generally we throw up all sorts of obstructions— nonbelief, incredulity, and so on. We pit our minds against the author's in a tug-of-war that results only in misconceptions and misunderstanding. The mind may critically examine, indeed that is one of its primary functions, but if that critical examination is based on preconceived notions, on prejudices, on psychological impediments, then there is not the true examination and certainly not openness to the pursuit or the perception of truth. To use a well-known phrase, we must "open the doors of the mind" to truth, and the interior evaluation proceeds from a deeper source than the examining mind itself. To study, then, is to align the truth without to the truth perceived within, utilizing every faculty of our being in this process of harmonization.

On this concept of study, the following suggestions for approaching *The Secret Doctrine* are based. For the end of our studies is not that we shall be able to say, parrot-wise, "HPB said . . ." or "*The Secret Doctrine* says . . ." Rather, the end (which is paradoxically the beginning) is that we shall have engaged ourselves wholly and without reservation in the creative encounter with truth that alone can carry us into that realm where the transcendental wisdom is perceived and known.

In the little work by the Countess Constance Wachtmeister and others, *Reminiscences of H. P. Blavatsky and The Secret Doctrine*, Bertram Keightley states:

> When studied thoroughly but not treated as a revelation, when understood and assimilated but not made a text for dogma, HPB's *Secret Doctrine* will be found of incalculable value, and will furnish suggestions, clues, and threads of guidance for the study of Nature and Man, such as no other existing work can supply. (Wachtmeister 1976, 82)

What, then, is *The Secret Doctrine?* This must be our first question if we are to find in it those "suggestions, clues, and threads of guidance" that will aid us in our quest of truth. HPB herself indicated that the written pages contain only a small fragment of the Esoteric Doctrine known to the higher members of the Occult Brotherhood. At that, it contains, as she pointed out, "all that can be given out to the world in this century," and she adds concerning the "Secret Archaic Doctrine" that "it will be centuries before much more is given out." Yet we must also remember that HPB warned us that her work contained many blinds, often concealing as much as was revealed.

In talks with her own class, given in London during the years 1888 to 1891, notes of which have come to us from one of her students, Robert Bowen, HPB said:

> Reading *The Secret Doctrine* page by page as one reads any other book will only end in confusion. The first thing to do, even if it takes years, is to get some grasp of the Three Fundamental Principles given in the Proem.

Then she says further:

If one imagines that one is going to get a satisfactory picture of the constitution of the universe from *The Secret Doctrine*, one will get only confusion from its study. It is not meant to give any such final verdict on existence, but to lead towards the Truth. Come to *The Secret Doctrine* without any hope of getting the final Truth of existence from it, or with any idea other than seeing how far it may lead towards the Truth. See in its study a means of exercising and developing the mind never touched by other studies.

We may conceive of *The Secret Doctrine* as a basic reference work, which one may approach again and again. To know and appreciate it fully, however, demands first that one be familiar to some extent with the life of HPB herself and the way in which she worked. At the outset of any individual or class study, it would be well to give some attention to this matter, acquainting oneself with some of the pertinent material concerning HPB. In this connection, one reference is highly significant for our understanding of *The Secret Doctrine*. In *Letters from the Masters of the Wisdom*, Second Series, edited by C. Jinarajadasa, four letters received by Dr. Hubbe Schleiden, an early member of the Society in Germany, are transcribed. One of these letters, dated 1885, contains this important clue for our study: "It is for his own satisfaction [that is, Dr. Schleiden's] that the undersigned is happy to assure him that *The Secret Doctrine* when ready will be the triple production of M., Upasika and the Doctor's most humble servant. K. H." (Mr. Jinarajadasa comments on this letter that the reference is to the first recension of *The Secret Doctrine*, the original manuscript which is at Adyar, and that the work as published was expanded by HPB to several times the original draft.) The letter from K. H. [Koot Humi] clearly indicates that, as HPB herself stated, she was aided in writing her major work by her Adept Teacher, Morya, and his great brother, K. H.

It has been said that *The Secret Doctrine* should be read with the will, and indeed one does find that it cannot be read with the ordinary mind. To say that it should be read by the will, however, does not mean that we should read it with bursting blood vessels. Rather we may take this to mean that the light of Atma, the illumination of the Self, should be allowed to shine upon our understanding. Our preparation must be such that we have invited the will to illumine our knowledge. Toward this end, our studies might be accompanied by meditation, contemplation, upon those immortal stanzas in *The Voice of the Silence*, which HPB herself recommended as a correlative study to *The Secret Doctrine*. Only with such preparation may one enter inwardly into the depths of the Doctrine. Again, it is not that the mind is set aside, but that the mind has become the pure reflecting mirror for the higher Self to perceive the universals of Reality.

As we come to the volumes with such outer and inner preparation as we can achieve, we may look a little more closely at the purpose of HPB's great work, perceiving also something of its meaning for us. HPB summarized her purpose in part: "The aim of this work may be thus stated: to show that Nature is not 'a fortuitous concurrence of atoms,' and to assign to man his rightful place in the scheme of the Universe" (1979, 1:viii).

In her *Studies in The Secret Doctrine*, Mrs. Josephine Ransom suggests a practicality of the art of dealing with ourselves. "Do not try to make that practicality fit only into the physical world, essential though that is. It is true of all worlds. Let us try to comprehend something of the inner worlds, of the operations of those worlds as suggested in these studies of *The Secret Doctrine*. Thus will we comprehend something of the stupendous inner values of the universe. Let us know something of the metaphysics of the universe, for there the Monad is at work in its own realm." It is with this in mind, with this inner attitude, that one is prepared to enter into that contemplation of eternals which is the study of *The Secret Doctrine.*

Four things the student may discover as he pursues his studies. First, *The Secret Doctrine* indicates that through the comparison of the cosmogonies of the ancients, a perception of true universals may be obtained. Next, it gives a clue with which to unravel the genuine racial history of mankind. Third, it lifts the veil of allegory and symbol to reveal the beauty of truth in all its manifestations. Finally, *The Secret Doctrine* presents to the eager intellect, to the intuition, and to the developed spiritual perception, the scientific secrets of the universe for our total apprehension.

Our approach, then, that we may explore and discover this fourfold vision, may well be in consonance with the method suggested by HPB herself. A thorough acquaintance with the Three Fundamental Propositions is necessary. Quite simply stated, these reveal to us the mysteries of Be-ness, Be-coming and Be-ing. Exploring these Propositions, we find ourselves entering the realm of Reality, from which emerge all laws, all principles, upon which the manifested universe is based. The conceptualizations of Theosophical knowledge find in these three majestic fundamentals, in this triumvirate of Truth, their final validation and confirmation. All principles, all the diversity of manifestation, are referable to these universals. So it is here, I think, we must make our beginning.

Madame Blavatsky then suggested that we "follow that up by the study of the Recapitulation"—the numbered items in the "Summing Up" at the conclusion of volume 1 (1979, 269–99). Here we find six outstanding ideas presented to us, which are necessary for our understanding of the entire *Secret Doctrine.* First, of course, is the fact that the Esoteric Doctrine is "the accumulated Wisdom of the Ages . . . an uninterrupted record" which has come down to us, traced in allegory and symbol, couched in myth and legend, perceptible always to those who desire perception. Second, we are reminded that the fundamental law of the esoteric philosophy is the unity of all things: "'Substance' on the plane of the manifested Universe . . . a 'Principle' in the beginningless and endless, abstract, visible, and invisible Space." We are next reminded of the universal principle of rhythmic unfolding, cyclic manifestation, taking place at every level. The fourth concept introduces us to one of the great mysteries of the esoteric philosophy, the ephemeral nature of all *ex*-istence, the doctrine of maya, unfortunately so often misunderstood. For maya is less illusion, in our ordinary understanding of that word, than it is the measured pace of manifestation. The root word here is *ma*, which means to measure, and the out-turned energies of a Creative Logos result, quite simply, in a measured order, which in the physical world reach their closest confinements in the measurements of time and space. Maya in its highest sense is the creative aspect of reality; not an illusion, it is the producer of all illusory forms, of appearance, change and transitoriness, and is actually the revealer of the spirit that inspires all forms. As HPB points out: "the Universe is real enough to the conscious beings in it" (1979, 1:274), for "the illusion of him who is in himself an illusion differs on every plane of consciousness" (ibid., 329). Consciousness is the measured perception of the one "Substance-Principle," and when measurement ceases, consciousness has moved into the immeasurable Absolute, becoming no-consciousness, the state beautifully described in the First Stanza and the commentary thereon.

The fifth concept of the Recapitulation reminds us that "Everything in the Universe . . . is conscious." It is the development of consciousness that provides the purposefulness of manifestation, and the doctrine of maya takes on new meaning for us. HPB points out later (1979, 1:296) that "the experience on any plane is an actuality for the percipient being, whose consciousness is on that plane." From this point, we may rightly move in our studies to a consideration of part 2 of volume 1, especially the section on

"Primordial Substance and Divine Thought," wherein we are brought face to face with the ordering of the evolutionary process, Cosmic Energy (*Fohat*) measuring out Cosmic Substance (*Akasha*) under the directives of Cosmic Ideation (*Mahat*). Thus the sixth great concept emerges, as HPB summarizes it in her Recapitulation: "The Universe is worked and *guided*, from *within outwards*."

Pondering the universals which are thus set forth for us, we may now move freely through the volumes, seeing the outworking of the great conceptualizations in terms of cosmogenesis and anthropogenesis, finding endless excitement in the correspondences that emerge as we explore the depths of meaning in the universal symbols of creation reflected in the life and heart of man. Pursuing our studies by exploring the many jewels of the wisdom or by tracing out the algebraic formula of creation given us in the Stanzas, we find ourselves, as the Rig Veda puts it, "gazing into eternity ere the foundations of the world were laid."

In our study, we come at last to the ultimate and sublime truth: the Cosmic Logos, the Creative Energy of our Solar System, and the Self in Man, the Inner Ruler Immortal, are ONE. This is the goal of yoga; this is the cosmic religious experience; this is the supreme vision of the mystic. As we remember this profound truth, the deeper awareness of our unity, not only with all manifested life but with the very sources of that life, becomes the abiding principle from which we move. We discover that the pattern of creation, of the Universe and of the Human, resides within the very fiber of our being. It is for us to reveal in conscious yoga that pattern of creation. *The Doctrine* is then our own secret, not so much because it is hidden, but because its very inwardness is inexpressible. The throbbing heartbeat of the Real is matched perfectly within ourselves, and humanity, the microcosm, mirrors the cosmic creative scheme.

A Japanese sage, half a world away in space, and centuries removed in time, said: "Do not try to do what your predecessors did; rather seek what they sought." To study *The Secret Doctrine* in its fullness, to enter creatively into the encounter with immortal wisdom, is to come to HPB's work with open heart and mind, seeking what has been sought by the wise ones through the ages, following the injunction given by HPB herself: "Follow not me, nor my Path, but the Path I show, which leads to the Masters."

WHAT SHALL WE STUDY?

Published in *The American Theosophist*, Volume 52, March 1964

Nowhere, as we have been reminded on many occasions, is there an official definition of Theosophy. Membership in the Society is not dependent upon the acceptance of any statement of creed; that one is in sympathy with the Three Objects is the sole declaration necessary for joining the organization. Yet we are told there is a need to study. Many are the admonitions to know Theosophy. If we would teach, we must first learn. But study what? What is it we must learn?

For the individual seeker, the question of what to study is usually solved by the dictates of personal interest. In the initial stages of Theosophical study, one is inclined to read widely, almost without discrimination, eager to explore in all directions, wading or swimming in that "shoreless ocean of truth" which Theosophy has been denominated. Later may come specific programs, developed out of need or interest or preference. One person may come to study only *The Secret Doctrine*, another *The Mahatma Letters*, while to yet another only the texts on meditation and the spiritual life seem to answer the inner need. For some, the works of Besant and Leadbeater are sources of never-ending inspiration and enlightenment. Others confine their studies to the writings of HPB and her Teachers. Yet others find Theosophy as much in literature published outside the Society as that issued within the organization. All the numerous individual approaches are reflected in the many modes by which Theosophy (or what is called Theosophy) is shared.

When we turn to group study, however, other considerations enter the picture. Individuals studying alone are free to pursue private interests, but group work demands a certain discipline that often seems to impose restraints upon individual freedom. Frequently individual differences in interest, preference, and background need to be resolved before the group can proceed. It may become necessary to place certain bounds on the study, to delimit Theosophy as it were, in order that the maximum benefit may be derived by the entire group. What, then, is to determine the bounds? What guideline exists by which we can say for group study, "This is the area of our concern; that is not"? Is there a measurement by which our studies may be said to approximate truth or deviate from the norm? To say that discrimination is necessary does not solve the dilemma that often confronts us.

Before the content of group study can be determined, it may be first necessary to define the purposes for which the group exists. The purpose of the Theosophical group may seem self-evident, but is it in reality? Since the individual members of the group have subscribed to the Three Objects of the Society, it may be assumed that these describe the uniting focus of the group work. But are the Objects descriptive of purpose? Many Theosophical groups would declare their purpose to be: "To study Theosophy in order to share the wisdom with those who are seeking understanding." Whether stated in such precise terms or not, it must be admitted that most Theosophical groups *do* study (in members' meetings) and *do* share (via public classes and lectures). Yet the Objects of the Society do not enjoin the study of Theosophy (for Theosophy is not even mentioned in them) nor advocate public work. Therefore, it may well be asked: "What is the essential purpose for which the Theosophical group exists?" Only when and as this question is answered may there be some approach to the nature and content of study in the group.

In line with the freedom of thought emphasized by the Society's official statements and the autonomy reserved to the groups, it may be suggested that it is for each group to explore its own inherent purpose. Beyond official statements of freedom and autonomy, however, there is a deeper consideration: purpose, to be truly valid, can never be imposed from without, whether it be in respect to individual or group purpose. This may be seen most clearly in relation to the individual, where it may be recognized that purpose is essentially integral to the nature of being human. What is imposed then is not purpose, but discipline in pursuit of purpose. As this may be applied to a group, we may say that purpose arises from within the nature of the group itself. If anything is imposed, it is not purpose—although it may masquerade as that—but disciplines, orders, injunctions, and even commands. The problems that most frequently arise are actually the resultants of a conflict between the inherent purpose (expressed or unexpressed, consciously recognized or unconsciously felt) and an outer command to pursue a given end.

Reflecting, then, upon the nature of purpose, we may come to understand the importance for examining this concept in our group activity. If the purpose of the group transcends the sum of the purposes expressed by the individual members of the group, the group itself takes on an existence and becomes an entity, over and above the individuals that compose it. Everyone who has participated in real group work has had an experience that verifies this view of a group as more than the sum of the individuals that compose it. The recognition of this fact is essential in defining the purpose of the group. At the same time, it aids in understanding that the purpose of one group may not necessarily be the purpose of another group, or of all groups, even of similar aims and ideals. Each Theosophical group may well ask itself: "Why do *we* exist as a group? What is our uniqueness?" As these questions are answered, the content of our study begins to come clear.

Expressing this in another way, we may suggest that purpose arises out of concern, in the sense of that in which we feel involved. In a very general way, we may posit that a Theosophical group has a certain concern, a concern that is Theosophical in nature. This concern relates itself to the Society, of which the group is an integral part, and also to those who come within the orbit of the group. As the concern of the group relates to the Society, it may be said that the Objects of the Society are the guidelines for study. As the concern of the group relates to those who may come within the orbit of its influence, it may be said that the study needs to be directed toward meeting the needs of those with whom we may come in contact. On this basis, group study is no longer an uncertain compromise of individual interests, but arises out of the dual nature of the concern or purpose the group exists to serve.

Group study, which arises thus naturally, is always related inwardly to first principles and outwardly to practical ends. Group work becomes marvelously harmonized and centered, for tangential interests, valid in individual work, are recognized as inappropriate to the group's task. In our studies as a group, we seek to explore the great universal principles of wisdom. No single member seeks to impose either their own particular interpretation or their own fancied "brand" of truth upon the group, however much any one may enjoy in private the fascinating byways of discovery. They bring to the group the enrichment of their own discoveries, of course, but not as possessions that the group must accept as binding truth. Such an attitude of possession usually means: *accept me and my idea*, or in refusing to accept my idea, you have rejected me and I must leave. Non-possessiveness of ideas is a *sine qua non* of group work. There is, of course, another aspect of this attitude, which is the reluctance to share ideas out of timidity or fear of non-acceptability. Is this attitude not really an outgrowth of over-protectiveness of oneself or, in other words, an inverted form of egotism? These considerations lead into the total realm of group action and must be faced by individual group members if the group is to achieve the larger harmony toward which its purpose leads. In view of this larger harmony, we seek to explore universal principles, and we find the counter-balance to our search in the effort to make these principles useful and workable in our lives and in the world about us.

The answer to the question of what we shall study lies, according to this analysis, not in formalized programs adopted by majority vote out of a compromise of individual preferences, but rather in that deeper perception of the nature of our work and the total group consciousness seeking to fulfill that basic nature or purpose. Specific programs develop out of the mutual group search to identify principles. Reading and discussion, sustaining and nurturing such programs, reflect individual interests and backgrounds, and serve to focus those principles upon the field of human affairs in terms of practical applications to the problems of life. When we mistake applications for principles, there is the danger of group disintegration, since this is the area in which differences may arise. Unless such differences are referable to basic principles, they can be the cause of separation.

It is not, of course, that group work represents uniformity of view or approach, but unity of aim. As this is recognized, there is the enrichment of mutual study and work as new insights challenge, and divergent interpretations stimulate, creative thought. What we shall study is not a categorical question separate from our mutual endeavors in a group, but represents the focal point at which universal principles meet practical needs, harmonizing interests and preferences, enlarging understanding, and providing exciting adventures across new continents of thought. In the paradoxical way truth has of revealing itself, the answer to what we shall study may be comprised in the words of *Light on the Path*:

> Seek out the way . . . Seek it by study of the laws of being, the laws of nature, the laws of the supernatural; and seek it by making the profound obeisance of the soul to the dim star that burns within.

The paradox, finally, is not that the question is unanswered by a specific this or that, but that the answer is itself a continuing question, for it is to seek.

THE CONSCIENCE OF
INFINITE CARING

Published in *The American Theosophist,* Volume 54, February 1966

In *The Voice of the Silence,* that priceless gem of meditation given to us by H. P. Blavatsky, reference is made to a "steeper path" which leads to illumination and liberation. This path, it is said, scales the "Paramita heights" up which the aspirant must ascend if he would achieve enlightenment, an ascent not for himself but for the benefit of all mankind. The Paramitas are those transcendental virtues that lead to Self-knowledge, virtues beyond the usual characteristics of the ordinarily good man. They are, by the very derivation of the word, beyond (*para*) the possibility of measurement (*mita*).

The first of these virtues of perfection is called "Dana, the key of charity and love immortal." Perhaps a clearer understanding of the meaning of Dana is gained if we interpret charity not in the ordinary sense of a giving of something to those less fortunate (certainly a measurable act), but rather in its deeper signification as a dearness which attaches to all things. The person of charity, then, is the one to whom all beings are dear. Such a one possesses a conscience of infinite caring.

Such a conscience is the urgent need of our day. It is the conscience toward which the Theosophist must always be striving, for it should characterize the believer in brotherhood. When all beings are dear to us, equally dear to us, when we care so much for life in all its multitude of forms that we hold all equally within our concern, when the welfare of another—whatever the race, the religion, color of skin, the circumstances—is as significant to us as our own, then brotherhood becomes more than an ideal or a convenient refuge in which we seek shelter from the needs of action. Brotherhood becomes the very mode of our actions; it is the dynamic motivator of every act, a reality experienced anew in every relationship. How is such a conscience awakened? How do we achieve that all-embracing concern which is an infinite caring for life?

"Blowin' in the Wind," a popular folk song by Bob Dylan, asks:

> How many roads must a man walk down before you call him
> a man?
> How many ears must one man have before he can hear people
> cry?

Such words are born of our present travail—the courageous search to find the extent of our humanness, to heal the wounds of racial discrimination, the scars of religious bigotry, the lacerations of war and violence. Such words reflect the beginning of a conscience of concern, the awakening of a conscience of infinite caring. They express the deeper longings of every individual to find their true stature as the Immortal One—Universal *Purusha*, the Divine One.

The steps on that ancient path, the "roads" we must walk down if we would achieve the stature of our immortality, have been called variously in the texts. Discrimination, dispassion, good conduct (including tolerance, cheerfulness, one-pointedness, confidence), and love: this is one way of naming the qualifications, and volumes could be, and have been, written in explanation of each step. But when our total concern is for the welfare of our fellow man, all steps, all qualifications, are comprehended under one mode of action: the conduct which proceeds from a conscience of infinite caring. Out of discrimination, then, arises the supreme unchoosing commitment to life itself—the commitment to serve life by acknowledging its unity no matter the form in which it manifests. Out of dispassion is born the ultimate passion of love.

Love, brotherhood, an infinite caring—however it be named, this is the conscience that must prevail if the world is to be made whole. Such a conscience must arise in each of us, for as the individual is healed and made whole, caring so much because all things are dear that we cannot wound or harm or injure, so does the world grow whole and brotherhood become the natural relationship that prevails. The Theosophical Society, dedicated to the task of creating a nucleus of the universal brotherhood of humanity, can be, in the world today, a clear and unmistakable voice of a collective conscience of infinite caring. It is a high destiny to which we have been called. It is a responsibility inescapable in its demand upon us. It is a calling each must heed, for the question sounds now, as always: "Hast thou attuned thy being to humanity's great pain, O candidate for light?" *How* we answer marks our response to Viet Nam, to India and Pakistan, to Harlem and Watts and Bogalusa—and to our neighbor in the house next door.

THE PATH FROM KNOWLEDGE TO WISDOM

Published in *The Theosophist*, Volume 95, February 1974

The study of Theosophy may be viewed as a journey, a journey from knowledge to wisdom. Now journeys, I think, are meant to be taken, just as roads are meant to be traveled, paths are meant to be walked, bread is meant to be eaten, and books are meant to be read. To take this journey from knowledge to wisdom, therefore, implies a certain movement. As with all journeys, some preparation is required, for one must equip oneself for the travel to be under-taken. In direct and simple terms, we are not meant to be armchair, or rocking chair, Theosophists, enjoying the journey vicariously.

There are some people in the world who, unable for physical or other reasons to travel far from home, go on armchair holidays around the world. They read all they can about a particular place, even view films or pictures of that place, and collect an enormous amount of information about it. Ultimately, they become very knowledgeable about that place and can even give lectures about it, as though they had been there. If they have accumulated suffi-cient information about some place and if they have given enough lectures or even written a book about it, they become known as authorities on that particular place, even though they may never have visited there. It is relatively easy for this to happen, for if people speak with sufficient emphasis and with an air of authority, we assume they must know what they are talking about.

In a world in which we rely so very much upon others, not only for the satisfaction of most of our physical needs but also for most of the data about the world's contents and processes, it is not surprising that we are generally content with the kind of knowledge that we can obtain without effort, the kind of knowledge that can be conveyed to us from outside without causing us any undue strain upon our own resources. Granted, of course, that much of our knowledge about the world must come to us from others who have become specialists in various branches of learning, we must not confuse that kind of informational knowledge about things and events with what may be termed essential knowledge. It is one thing, for example, to rely upon others for statistics on how many of the earth's peoples go to bed hungry every night, but it is quite another thing to contact directly, for ourselves, the nature of human suffering and to search out, as did the Buddha, the causes of suffering and the path to the alleviation of suffering.

The distinction made amply clear in *The Voice of the Silence* by H. P. Blavatsky between "head-learning" and "Soul-Wisdom" is precisely the distinction between the second-hand knowledge, which is derived from external sources, and the essential knowing which arises when we have embarked upon the inward journey to wisdom. The journey about which I am speaking, this path from knowledge to wisdom, which must be walked by each one who is concerned for the world's redemption, may be described in a number of ways. We are all embarked upon the journey, whether consciously or unconsciously, and I would make it very clear at the outset that I am not speaking from some vantage point well along on our travels, but rather out of a conviction that there is a path, that it must be trodden, that all humanity is involved in the journey, and that it does not matter very much where we are on the road so long as we have set our course surely and truly, and that, finally, as we walk, we come to know that we are in a most glorious company. Perhaps somewhere along the way, too, we may discover a most amazing truth: "Thou canst not travel on the Path before thou hast become that Path itself."

One way of delineating the path from knowledge to wisdom is by reference to the Three Objects of The Theosophical Society, for they represent the progress that is implied in our journey. The Third Object particularly relates to a developmental pattern that may be defined as the way from knowledge to wisdom. For the knowledge we are to seek pertains to the laws of the universe, whether known or unknown, the universal processes in terms of their fundamental lawfulness, in their essential orderliness. But it is each person who makes conscious those processes, each individual who is the self-conscious operative element within the universal processes. Therefore, each one of us must awaken within ourselves those deific powers which alone lead to a comprehension of universals, a comprehension which is of the nature of wisdom, of the inherent truthfulness of all external things and processes.

For the truly human powers—the powers latent in humanity—are the faculties whereby we perceive universals, the wholeness of things, and the reality underlying the manifold aspects of existence. They are the powers of love, understanding, and compassion, out of which wisdom arises as a fragrance arises out of a rose to perfume the air about it or, to use another metaphor, as a light which illumines everything upon which it shines.

The inherent truthfulness which emerges from an investigation of universal law through the awakening of humanity's latent spiritual and human potentials is the realization, the recognition, of brotherhood. The First Object, then, becomes not only a statement of an ideal but a reality basic to all existence which can be experienced directly. The ideal of brotherhood is supported and validated by an examination of all the religious traditions. It is a philosophic necessity. It is scientifically verifiable. So the Second Object, with its emphasis on study, which inevitably results in the acquisition of knowledge, refers to a most important aspect of our journey to wisdom. But the accumulation of facts about religion, philosophy, and science will not produce wisdom nor will it reveal the reality of brotherhood. Yet such study has its place, a most significant place, on the path from knowledge to wisdom, and without it, the truth of brotherhood will lack, as it were, an anchorage in humanity's cultural experience.

The Three Objects, then, may be viewed as intimately interrelated, and it is unwise, I suggest, to see them as merely three separate statements. It does not make very much sense, from this point of view, to say that one can accept one or even two of the Objects and simply disregard the others. Together they constitute a splendid directional light focused on the path that leads from knowledge to wisdom. They point towards the one great purpose which has been said to constitute the true work in which we are engaged as students of Theosophy—the spiritual regeneration of humanity. That regeneration is possible only when the essential truth of brotherhood is experienced, not merely talked about as a rather nice ideal but acted out in every relationship in our lives. That experience, that realization, is possible because there are latent in every individual those powers of comprehension which give rise to a true knowledge of universals, of first principles, of primary truths. Those are the powers hinted at in our Third Object. It is for this reason that I suggest the Third Object is the operative one that should move us onto the path from knowledge to wisdom.

Another way to state this interrelationship of the Society's Three Objects is to note that the study of the various branches of learning—the religions, philosophies, sciences of the world—can well lead to a sense of separateness, for such a study inevitably emphasizes the difference between one religion and another, between one philosophy and another. When differences are emphasized, comparisons arise, and when comparisons arise, value judgments are made, so that very soon one religion or philosophy is perceived as superior to all other religious or philosophical systems. But the Second Object, encouraging the kind of study that it does, is not meant to stand alone, separated from the First and Third Objects. Placed as it is between the First and Third Objects, the Second Object should be seen as encouraging study for a particular purpose. That purpose is the recognition of an underlying brotherhood, which simply means an underlying relationship obtaining throughout the universe, a relationship which in human terms is known as brotherhood. This purpose is fully revealed, however, only when there is an investigation of universal processes which operate in a lawful manner and which are made conscious through each person.

The progress that is implied in the movement from knowledge to wisdom may be compared to the usual developmental stages in our own growth when we come into contact with the mind-transforming and heart-inspiring concepts of Theosophy. For the most part, entry into the Society after an encounter with the wisdom-tradition results from a kind of rebellion against the established authority of religious or scientific dogma. We demand the right to say "no" to the conventional modes of thought. We reject the authoritarian dogmatism in which we may have been raised. We eagerly embrace the Theosophical philosophy in an effort to free ourselves from past conditioning, for our studies open new vistas that promise true freedom of thought.

But we may fail to realize that our new studies can constitute a subtle trap. We may find ourselves free from one set of ideas only to be enslaved by another set. We may exchange one external authority for another external authority. Now instead of quoting scripture or the latest scientific discovery to bulwark our arguments, we quote H. P. Blavatsky, Annie Besant, C. W. Leadbeater, the Mahatmas, *The Secret Doctrine*, and a whole host of new authorities. If we become stuck at this point in our studies, believing we are free when we have only exchanged one authority for another, we will soon find that we are stalled on our journey, and that we are no closer to wisdom than we were before our encounter with Theosophy.

From the no-saying stage of rebellion against dogmatic authority of the past to the yes-saying stage of acceptance of the immortal ideas of Theosophy, we must be prepared to move on to the discovery that the only authentic authority is our own interior knowing. This is the authentic authority of one's being, the authority of one's presence. The authentic authority of which I am speaking is not the authority which commands another to do some particular thing, nor is it the kind of authority that interposes between the individual who possesses it and the one who is seeking some answer, a veil of words from some supposed source of wisdom. The authority to which I am referring may best be defined as the ability to be wholly present where one is.

Let me illustrate this. Usually when someone asks us a question or poses a problem on which they wish our views, we become occupied not with the person before us but with a great number of other matters. We are not present where we are, for our minds may be leaping ahead to consideration of how we can best dispose of this person, get them out of our way, so that we can continue whatever else we were doing. Or we are searching about in our minds for some suitable quotation from our studies, so that we can reply to our inquirer: "HPB said . . ." or "Annie Besant said . . ." or "The Upanishads say . . ." or whatever other source of information we find lying about in our mental cabinets. If we can find just the right authority, then we will feel we have given something to the person before us. The fact is we will have given nothing, for we will not have given ourselves. Only when we are present with the person before us, present authentically where we are, can we give of ourselves, of our own knowing, and it is such giving that constitutes the only true answer to any question that may be asked of us.

Authentic authority resides in the individual who has made his own journey from the studies that produce knowledge to the comprehensive insights that collectively symbolize wisdom. In the first issue of her journal, *The Theosophist*, H. P. Blavatsky addressed herself to the question, "What is Theosophy?" Following an examination of the various strands in the fabric of the mystery-tradition, she stated: "Theosophy develops in man a direct beholding." She continued by suggesting that "under the influence and knowledge" of the Theosophical philosophy "man thinks divine thoughts" and "views all things as they really are." HPB's statement implies that there is a way of viewing everything which is in its essence a Theosophical outlook, and that this manner of looking at life follows upon the development of a mental condition in which consciousness is free, free from attachment to anything, free even from the notions and ideas which may have initiated the process of the liberation of the mind.

Indeed the process is clearly defined by HPB, in the article referred to above. She summarizes the teachings of Plotinus, pupil of the "God-taught" Ammonius, who related that "The secret gnosis or the knowledge of Theosophy, has three degrees—opinion, science, and *illumination*." These are the three stages on the path from knowledge to wisdom, and it is only when there is that kind of insight, which may be described as interior illumination, that knowledge has moved to wisdom. In that condition, there is an authentic authority because it is an internal authority. The individual who bears this about him as an aura of authentic presence looks at all things in a new way, a way that may be called, as HPB defined it, "direct beholding."

How can we gain that "direct beholding" that will put all things in a new perspective, that will enable us to see things as they *truly* are, which is not a psychic viewing any more than it is a physical viewing? Since what we are talking about is a way of perceiving the world, the key by which we can answer our question must lie in the quality of the mind which is doing the perceiving. The mind, as we well know, is a most interesting faculty, for it has the remarkable capacity of attaching itself to whatever it observes and consequently transforming itself into the likeness of the object that is perceived. In fact, one may say the mind has within it a substance which glues it, sticks it, to whatever comes within its purview, so that there develops within the mind a host of images, a great range of likes and dislikes, and the mind takes on a multitude of forms, shapes, colors, so that perception becomes clouded, distorted, obscured.

The first task confronting us, if we are to develop that "direct beholding" which is the nature of wisdom, is to free the mind from its tendency to adhere to things. We must remove, if we can, the stickiness, or at least the tendency towards stickiness, so that the mind can move freely, without prejudice, without attachment, perceiving things as they are, without any cloud of like or dislike shrouding the object. Truth then arises as a natural condition within consciousness. We no longer look outwards and say, "That is true," or "This is true," as though truth were in an object, an idea, an experience. Truth is not external, residing in things, but is a quality of mindfulness which is present when the mind is free. It is in this condition, I suggest, that "direct beholding" is possible.

To the one who looks out upon the world in this manner, with a "direct beholding," all things are perceived as divine in essence. Behind and beyond all phenomena, there abides the noumenon, the One Reality, and this alone is seen. To see That, to awaken the divine in every human heart—to perceive, not the coruscating colors of psychic auras, but the white light of Spirit, and to read, not the past series of one's own or another's incarnations, but the message of the One Life writ large through all manifestation—here is the essence of that "direct beholding" which Theosophy can awaken in the student. So, as HPB reminded every would-be Theosophist: "Without ever becoming a Mahatma, a Buddha or a Great Saint, let him study the philosophy and the 'Science of Soul,' and he can become one of the modest benefactors of humanity, without any 'superhuman' powers." This is the way to wisdom, the way of "direct beholding," which, leading from knowledge, awakens in the student the realization that, to continue with HPB's words, *true Occultism or Theosophy* . . . is ALTRUISM," and it throws him who practices it out of calculation of the ranks of the living altogether. "Not for himself, but for the world, he lives," as soon as he has pledged himself for the work.

Again and again, the Theosophical student is directed towards the essential work which is epitomized as a path from knowledge to wisdom and to which he must commit himself, his entire nature, all his resources and energies, wholly and without reserve. In the course of that remarkable correspondence which took place between A. P. Sinnett and those who have been regarded as the Inner Founders of the Society, there are innumerable hints as to the studies to be undertaken and to the primary work to be accomplished by anyone desiring to qualify themselves not merely to enter the precincts of occult knowledge but more importantly to become a force in the spiritual regeneration of humanity, an active worker in the cause of human brotherhood.

In Letter 68, in the series of *The Mahatma Letters to A. P. Sinnett*, Mr. Sinnett is advised by his Adept-correspondent to study well the twin doctrines of *karma* and *nirvana* as it is on a knowledge of these that all the rest of the philosophy depends. An analysis of this statement reveals, I believe, that here is but another way of encouraging the student to move from a knowledge of the orderliness and lawfulness of universal processes to that wisdom which is a "direct beholding" of the one universal Reality underlying all processes. It is, in this sense, a movement from non-freedom, a state in which we are bound by inexorable law, to the true freedom of lawfulness that arises when we know ourselves to be one with all life.

Karma, of course, is usually translated as the law of cause and effect. Studying karma reveals the lawfulness of all processes in the realms of manifestation. It relates to the sequential and orderly progression of all things, for it is the essential principle of balance, equilibrium. Every action is both causative and effective. Action is movement, at whatever level the action takes place, and movement contains within itself an ongoingness in terms of sequence. Karma, therefore, is the law dealing with the world of manifested existence, the sequential world, the world of *Samsara*, as it is called in Buddhism. A knowledge, an understanding, of the lawfulness inherent in the universe, gives us knowledge about truth, an understanding about things and about relationships. We know about this and that, and how this and that are related or interconnected.

Nirvana, on the other hand, is that realm of consciousness— that perception—which is present when all else is blown out, as it were, extinguished in its separateness, in its sequentiality. It is the realm of wisdom, in which knowing is no longer *about*, but *is*. Nirvana reveals the presence of the universal sub-stratum of One Reality underlying all process. Here is illumination, direct beholding, immediate insight, so that one perceives or becomes aware of the all-at-onceness of life rather than its sequential succession.

In *The Voice of the Silence*, there is a very beautiful phrase, "Once thy foot hath pressed the bed of the Nirvanic stream . . ." that suggests there may be a current in consciousness which is pure, free, unsullied. The foot may be representative of understanding, so that when our knowledge is rooted in the nirvanic stream, when our understanding is based, pressed, upon the bed of that stream, there flows through consciousness a fundamental awareness of the abiding Real. Everything that is perceived, then, is bathed in that pure stream of Reality. The perceptions of the mind and the intuitions of the heart flow together in that Wisdom which is Love, embracing all things. In such a state of perception, Samsara and Nirvana become one. The world of existent things is seen as but the outward revelation of the realm of the Immortal Presence, the eternal Presence of the One.

So from knowledge, we move to wisdom. But as we have already pointed out, we must come, sometime on this journey, to the realization that "Thou canst not travel on the Path before thou hast become that Path itself." What, then, is this becoming, and how do we become the path on which we would move out of the Hall of Learning to the Temple of Wisdom? In *The Key to Theosophy*, H. P. Blavatsky refers to the Eclectic Theosophical System of Ammonius Saccas and his disciples. In this system, which HPB indicates is the basis for the modern Theosophical presentation, there were three aspects. The first two are concerned with a knowledge of the nature of the "one absolute, incomprehensible and supreme Deity, or infinite essence, which is the root of all Nature," and a knowledge of man's eternal immortal nature, because, being a radiation of the Universal Soul, it is of an identical nature with it. The third aspect of the Theosophical system of Ammonius, an aspect very much present in the writings of HPB as well as in the letters received by Sinnett and others from the Adept Teachers, is called "Theurgy," "divine work," or "producing a work of gods." As HPB states in *The Key*, this is the mystic belief "that by making oneself as pure as the incorporeal beings, i.e., by returning to one's pristine purity of nature, man could move the gods to impart to him Divine mysteries" (Blavatsky 1972b, 2).

It is only as we step on the bed of the nirvanic stream, as it were, that we are enabled to recover the pristine purity of our original nature, the quality of consciousness in which there is that direct beholding which is of the nature of wisdom. The human being has been called the transformer of energies and it is the function, and indeed the responsibility of the human, to engage in the great alchemical work by which the transformation of the material into the spiritual is effected.

A study of the classical principles concerning the universe and the human, Theosophical principles enunciated from time immemorial, must be validated, authenticated, by our lives. They must be tested in the crucible of daily existence. The would-be Theosophist must be the modern alchemist, transforming first the lead of the lower nature into the pure gold of essential being and then transforming the base metal of the world's sorrow into the golden elixir of universal brotherhood. For this divine work, the great theurgical task to which we are called, we must submit ourselves to a kind of deconditioning process by which we remove from our conscious or unconscious experience those elements which make for separateness in our relationships with others, in our cultural life, in our approach to all Nature's kingdoms, in our attitudes, feelings, words, actions.

In this deconditioning process, we must pledge allegiance only to that one integrating principle in the universe, recognizing that there is but one source, one life, one law, and its name is Love. The process to which I refer is similar to the work undertaken by the sculptor who, perceiving in the crude marble before him the form of beauty, does not add anything to the marble, but skillfully chips away all that is non-essential, all that is extraneous, permitting the shape of beauty to emerge naturally, gracefully, harmoniously, happily.

This alchemical task is not the work of a day nor of a year, but of centuries of growth. It is one in which, as we have been told, our whole nature must be used wisely: every faculty, every power, every aspect of our humanness committed irrevocably and absolutely. So do we become the Path, as we undertake the true burden of existence, to become authentic individuals, present where we are, theurgists and alchemists who are constantly transforming the world because we ourselves are inwardly transformed. If we are aiming at a certain perfection of the soul in a life that has some degree of completeness, we cannot entertain priorities that give rise to differences. The advance to an enlightened brotherhood must be on all fronts, and the grand strategy of Theosophical endeavor demands that we perpetually broaden our understandings and deepen our sympathies. It is not a matter of "head-Theosophy" or "heart-Theosophy," as some would suppose, but that out of the experience of the unity of our own nature we discover our intimate kinship with all living things. So the world's sorrow in all Nature's kingdoms must find an echo in the heart of the disciple—our circle of compassion must ever be extending its circumference. And we must know, with a direct beholding past all knowledge and study, that within the heart of every living thing is an "imprisoned splendor," reflecting the greater Splendor of the One Reality.

Speaking of this very experience, the heart and core of Theosophy, Bhagavan Das once wrote:

> When we can weep with one eye for the woes of the world and smile with the other for its joys; when we know the comedy of knowledge and feel the tragedy of feeling simultaneously; . . . when we feel at once sad over breaking bodies and glad over the deathless Spirit; when we know and feel that the insect's flutter, the river's roll, the ocean's surge, the wind's unceasing sigh, the march of the moon, planets, suns, stars—is all part of One and the self-same Life, Life, one continuity of living motion, the endless manifestations of One Living Energy, the incessant transformations of One Living Substance which is Consciousness—then indeed we sense *Nirvana* even in the flesh. (Das, 1921)

This is the royal road to wisdom, the path we are all walking together, the path which in essence we are. Here is the great work, the work of theurgy to which we are called, the true work of Occultism which is altruism. Its accomplishment is brought about not by the change of many conditions, the alteration of externals, the reformation of the world, but by the change of one condition only. The mental vision that has been turned outward must now be turned inward. We must regain our oneness with a living universe. As students of the Esoteric Philosophy, we must follow the ideal of pure knowledge, which is wisdom by seeing things as they are, not as we presume them to be.

Through the Theosophical Society, we have been brought into communion with the spiritual force generated by the Great Brotherhood, a Brotherhood of Knowers, a Brotherhood of the Teachers of Humanity. We have been invited by them to participate in the work of that fraternity for the regeneration of the world. In order to participate fully, we must learn the nature of our own soul, and in the experience of its pilgrimage through the inner and outer worlds of its being encounter the reality of its source. As the followers of Ammonius were called "*theodidaktos*," the God-taught, so the modern student of the Ageless Wisdom must be taught by the Immortal Self, the God within. A recipient first of a revelation that appears to arise from the outside, a knowledge of things and processes which is vouchsafed us, the student must move towards the wisdom whose source is within. In the familiar words of Robert Browning:

> *Paracelsus*:
> Truth is within ourselves; it takes no rise
> From outward things, whate'er you may believe.
> There is an inmost center in us all,
> Where truth abides in fullness . . .
> . . . and to know

Rather consists in opening out a way
Whence the imprisoned splendor may escape,
Than in effecting an entry for a light
Supposed to be without.

This is not essentially different from the remark of the Mahatma K. H. to Mr. Sinnett who, impatient for the final secrets of the occult philosophy, was reminded that "The illumination must come from within." For the true "*theodidaktos*," Theosophy is no longer simply a set of beliefs, a knowledge however lofty of the nature of the human entity and the universe. It is an experience, the supreme experience of wisdom, essentially incommunicable and yet forever communicated by the authentic presence of the one who has been possessed by the experience and been transformed thereby. For we do not possess the experience, holding it, clutching it, owning it as our own. Rather the experience that is Theosophy comes to possess us, shaking us to our very roots, stirring us, moving us, at times making us very uncomfortable, but ultimately transforming us so that we may, in our turn, transform the world.

To every seeker on the path from knowledge to wisdom, to all who journey on the great quest for the light, the words spoken to the neophyte in *The Idyll of the White Lotus* ring true now as ever:

Life has in it more than the imagination of man can conceive. Seize boldly upon its mystery, and demand, in the obscure places of your own soul, light with which to illumine those dim recesses of individuality to which you have been blinded through a thousand existences.

This is to awaken the direct beholding, the unveiled spiritual perception, which recognizes in the world of karmic events, the world of samsara, the background and the essential presence of nirvana.

And traveling onwards, one with the Path itself, we hear the eternal paean as in *The Voice of the Silence*: "Behold! Thou hast become the Light, Thou hast become the Sound, Thou art thy Master and thy God."

INAUGURAL ADDRESS:
THE INTERNATIONAL CENTER
OF THEOSOPHICAL STUDIES
AND RESEARCH

Published in *The Theosophist*, Volume 97, November 1976

In the thirteenth chapter of the Bhagavad Gita, Arjuna asks of Sri Krishna: "What is that which is worth knowing?" That question has been asked by every earnest seeker since time immemorial. Today it is undoubtedly one of the most relevant questions we can ask, for we are so bombarded by knowledge about every conceivable thing, from the composition of Martian soil to the sex life of the fruit fly, that it is proving exceedingly difficult to determine what information may have some lasting value and what facts are of transient interest only. Is there, indeed, anything worth knowing?

Perhaps some of the rebelliousness of modern youth can be directly traced to our increasing inability to answer the question of what is worth knowing. We have been content to gather more and more information about all manner of things and to insist that succeeding generations learn as much of it as possible without regard to its meaningfulness or significance, without regard to whether what we are presenting is worth knowing at all.

The Theosophical student, the student of esoteric philosophy, must inevitably answer Arjuna's question in terms of that knowledge which comprises an understanding of the essential nature of all things. For there is indeed that which is worth knowing, although it cannot be said in a word, in a sentence, or even in a book. Paradoxically, it may never be capable of complete expression in language, though words will always be used to approximate it and to provide insights that awaken intuitive understanding of the one thing worth knowing at all. It is the very nature of our humanness to endeavor constantly to clothe the spirit of Truth in the garb of human speech. That which is worth knowing is that which imparts meaning to existence, which reveals the Ultimate Reality and the path to it, which restores to humankind an enduring vision of its own Immortal Self. As Sri Krishna informed Arjuna, "Wisdom as to the Field and the Knower of the Field, that in my opinion is the wisdom."

In inaugurating this International Center of Theosophical Studies and Research, we are continuing a tradition that has been present in the work of the Theosophical Society since its inception. It is the tradition of seeking that which is worth knowing and of applying our knowledge in the market place of daily existence. More than that, it is the tradition of encountering, through study, contemplation, and service, the age-old and ageless Wisdom that we call Theosophy. That tradition has been given expression in various enterprises throughout the Theosophical world. Here at Adyar we have had the Brahma Vidya Ashram and the School of the Wisdom, to mention but two of the predecessor institutions to this new Center of Theosophical Studies. The tradition of which I speak is one in which both a teaching and a teacher are present, a tradition that is dedicated to awakening in students their finer sensibilities, their innate creative potentials, not for any gain that may accrue to the individual but solely for the benefit and welfare of the whole of which each one is an integral and indivisible part. It is, in brief, the tradition of self-education, self-knowledge, and self-discipline. From the earliest days of the Society, the members have been described as a group of students, and it is that aspect of studentship that is again being given outer expression through this new undertaking.

The name selected for our current educational venture is significant in understanding the aim of our endeavor. Not a school, this is to be a *Center* of Theosophical Studies. The word "Center" implies not only a place but also a process. The place, of course, is here at Adyar, the hub of the Theosophical world. It is, symbolically, the heart of our movement and by reflection there is an Adyar in the heart of every member, which is the center of our own understanding. As a process, the term *Center* indicates a primal need in every human being to find that point within from which the individual can view all the manifoldness of phenomenal events. Our basic task is to come to that interior center, to center or nest ourselves at the heart of the universe. Only from that still point within can we gain true perspective on all that occurs about us. On the periphery of the wheel, as it were, there may be numerous courses presented here, various programs of one kind or another, talks, symposia, etc., but the underlying purpose and the fundamental aim of all that is done here will be to help all who come within the orbit of this enterprise to center themselves, to move on their own roads to Self-Realization. The greatest flexibility in subject matter and presentation will guide our efforts. And the ultimate value will rest with each one who comes for a longer or shorter period. If the centering process can be stimulated, encouraged, nourished, and fostered, then it will be seen that this process is not dependent upon time or place, but is a continuing movement of the soul, of the mind, the entire being, towards that in which we are all eternally rooted.

Then our enterprise has been named a Center of *Theosophical Studies*. There is a vast difference between the study of Theosophy and Theosophical study. The study of Theosophy will certainly have an important and vital place, a central place, in the work to be undertaken here, for unless we are familiar with the Theosophical philosophy we can scarcely embark upon Theosophical studies. But Theosophy is not to be viewed as just one course among a multitude of courses, one subject among numerous other studies, that may be taken up. Rather it is our view that Theosophy furnishes, and must furnish, the context in which all other studies are pursued, the perspective which gives to all study its meaningfulness and significance, which puts proper value, in other words, on that which may be known because it points up what is worth knowing.

As has been pointed out by many students, most recently by Mrs. Emily Sellon in her Centenary Convention talk on "Theosophical Education," Theosophy provides, or should provide, the "unifying context," the uniquely holistic perspective or "esoteric worldview" within which all studies, all human concerns, all activities, can be accommodated. In this sense, the study of Theosophy should lead us inevitably to Theosophical study, which is to say to that centering process which is a life-long undertaking of our studentship.

How we view the world, how we perceive ourselves and others, will finally determine the kind of world in which we live. The kind of study, for example, that is encouraged by the Second Object of the Society, reveals the great variety of worldviews which have influenced the cultural experiences of nations and ethnic groups. Ultimately, cultural background and experience have found expression in politics, in social conditions, in education, in economics, and in all the other activities in which humankind engages. Without providing detailed substantiation for such a statement, and at the risk of oversimplification of the matter, I would merely call your attention to the differences between what may be called the Western approach to life and the Eastern approach.

To cite one small but highly significant example: witness the manner in which time has been traditionally viewed in the West with the way in which time is usually seen in the East. Western people, steeped in the cultural tradition of the Greco-Judaic world in which time is conceived of in a linear movement, have felt the urgency to achieve as much as possible in the years allotted to them, for progress implies a forward thrust in an existence that is a non-repeatable experience. Eastern people, on the other hand, immersed in a cultural tradition that views time as cyclical and existence as not only repeatable but doomed to repeatability through an inexorable law, have been less concerned with material progress and far more with that progress of the soul, which can ultimately end the repeatability of existence.

A holistic worldview must encompass all worldviews, and yet transcend them. In just such a way, Theosophy is neither an eclectic system nor one system among many others. Theosophical studies, then, are studies in which Theosophy provides, as we have proposed, the unifying context by revealing the universal patterns underlying all phenomena. Only by understanding that context (by a familiarity with the esoteric worldview) can we approach the study of any subject meaningfully and recognize the true relevance of such study in terms of any and every experience that comes to humankind.

If we are to be Theosophical students, we may well begin by being students of Theosophy, but we cannot rest content with studies that expose us to the same risks of parochialism and dogmatism as are present in the study of any subject in isolation. It was this very danger of which H. P. Blavatsky warned the members of the Society when she wrote, in *The Key to Theosophy*, that "Every such attempt as the Theosophical Society has hitherto ended in failure, because, sooner or later, it has degenerated into a sect, set up hard and fast dogmas of its own, and so lost by imperceptible degrees that vitality which living truth alone can impart." Our studies then must be, in the widest and fullest sense of the word, Theosophical. They must be infused with the vitality of a living truth, a truth that lives because it works within us in a kind of spiritual fermentation process.

Early in the history of the Society, Mohini Chatterjee pointed out that the esoteric doctrine "teaches with special emphasis that there must exist at every moment of the history of human evolution a class of men in whom consciousness attains such an expansion in both depth and area as to enable them to solve the problems of being by direct perception and therefore with far more certainty and completeness than the rest of mankind." This Center of Theosophical Studies is dedicated to the premise that the Theosophical Society was founded for the express purpose of awakening in all people their spiritual potentials, of bringing about the growth of that consciousness which can indeed solve the problems of being by direct perception, and thus ensuring that there will always be in the world such individuals who have attained the kind of awareness of which Mohini wrote. Only in such awareness can true brotherhood be established, for it is not based on a sentimental or superficial recognition of human solidarity, but upon knowledge of the fundamental Source in which all life is eternally rooted. The existence of an Inner Brotherhood of Adept Teachers, of just men made perfect, Bodhisattvas, Masters of Wisdom and Compassion, provides the pattern for the establishment in the world of external affairs of a genuine brotherhood of humanity.

A modern Jungian psychologist, Dr. June Singer, has suggested that there are two ways of thinking: convergent and divergent. In convergent thinking, one perceives existence as composed of problems to be solved, and to each problem there is one right solution. Divergent thinking, on the other hand, recognizes life as a journey, in which many paths move outward from the given of any moment, from the core of the situation. We have surely had enough of convergent thinking; the syndrome of one problem, one solution, has left us still in a state of confusion, in a world in which political leaders, scientists and technologists, religious and philosophical thinkers, each proclaim a single right answer, with a multitude of solutions thus vying for support and only producing continued war and conflict. We need desperately to cultivate divergent thinking, which recognizes as J. J. van der Leeuw so beautifully put it in *The Conquest of Illusion*, that "The mystery of life is not a problem to be solved, it is a reality to be experienced." If in this Center of Theosophical Studies, and in similar centers throughout the world—centers such as the Krotona School of Theosophy, for example—we can encourage that kind of thinking, provide the setting for true Theosophical studentship in which each who comes into contact with the wisdom-tradition gains new insight and greater understanding for alleviating the sorrows and ills of the world, then surely what we have begun today will bring to this Society a new vigor, a fresh enthusiasm, a recreative and recreating spirit in the pursuit of truth to which the genuine theosophist must ever aspire.

Finally, as it is my privilege to have had some part in the conception of this new program of studies and to have set forth something of its aims during what may be termed its prenatal life, let me conclude with a statement of personal conviction. I suffer—and I freely confess this—from what some may consider a near fatal flaw. I am primarily an optimist, although today it may be more fashionable to be a pessimist or at least a cynic. I do not believe that humanity is doomed to extinction nor that our fragile, small, yet beautiful planet will soon be laid waste and made uninhabitable for all except bacterial growth. I believe, as have so many far greater than I, that it is better to light a candle than to curse the darkness. I am naive enough to believe humanity will ultimately triumph. I am proud enough to feel that my small efforts may help achieve humanity's final victory, but I am humble enough to recognize that not one of us can accomplish much alone, and I have full faith that no one who works for the cause of "orphan humanity" ever works alone.

I have confidence that there is an Inner Government of the world, and I have an absolute and unwavering conviction that if we do our part, the Great Ones will not desert us or withhold their strength from our efforts. I do not believe that the Theosophical Society has lost its way, as some of our critics both within and without the movement are telling us, nor do I think it is no longer relevant, as other voices proclaim. Neither do I believe that relevance is achieved by patterning ourselves on every other occult or pseudo-occult organization nor by following every popular slogan in the guru-ridden market places of human concourse. I am not so sanguine as to believe that this International Center of Theosophical Studies will, in some mysterious but overwhelming manner, become the most blazing and brightest star in the Society's diadem of jeweled achievements. But I do earnestly hope that it may, as the initial brochure of our program states, "encourage each participant to become a genuine student and not merely a listener, so that through individual study and reflection in the rich atmosphere of Adyar creative insight, loving understanding, and deeper comprehension may develop." Perhaps if that aim is realized, the Society will be a little richer for the work we attempt in this Center, and the world at large will be a little brighter because we have lit here a few small candles of true understanding to dispel the darkness of ignorance.

A Clean Life

Published in *The Theosophist,* Volume 97, December 1976

Behold the truth before you: A clean life, an open mind, a pure heart, an eager intellect, an unveiled spiritual perception, a brotherliness for all, a readiness to give and receive advice and instruction, a courageous endurance of personal injustice, a brave declaration of principles, a valiant defense of those who are unjustly attacked, and a constant eye to the ideal of human progression and perfection which the secret science depicts—these are the golden stairs up the steps of which the learner may climb to the Temple of Divine Wisdom.

—H. P. Blavatsky

The tendency to repeat certain familiar words or phrases without considering the depth of meaning or inner significance they may possess is most marked in regard to well known aphorisms. The more familiar we are with a passage from scripture or a poem or lines written by a great teacher, the more we tend to use the words without thinking of their content. We may take H. P. Blavatsky's famous words, which have been called "The Golden Stairs," as an example. Consider, in this regard, just the first step, "a clean life."

If we are repeating the "Golden Stairs" aloud, either in a group or to ourselves, we tend to rush past this first step to others that occur later in the sequence and which may seem more exciting or at least more challenging. Quite obviously, as students of Theosophy, we feel we are living what is termed a clean life, but when we come, for example, to "a courageous endurance of personal injustice," then we begin to feel an inner excitement. Those words sound so heroic. We visualize ourselves in desperate situations, unjustly accused of all sorts of things, and we see ourselves enduring the conditions with tremendous courage.

Or to take another example, we say, "a brave declaration of principles," and then picture ourselves on some platform expounding the Theosophical philosophy amidst catcalls of ridicule and shouts of abuse, while we bravely continue to declare the principles we know to be right. Even so beautiful a phrase as "an unveiled spiritual perception" seems far more significant than "a clean life."

So we may tend to overlook the first step, but if we examine the matter a little, we may discover that the first step may be the most important and perhaps even the highest to ascend. If I may use an analogy, I recall my astonishment when I first saw the steps built by the Incas in such places as Machu Picchu in Peru. There, it seemed that the first step was much higher from the ground than the succeeding steps were from each other. It was as though if one could make the climb to the first step, the others, while steep, were easier to ascend. This may indeed be a very apt analogy, for if we consider the depth of meaning in this very first step of the Golden Stairs, we may see that it provides a firm base upon which the rest of the steps must rest.

Socrates, we are told by Plato, emphasized that the unexamined life is not worth living. The examined life must mean that we look at every aspect in our lives to determine whether we are moving in the direction we have set for ourselves. Are we, in other words, climbing the Golden Stairs that lead to the "Temple of Divine Wisdom," which is the achievement of full Self-Realization? To change the simile, we may say that we have embarked on a kind of sea voyage, the goal of which is a harbor of enlightenment. We cannot set sail without reference to an interior compass and we must, again and again, true our course in accordance with that compass.

N. Sri Ram, in his work *An Approach to Reality*, phrased the matter in these words: "The vital questions to be put to ourselves in each and every situation are: What should be the nature of our approach to it; what the nature of our thoughts and feelings therein; what action shall we perform? In the mass of circumstances which beset us on every side, what is the direction of true progress?" If we ask these questions, if we check the compass to be sure of our direction, we find we are leading the examined life.

The examined life may be said to be the first requisite for a clean life. Indeed, the examined life *is* a clean life, for it is a life that is orderly, a life that is stripped of all nonessentials, a life in which we are willing to examine ourselves and reset our course, if necessary, in accordance with that interior compass whose north always points to the goal we seek. A clean life, in other words, is far more than just taking a bath every day, although physical cleanliness is certainly essential. Certainly we must give care and attention to the condition of the instrument we use in the world of action. The physical has its own importance, and if it is clogged with impurities it can scarcely serve us effectively or efficiently.

Sometimes it has been said by those who would defend habits of meat-eating or smoking or the taking of an occasional cocktail before dinner that, after all, it is far more important what comes out of a person's mouth than what goes into it. Such an argument seems to have a certain plausibility when one considers the many outstanding people in the world, good people, useful people, who indulge in such habits. Perhaps the argument is even strengthened by the fact that we often find vegetarians and teetotalers engaging in the most incredible gossip, spreading rumors, etc. It should be obvious that a clean life should include both what goes in and what comes out of the mouth, for the basic meaning of "clean" is to be without impurities, unsoiled, unstained, having no obstructions. It also means neat and orderly, so that a physical body, which is given its proper due and attended to in an orderly manner, is implied by the phrase "a clean life" in so far as it applies to the physical plane.

A clean life, then, begins with the physical. In addition to the care of the vehicle, cleanliness must embrace our actions, our words, and our gestures. These also must be without any impurities attached to them, which means they must be unstained by any selfish thought, any motive for self-aggrandizement, any feeling of vindictiveness or jealousy. Action, as the Bhagavad Gita so beautifully reminds us, must be performed without thought for its fruit. It must be pure, which is to say, clean, uncluttered, unsoiled by desire for reward or praise. Can our actions, in other words, flow directly from that interior center of the Immortal Self, so that they are in no way obscured by personal interest, stained, or polluted by personal desire? Can our words have about them a radiance of loving compassion because they are cleansed of all hurtful intent?

Then just as we bathe the physical body each day, putting on clean clothing, so in the examined life, the *clean* life, we may learn to bathe the emotional and mental vehicles. At those levels also we need to don the clean apparel of right feelings and right thoughts. Meditation and study provide emotional and mental baths required for the clean life. Meditation especially immerses us in the light of the Immortal Self, bathes us in the radiance of the One, removing the impurities that result from our forgetfulness of our Source.

What does such an interior bath imply? It must mean that there can be a freshness in all we think and feel, a certain unobstructed inner flow which pervades the day, for the waters of life within us are not stagnant or polluted. Our lives move from an inner source that is always fresh and clear, an inner spring that is constantly renewing itself, and we put up no obstructions to the flow of life itself. There is a naturalness, a spontaneity, a joyousness about our lives. Thought, feeling, and action are in harmonious accord.

A clean mind is an orderly mind, a mind that is not in a state of confusion nor polluted by extraneous ideas, opinions, or beliefs. Such a mind is able to sort out at once whatever presents itself to it throughout the day, and to look at everything in a fresh and clear manner. Clean feelings are feelings that arise spontaneously from the inner springs of compassion and love. There are no whirlpools or eddies of self-pity or self-concern, no muddiness of emotional tantrums and unhappiness in the emotional vehicle that has been bathed in the pure light of Love.

To ensure that clean flow within, we need to examine our motives. What is it that motivates us to action? A clean life surely must mean that our motives are as pure as possible, but this is dependent upon our ability to be aware of our motives. When we are aware, we can no longer do or say anything unthinkingly or unfeelingly. If we are prone to say, when some action of ours has produced an undesirable effect, "Well, I did not think of that," it means we have not been alert, clean or purified within, but rather that we have been content to exist in a kind of stagnant pool of unconsciousness. Sometimes words seem to burst forth from us, as though they had no roots in consciousness. Much of our time may be spent in explaining ourselves, in saying, "But I did not mean *that*" and so in excusing ourselves.

In a clean and orderly life, in which motive has been examined, there is an awareness of every thought, every feeling, every word and action, but it is an awareness that in no way detracts from the spontaneity of thought, feeling, and action. When we lead the clean life, through and through, spontaneity and freshness characterize all our actions; the word that is needed at the moment is spoken, the act that is the pure act is performed, because we have participated in, and are part of, that inner flow of Reality which emerges from the Self through the self, unimpeded, clear, unobstructed.

So a clean life means a life without any impurities, unpolluted at any level of our existence. If there is genuinely the clean life, if we can take this first giant step on the Golden Stairs, the stairway to Self-Realization, then surely all the other steps must follow naturally. For a clean life means "an open mind, a pure heart." It means a life lived from the center, a life in which there is "a willing obedience to the behests of Truth," because one is ever obedient to that interior center where truth takes its rise and no impediments are placed in the way of our perception of the One Reality. Action flows pure and unobstructed from that interior center of the Immortal Self.

St. Paul spoke of the clean life as it concerns our thoughts: "Finally, brethren, whatsoever things are true, whatsoever things are honest, whatsoever things are just, whatsoever things are pure, whatsoever things are lovely, whatsoever things are of good report; if there be any virtue, and if there be any praise, think on these things." A mind so absorbed is a mind in which none of the dust of selfish concern can settle.

Annie Besant once wrote, "Not out of right practice comes right thinking, but out of right thinking comes right practice. It matters enormously what you think. If you think falsely, you will act mistakenly; if you think basely, your conduct will suit your thinking." A clean life reflects the purity of thought and emotion which gives rise to right action, beautiful action, action that is truly for others and without thought of reward.

The ideal has been beautifully summed up in the words of N. Sri Ram: "There is a way of living so vitally, freshly, originally, spontaneously and dynamically that life becomes a transformation, a state of perpetual joy, a native ecstasy which nothing can take away." Living such a life, a *clean* life, a life in which there is no impurity in the flow of energy from the center, we know and experience that "native ecstasy" which nothing can ever obscure or destroy.

THEOSOPHY:
PHILOSOPHY OF
RIGHT VIEWING

Published in *The Theosophist,* Volume 101, October 1979

When H. P. Blavatsky inaugurated her first journal, *The Theosophist,* it was inevitable that she should begin the venture with an article entitled, "What is Theosophy?" Through the years, since the appearance of the initial issue of that journal in October 1879, that question has continued to be asked, as much by members of The Theosophical Society itself as by casual inquirers. Undoubtedly, the question is a perennial one, and no answer will be fully satisfying to everyone. The diversity of response is itself an indication of the richness of meaning to be explored in so singular a word. Ultimately, each serious student comes to his own definition (or definitions) which may, in the course of years or in the process of deepening study, undergo change, either narrowing or expanding its meaning.

Although HPB identified the various threads in the fabric of the wisdom-tradition of the ages, she seemed as much concerned with the consequences of a knowledge of Theosophy as with the knowledge itself. In the article referred to above, she states, for example, that "Theosophy develops in man a direct beholding." It is immediately clear from a further reading of her comments as well as from a study of her major works, that the "direct beholding" which results from contact with Theosophy is neither clairvoyance nor some other kind of psychic perceptivity. Rather, as HPB states further, "under the influence and knowledge" of the Theosophical philosophy, "man thinks divine thoughts" and "views all things as they really are." Theosophy, then, may be identified as the philosophy of right viewing.

The Theosophical philosophy comprises fundamental principles—those ultimates that denote the nature of the human being and the universe, pointing to a central Reality undergirding all existent manifestation. Encountering those principles, recognizing their inherent reasonableness and validity, we come to think in a certain manner, act in certain ways, and view all experience from a certain standpoint. We may not always be able to verbalize our realizations or even communicate the depth of our understanding to others, but our lives must finally reflect what we know. The individual who *knows* that all life is one in essence treats all living things with reverence. Such a person *is* brotherly, whether they lecture about brotherhood or not. The individual who has tapped the springs of peace within, having come to a knowledge that life in its ultimate essence is bliss, *is* peaceful. That person does not need to tell everyone around that peace has been found, because their very life exhibits that discovery. Not that we live our ideals (or even our knowledge) so perfectly, but that the manner of our living inevitably reflects, in some unspoken way, the fact that we do have ideals, that we have encountered a certain knowledge which is the wisdom-tradition known as Theosophy.

LIVE WHAT YOU KNOW

The intellectualizations involved in describing or defining what Theosophy is, are resolved into a mode of life that is continually transformative. Here is the living power of Theosophy by which textbook knowledge is transmuted into dynamic experience. It is to this task that HPB, as well as her Teachers, point on numerous occasions. A study of *The Mahatma Letters to A. P. Sinnett*, for example, reveals, among much factual information about the esoteric philosophy, that "The Occult Science is *not* one in which secrets can be communicated of a sudden, by a written or even verbal communication" [Letter 20]. *Something*, in other words, must take place within the aspirant, and that something has to do with a development which can only be described as an alchemical process whereby the elements of factual knowledge are placed in the retort of the personality, there to be transformed by the fire of experience into the gold of a life lived from a new point of view. So in the letter just quoted, the Mahatma K. H. continues: "The truth is that till the neophyte attains to the condition necessary for that degree of Illumination to which, and for which, he is entitled and fitted, most if not all of the Secrets are incommunicable." In an earlier communication, Mr. Sinnett is informed that:

> The truths and mysteries of occultism constitute, indeed, a body of the highest spiritual importance, at once profound and practical for the world at large. Yet, it is not as a mere addition to the tangled mass of theory or speculation in the world of science that they are being given to you, but for their practical bearing on the interests of mankind. (1993, Letter 12)

Much more could be cited, but the implications are always quite clear: one must live what one knows, and one will know more only as one puts into practice, *uses*, the knowledge which one has already gained.

The Path of Seeing

The Path of Seeing may be approached from another point of view. In the Mahayana schools of Buddhism, the Path which leads to enlightenment has often been described as dual in its essence: the path of seeing (*darsanamarga*) and the path of attention, sometimes translated as the path of practice (*bhavanamarga*). As Herbert Guenther points out in his excellent study, *Philosophy and Psychology in the Abhidharma*, the path of seeing involves the destruction of wrong views, "because the Truths have been caught sight of"; hence, the first step is the perception of "things as they really are," to quote HPB's statement. Only when wrong and distorted views concerning the world and ourselves are abolished, are we able to give attention to the reality that underlies all the phenomenal maze of existence. The path of attention, therefore, has been identified also as the "Path of Practicing the Truths," because, ultimately, to give attention is to act on that which has been seen. As Guenther comments further, the two paths are actually coexistent "since we cannot help acting on what we have seen unless we are moving corpses."

Thus the Noble Eightfold Path of Buddhism—the fourth of the great truths enunciated by the Buddha—may be summarized under two aspects: correct viewing of Reality and correct action or mode of life. It may be salutary to mention that, as Guenther reminds us, the *Vijnanavadins* declare that "to walk the Path of Practice takes already two *Asamkheyas* (one Asamkheya being equal to the lapse of as many years as we would express by a 1 followed by 140 zeroes) to say nothing of the time that is needed for arriving at this particular stage of the Path." Our first task is indeed to see the truth; perhaps, more precisely, we should say that our initial task is to fit ourselves to see the truth.

DIRECT BEHOLDING

How, then, can we gain that kind of "direct beholding" that will enable us to "view all things as they really are," to enter the path of seeing? Here, quite obviously, is the crux of the matter, not so easily answered as might seem apparent. Since we are concerned neither with a physical nor a psychical mode of perception, the "how" of the work to be undertaken must lie in a process that encompasses our total nature, but with an emphasis more especially on bringing into operation those deific powers which belong to the spiritual nature. Each one, of course, must take up the task for themselves. No one can open the eyes of another, although those who see can encourage those still blinded by the haze and smoke of the phenomenal to recognize that there is a realm of clear light. For the path of seeing involves the destruction of wrong views for achieving the goal. Hints about the requirements for entering that path have been given in many places, often veiled in allegory and legend, often stated openly, sometimes presented in ritual and symbol. Perhaps one of the most direct and simplest of all the statements depicting the process is that expressed in the Beatitudes: "Blessed are the pure in heart for they shall see God." To "see God" is indeed a "direct beholding." It is to see, wherever one looks, the Godlike, the divine nature revealed in all its potential glory. It is to know, with utter and complete assurance, that behind and beyond all phenomena there abides the noumenon, the One Reality in its entire splendor. To see THAT, to awaken the divine in every human heart, to perceive, not the coruscating colors of psychic auras but the pure white light of Spirit in every living thing; to read, not the past series of our own or others' lives but the message of the One Life writ large through all manifestation; here is the essence of that "direct beholding" which Theosophy engenders in the student-aspirant. And the way is always through a purity of heart, which seeks no return, asks only to see things as they really are, and is turned only to the service of life itself. The heart in which no self-interest can arise is the pure heart. The heart that pours forth love in ceaseless giving of itself for the healing and happiness of all is free of all selfish entanglements.

THE PROMISE AND THE VISION

Dr. Bhagavan Das, in *The Science of Peace*, summarized in this manner the essence of that "direct beholding" which is the fruit of Theosophical knowledge:

> When we can weep with one eye for the woes of the world and smile with the other for its joys; when we know the comedy of knowledge and feel the tragedy of feeling simultaneously; . . . when we feel at once sad over breaking bodies and glad over the deathless Spirit; when we know and feel that the insect's flutter, the river's roll, the ocean's surge, the wind's unceasing sigh, the march of the moon, planets, suns, stars—is all part of One and the self-same Life, My Life, one continuity of living motion, the endless manifestations of One Living Energy, the incessant transformations of One Living Substance which is Consciousness—then indeed we sense Nirvana in the flesh . . . For surely the Spirit is no more distant from, no less near to, any form of matter, gross or subtle, than any other. All planes and grades and shades of matter are equidistant from It, all equally within Its consciousness. (Das, 1948)

When we embrace that vision totally, looking with the eyes of Spirit upon the things of matter, perhaps then we shall understand fully what Theosophy is. When we are asked the question, our lives will exhibit the answer that words alone can never wholly express. Yet we will go on asking and being asked, "What is Theosophy?" Answering is only a continuation of the quest, as we invite all who seek to join us on the journey, for as the neophyte is told in *The Idyll of the White Lotus*:

> Life has in it more than the imagination of man can conceive. Seize boldly upon its mystery, and demand, in the obscure

places of your own soul, light with which to illumine those dim recesses of individuality to which you have been blinded through a thousand existences.

Let us, then, open our eyes and see: in right viewing lie the promise and the vision of the Theosophical life.

WHAT'S PRACTICAL
ABOUT THEOSOPHY?

Published in *The Theosophist*, Volume 103, August 1982

A question, which seems to recur in a variety of forms, points to the issue of the practicality of the Theosophical philosophy. One form of the question is simply that of the title of this article, while another directs the matter to the individual: "But what do Theosophists *do?*" Yet another form of the query involves the membership as a whole: "Why doesn't the Theosophical Society *do* something?" Whatever form the question takes, it is obvious that the inquirer does not consider study, meditation, lecturing, or the publishing of books to be practical activities.

Those who ask such questions usually point to the numerous fine organizations that are actively engaged in what used to be called "good works"—service which must be applauded for the benefit it brings to those who lack basic material necessities. People who stand in the front lines of causes are thought to be involved in the most practical of all activities, that of "doing something." Meditators and lecturers are obviously "doing" nothing, since there is no visible or measurable service. This is not to say that many Theosophists are not engaged in efforts to alleviate the suffering that exists everywhere, not only in the human kingdom but among animals and, indeed, all living things.

But what of Theosophy itself? Is Theosophy practical? Will its study result in any lasting benefit, either to ourselves or, more importantly, to the world about us? Is not philosophy a luxury which a world rapidly propelling itself to the brink of disaster can ill afford? Unfortunately, at this time when there is such a hankering after gurus who will solve all our problems with one swift gesture of hand or head, and such an absorption with phenomena that will satisfy our external cravings or bring us personal enlightenment, the study of Theosophy appears to lack a certain glamour or fascination that attracts and holds. Therefore, say our disparagers, it may be dismissed while we get on with the world's work.

It has been said, in regard to Buddhism, that just because its subject is everywhere one should not claim universal manifestation for it. The same may be truly said of Theosophy: just because Theosophy is everything, we should not make the mistake of assuming that everything is Theosophy. Professor Cheuk-Woon Taam, writing about Buddhism, points out that "it does not pervade the universe. It presents universal nature—universal mind—but it does so as a particular teaching. Confusing the specific teaching with its vast and undifferentiated subject is a trap that has caught several tigers." This is an apt description of Theosophy as well, and gives its students a useful warning!

In other words, before we can assess the practicality of Theosophy, we must be very clear what the Theosophical worldview is. We can perceive the practicality of Theosophical concepts only when we have, to some extent at least, begun to assimilate its eternal verities through a genuine contact (which involves mind, heart, reason, and intuition) with those universal verities.

True, Theosophy has not been officially defined, nor can it be, at least in terms that comprehend its universality, for every interpretation is by its very nature limited by the mind and under-standing of the one who offers it. But the fact that Theosophy is not subject to some one official and final definition does not mean that it is either an amorphous, vague notion or a concept that is limited by whatever anyone wants to make of it. It is a specific *darshan*—a view into the realm of Reality, a view across the plains of existence, which are all too often obscured by the mists that arise from them and which, in our ignorance, we may attribute to sources outside ourselves. It is precisely our view about existence and ulti-mate Reality that determines our action in the world. We may say therefore that the practicality of Theosophy lies in the extent to which we have permitted Theosophical ideas and ideals to work upon us in clearing up our perceptions so that we may see things whole and unobscured.

Every effort to define or re-define that worldview which The-osophy constitutes must inevitably carry us further into the domain of Wisdom, since our very efforts involve us in an understanding of precisely what is contained under the term Theosophy. Certain fun-damental principles begin to emerge, although they may appear in numerous contexts and under a number of guises depending on whether they are approached via the great religious traditions or in terms of philosophical concepts or, yet again, by means of truths revealed by science. They are fundamental—radical, in the original sense of that word—because they apply with equal validity to nature, humanity, and society. Open to a wide range of interpreta-tion and capable of re-embodiment in language suitable for the times, these ideas or principles affect the very fabric of collective and individual existence by providing spiritual values that translate into personal attitudes of motive and action. For the Theosophist, they should be no mere theoretical abstractions, but the very stuff of life as we struggle to realize their truth in our own experience and dis-cover their transforming power.

The practicality of Theosophy is emphasized in one of the most remarkable documents to be received during the early years of the Society's existence—a letter sent to A. P. Sinnett and said to be "an abridged version of the view of the Chohan on the T. S." C. Jinarajadasa, one-time president of the Society, wrote of the communication that "This is certainly the most important Letter ever received from the Adept Teachers," adding that it "is practically the charter for the work and development of the Theosophical Society throughout the ages." In that document, we read these significant words:

> For our doctrines to practically react on the so-called moral code, or the ideas of truthfulness, purity, self-denial, charity, etc., we have to popularize a knowledge of theosophy. It is not the individual and determined purpose of attaining oneself Nirvana (the culmination of all knowledge and absolute wisdom) which is after all only an exalted and glorious *selfishness*, but the self-sacrificing pursuit of the best means to lead on the right path our neighbor, to cause as many of our fellow creatures as we possibly can to benefit by it, which constitutes the true *Theosophist*. (Jinarajadasa 1973, 3)

At the risk, then, of oversimplifying the Wisdom that is true Theosophy, of providing yet another rephrasing of those fundamentals of an immortal truth, we may ask what are the ageless principles, which compose the Theosophical worldview? Let us for the present suggest five-fold delineation:

1. The universe and everything within it are one interrelated and interdependent whole, because

2. Every existent being, whether mountain, molecule, or human being, whether animal or atom, is rooted in the same universal spiritual Reality which is all and everywhere and yet transcends all its expressions.

3. Consequently, that one Reality may be perceived everywhere, in the order, harmony, beauty, and meaning of
the natural world as in the deepest recesses of mind,
heart, and spirit.

4. Therefore, the unique value of every living being is recognized and honored. That recognition expresses itself
in reverence and compassion for all living things, sympathy for the needs of each, encouragement of every
individual to find truth for themselves, and respect for
all paths that lead man to spiritual enlightenment.

5. Finally, all are engaged in one common enterprise—the
search for understanding, and growth towards self-realization. It is this process of inner growth that is the real
mark of being human. The whole of human experience
is indeed a process of self-unfolding, of an ever-deepening awareness of one's own true nature. Our root in
universal Reality endows us, therefore, with infinite possibilities for creating a future for humanity "whose
growth and splendor has no limit."

The practicality of such a world-view should be immediately
apparent, for it gives meaning and substance to existence and awakens
in those who perceive its essential truth the altruism which, according
to H. P. Blavatsky's definition, *is* occultism or pure Theosophy.

Anyone who reads the history of civilization will recognize the
validity of the axiom referred to on many occasions by the Adept
Teachers in their letters to A. P. Sinnett, that "ideas rule the world."
The force of ideas can never be underestimated, for our own lives
exhibit the ideas which shape our actions. A philosophy that is
based, for example, on the concept that within God's creation there
is an original structure by which a number of independent spheres of
life exist, each with its own rights, leads inevitably to actions which

separate and divide classes, nationalities, ethnic groups, creating antagonisms and conflicts. Such a philosophy, based on the views of Rousseau and the eighteenth-century Dutch Calvinist theologian and politician Abraham Kuyper, has dominated much of European history in this century and contributed greatly to the philosophy of colonialism from which the world is not yet fully liberated.

It has been said repeatedly, from the earliest days of the Society, that our task is to change the thought-patterns of the world. When we see the devastating effects caused by a philosophy of separatism and when we perceive the outcome of philosophies and views that are concerned only with special interests or with temporary results (the so-called "one life" views), we should be alert to the need for just such a change as the Theosophical philosophy can bring about. The task is not an easy one, nor can it be accomplished overnight. Yet it would seem to be the only worthwhile endeavor and one to which we should give all our efforts and our constant attention. It is far easier to be caught up in the maelstrom of current events which appear to be leading our present civilization downwards to annihilation than to stand against the current of circumstances and attempt to stem that "tidal wave" to which HPB once referred in speaking of the Theosophist's aim. What is demanded is a bravery of soul and a courage of the spirit that we must develop at all costs. There is really no other way, if we would be true to our ideals and loyal to the vision we have seen.

Dr. C. G. Jung, the eminent Swiss psychologist, is reported to have said on one occasion: "To the constantly reiterated question 'What can I do?' I know no other answer except 'Become what you have always been,' namely, the wholeness which we have lost in the midst of our civilized, conscious existence—a wholeness which we always were without knowing it."

Just so we must learn to answer that nagging question, "What's practical about Theosophy?" Studying the Theosophical philosophy, embracing the Theosophical world-view, we must learn to live out that wholeness, becoming whole ourselves, and instilling into the world about us those life-transforming ideas and values which alone can lead humanity to a new dawn of understanding, heralding a day of peace and unity.

No better answer to our question can be found than that given by H. P. Blavatsky when she wrote of the Theosophist's duty:

Without ever becoming a "Mahatma," a Buddha or a Great Saint, let him study the philosophy and the "Science of Soul," and he can become one of the modest benefactors of humanity, without any "superhuman" powers . . . Let [him] know at once and remember, always, that *true Occultism or Theosophy* is the "Great Renunciation of SELF," unconditionally and absolutely, in thought as in action. It is ALTRUISM, and it throws him who practices it out of calculation of the ranks of the living altogether. (1981)

LANDMARKS OF THE ESOTERIC TRADITION

This talk was given at the Parliament of the World's Religions, Chicago, August 1993 and published in *The Theosophist,* Volume 115, February 1994

In his introduction to the revised edition of Fritjof Schuon's classic work, *The Transcendent Unity of Religions,* Dr. Huston Smith refers to the manner in which Schuon draws a distinction between the esoteric and exoteric features of the various religious traditions. As Dr. Smith points out:

> The fundamental distinction is not between religions; it is not, so to speak, a line that, reappearing, divides religion's great historical manifestations vertically, Hindus from Buddhists from Christians from Muslims, and so on. The dividing line is horizontal and occurs but once, cutting across the historical religions. Above that line lies esoterism, below it exoterism. (Schuon 1984, xii)

Schuon's concept is not particularly original, but it does point to a very significant distinction in considering the several traditions. Commonalities among the faiths of the world cannot be sought in the realm of the exoteric, that area which concerns creeds, forms of worship and all other outer expressions. Rather one must look to underlying principles, ideas that in the abstract may be found to be significant as central to all traditions. If one could identify those basic principles, one would then come to the heart of religion itself from the esoteric point of view. It is to that task that we propose to address our present inquiry.

With the advent of the Theosophical Society into the world over a century ago, three essential features of the esoteric traditions were given an exoteric expression. These three features may be briefly summarized as:

1. There is a wisdom-tradition, a teaching or a doctrine, essentially esoteric in nature, once taught in mystery schools and found at the heart of every religion;

2. There are now and have always been those who know, those who by intensive study, meditation, and training have become initiates in the wisdom-tradition. They have been known by many names: the magi or wise ones, the Christs and the Buddhas, the sages and mahatmas, the rishis and the theodidaktos of the ancient mysteries. They have become both the guardians and the transmitters of the esoteric tradition.

3. Finally, there is a way, a path, a road that leads to the wisdom. There may be many approaches, but ultimately the way itself is one. And the way involves a mode of life, a discipline, a willingness to learn which also means an obedience simply not to an outer teacher, but to one's own highest and most inviolate Self.

Within each of these three divisions of the esoteric tradition, four major areas of concern may be identified: (1) the Ultimate

Reality or source from which all existence emerges; (2) the nature of the human state; (3) the ethos which defines the relationship both between the human and the source and between the human and all else in the universe; (4) the goal or end and aim of human existence. The further one goes in discussing each of these areas, the further one moves into the realm of the exoteric, where divisions are more apparent and agreement becomes more difficult. Yet it may be suggested that while the "knowers" of the wisdom-tradition have necessarily addressed these four areas in terms consonant with the language, culture, and mores of the historical periods in which they lived and spoke, the underlying wisdom, its esotericism, has been the same and consequently the way to it has also been fundamentally the same.

Is it possible, then, to identify the major landmarks of the esoteric tradition in such a way as to avoid religious sectarianism on the one hand and metaphysical reductionism on the other? Within the esoteric tradition there has been, and perhaps continues to be, a rich flowering of diverse expressions, each seeking to address itself to the major questions of our source, our identity, our action, and our goal. As those many expressions have taken on more and more exoteric clothing in terms of creeds and established belief systems, they have crystallized as the great religions of the world, all too often claiming exclusivity and thereby denying the true nature of religion itself. For religion by its very nature acknowledges the spiritual dimension in life and our connectedness (through *re-ligere*, or a re-binding) with it. This acknowledgement must first and foremost characterize the esoteric tradition and provide its total *raison d'être*.

"Religion . . . in its widest meaning," wrote H. P. Blavatsky in her journal *Lucifer* (November 1888), "is that which binds not only *all* MEN, but also *all* BEINGS and all *things* in the entire Universe into one grand whole." And she added,

> Unity of everything in the universe implies and justifies our belief in the existence of a knowledge at once scientific, philosophical and religious, showing the necessity and actuality of the connection of man and all things in the universe with each other: which knowledge, therefore, becomes essentially RELIGION, and must be called in its integrity and universality by the distinctive name of WISDOM-RELIGION. (1888, 182)

As that "Wisdom-Religion" may be seen as the source from which all the various religious systems have come, we may look to that "Mother-Source" as HPB once called it, for the unifying elements that will carry us beyond the external or exoteric forms which divide the many faiths to those internal and esoteric realities which inspire the religious spirit. It is those unifying elements that may comprise the landmarks of the esoteric tradition, although not everyone will agree upon the words which define them.

At the risk, then, of seeming to define that which—since it deals with the esoteric—is ultimately undefinable except as it is known in experience, I propose to list those landmarks in the language which Blavatsky used in summing up her exposition of the "Wisdom-Religion" or esoteric philosophy, as she presented it in her major work, *The Secret Doctrine*. Having identified that presentation as the "accumulated Wisdom of the Ages," she then set forth certain fundamental ideas which, in her judgment, constituted primary "laws" or essential truths inherent in that "Wisdom" (Blavatsky 1979, 1:272–76).

First and foremost is the recognition of "One Homogeneous Divine SUBSTANCE-PRINCIPLE, the One Radical Cause," which undergirds all existence. "It is," as Blavatsky put it, "the omnipresent Reality, impersonal, because it contains all and everything . . . It is latent in every atom in the universe, and is the universe itself" (ibid., 273).

The second principle, or landmark, of this tradition follows inevitably from the first: "The universe is the periodical manifestation of this unknown Absolute Essence" (1979, 1:273). The One Reality is "neither Spirit nor Matter, but both," though we perceive them as distinct, assigning to the ultimate the designation "spirit" and to manifested existence the term "matter." Yet if the ultimately Real pervades all existence, then It (or whatever other term is used for That which is beyond all terms) must embrace both spirit and matter. At the same time, the manifestation of That, the ultimate or the ultimately Real, is subject to continual change. Hence, the third axiom of this tradition:

"The universe is called, with everything in it, MAYA, because all is temporary therein . . . Compared to the eternal immutability of the ONE, and the changelessness of that Principle" (ibid., 274), the perceivable universe (perceivable not only at the physical level but by whatever mode of conscious perception) is subject to continual change. "Yet, the Universe is real enough to the conscious beings in it, which are as unreal as it is itself" (ibid.). Stated in another way, we begin to recognize a supreme mystery. While every existent thing, every existent being, is undergoing continual change, even its momentary exhibition has a reality for the perceiver. At the same time, the ultimately real is not in the *form* but in That which is beyond all forms and which can exhibit Itself through the transitory.

Essential to the esoteric philosophy is the recognition that "Everything in the universe, throughout all its kingdoms, is CONSCIOUS, i.e., endowed with a consciousness of its own kind and on its own 'plane of perception'" (ibid.). Such concepts as "dead" or "blind" matter, as Blavatsky points out, "find no place among the conceptions of Occult Philosophy." At the heart of this idea, of course, is the definition of consciousness and the distinction between rudimentary consciousness or life-responsiveness, if we may call it that, and self-awareness or self-reflective consciousness as we know it in the human kingdom.

Because consciousness or life is present throughout the universe, at the heart of all that exists, a further principle must be recognized: "The universe is worked and *guided*, from *within outwards*." This follows the well-known Hermetic principle or axiom that as it is above, so it is below, for even in our own experience, we realize that our actions are "produced and preceded by internal feeling or emotion, will or volition, and thought or mind." There is always the movement of consciousness from within outwards.

While others will inevitably define landmarks of the esoteric tradition differently, the principles just enumerated must be held to be basic. I have used the language in which HPB couched the ideas because I would contend that it was she who opened the door of the Wisdom-Religion to all who would seek behind the outer forms the hidden realities of existence. Her work bore testimony to the fact that there has always been in the world an esoteric tradition, part of every faith, taught under the veils of symbol and allegory in the mystery schools of past ages, accessible to those who would tread the ancient way to enlightenment. Always too there have been the Self-realized ones, the sages and seers of every culture, the saviors of humanity, those who live but to be of service and point the way to all genuine aspirants.

Ultimately, beyond all words and definitions, all statements regarding the esoteric tradition, lies the religious experience itself. In discovering our own spiritual center, that deep center at the heart of our very being, we move toward a genuine religious understanding, toward the One Truth which we may know, with utter certainty, lies behind and beyond all outer and partial expressions of it. As we journey inwards or upwards (spatial dimensions are irrelevant in the domain of the spirit), toward Truth itself, we move beyond all forms of worship, all creed systems, all differences of terminology, to the realization of that One Self, the Universal Self, the One Life, which is immanent in the heart of every being, and transcendent to all as the Supreme Reality, embracing everything.

Perhaps it is enough to know that there is an esoteric tradition which we may explore as we venture forth onto the domain of the spirit. It is enough to know that there have been, in all ages, the "knowers" of that Wisdom. And it is enough to know that we too may walk the way that leads to transformation, to peace, and to a healing of ourselves and of the world.

THE SECRET DOCTRINE: IS IT RELEVANT TODAY?

Published in *Theosophy in Australia,* Volume 58, December 1994

It has been said that we are born into the world we have made. This may be interpreted in many ways, but a number of contemporary thinkers are speaking of a *participatory* world, suggesting that we are cocreators in an ongoing evolutionary process. Such a concept echoes ideas presented well over a century ago by H. P. Blavatsky in her mind-stretching work, *The Secret Doctrine.*

When the question is asked as to whether those volumes are still relevant today, we could respond by acknowledging that one of the great mythical archetypes given unique emphasis by Blavatsky is that of human participation in the cosmogonic act. Participation in the creative processes of cosmogony constitutes the renewal both of the world and of ourselves. At critical junctures, it involves transformation. The stages in the cosmogonic act constitute in actuality the stages in our own development, the development focused through the psyche or soul. The contemporary writer—philosopher and psychologist—Jean Houston, has cast this thesis in dramatic form in her richly textured work, *Life Force: The Psycho-Historical Recovery of the Self.*

Beyond or, more properly, within the larger canvas of the cosmogonic process, with its several stages, lies the picture of our human endeavor. In exploring the relevance of *The Secret Doctrine* in our contemporary world, one could easily focus on those stages in the unfolding of a cosmos so beautifully and poetically delineated in the *Stanzas of Dzyan* which provide the skeletal structure on which Blavatsky hung the garments of occult wisdom, those eternal archetypal ideas to be found in every spiritual tradition. A sevenfold pattern is unfolded through the initial seven Stanzas of the ancient text of *Dzyan* (a word cognate with both *jnana* or knowing and *dhyana* or contemplative insight). Out of the formless, nondifferentiated matrix or womb of Space arises a cosmos, expanding from within without, reawakening the seeds of form and energies from previous universes. From a condition of nonspecificity arise all the specifics of a new universe, grounded in Universal Mind or Consciousness ever tending toward its own expression in the multiplicity of forms and images that derive from the archetypes inherent within it.

These stages of the cosmogonic process, as suggested, are repeated in the psychic processes of our own evolutionary journey. Sri Krishna Prem and Sri Madhava Ashish, in their work, *Man the Measure of All Things*, a most remarkable and perceptive commentary on the Stanzas, point clearly to the fact that those archaic presentations *are about us, our origins, our development, our conscious selves, and our bodily forms.* Summarizing the message contained in the Stanzas, Prem and Ashish add:

> If we have read aright the Stanzas' message, it is that this great universe and all that it contains . . . is a shining being, the unity of God spread forth before Him on the web of Time and Space. The study of it is the study of ourselves. He who experiences

the whole is Man. Cosmogony is Man writ large upon the Heavens.

We do not speak of such potential men as we are now, though even we, alone among all beings, have in our hearts the power to grasp the cosmos in our fists, to fuse again the mass of scattered splendour into a gleaming Pearl within the heart. (1969, 352)

If, then, the cosmogonic process is, to quote Prem and Ashish further, "entirely a movement within the unity of conscious being towards the achievement of self-conscious experience," the essential relevance of *The Secret Doctrine* is today, as it has always been, in terms of the practical application of a universal wisdom to our daily lives. For, again, to be conscious cocreators of the universe means ultimately that if we would transform the world, we ourselves must be transformed. So, whether we consider the *Secret Doctrine* to denote only the volumes by that name or to refer to that wisdom-doctrine which is ever *secret* until we reveal it in our lives and in the very fabric of our knowing selves, the relevance of our studies must be examined in terms of the lives we lead—lives that, acknowledging their source in the One Life, contribute meaningfully to the conscious building of a world in which all acknowledge their inter-relatedness in a genuine brotherhood.

In describing what he calls the "new paradigm thinking," the physicist Fritjof Capra, in his book, *Belonging to the Universe* (co-authored with Brother David Steindl-Rast), emphasizes that fundamental to the current world-view in science is the fact that "properties of parts can be understood only from the dynamics of the whole. Ultimately there are no parts at all. What we call a part is merely a pattern in an inseparable web of relationships." Extrapolating from this fundamental reversal of Cartesian and Newtonian thought, we must recognize that such a statement not only echoes the Theosophical world-view, but that it also defines the very basis of our human responsibility. The words of the preacher-poet, John Donne, *No man is an island*, spring to mind, as well as many other cryptic expressions of our interrelatedness not only with our own kind but with all existent beings and with the universe itself.

It could be argued that as the new paradigm thinking fostered by contemporary science (and reflected in many other fields of thought today) is making us aware of our interconnectedness with all life, that the current paradigm can be described as holistic, ecological and systemic, it is scarcely necessary to study the complexities of the cosmogonic and anthropogonic processes elucidated in *The Secret Doctrine*. What then is added in speaking of the relevance of that work to today's thought?

To answer that question, we may first state that *The Secret Doctrine* undertakes to describe the principles and sequences by which the periodical, perishable, phenomenal universe came into existence from and within the deathless, unmanifested, noumenal reality. As part of that undertaking, the work also expounds the essential nature and cosmic origin of our humanity, as well as the journey that must be taken in consciousness toward a destiny whose splendor we can scarcely comprehend. In brief, *The Secret Doctrine* supplies the metaphysics of a world-view that is being increasingly accepted today. However, to understand a rational, orderly, dynamically interconnected manifested universe is not the final object of HPB's work, although such an understanding will inevitably be gained from a study of her volumes. What is aimed at is simply a complete transformation of consciousness marked by the awakening of a new mode of thinking.

We can put the matter in another way. *The Secret Doctrine* declares that since the world is made out of spiritual awareness (*element principles* or *tattvas* to use the technical term, a "cascading of Thatness," to use a phrase coined by Prof. Hussein Nasr), the greatest truths have always been knowable and have been taught on this planet for millennia. Wisdom is primordial, embedded in the system, as it were, by virtue of the fact that all emerged from Universal Mind. Matter, life, and consciousness are functions of the nonmaterial or spiritual Reality. Understanding does not depend solely on physical evolution or the developments of human history. Understanding, in terms of *The Secret Doctrine*, means *insight conjoined with self-disciplined right conduct.* The new mode of thinking to which HPB's work refers is not the result of external factors (either physical or psychic stimuli to growth, the accumulation of knowledge, etc.). It is clearly the fruit of a life lived progressively in consonance with that Reality which is the ultimate cause of all existence.

The best we can do in an effort to characterize such a life in terms of HPB's dictum, that if you would come to the wisdom you must live the life, is to use such words as compassion, caring concern, and love. The awakening of the Buddha-mind, the Christ-mind, the Krishna-mind, demands not less than everything. In the furtherance of that aim, *The Secret Doctrine* is as relevant today as it was a century and more ago. It will continue to be relevant so long as there are those individuals willing to engage themselves in hastening the human journey toward the Light. That perceiving the Light, they may transmit its warmth and splendor for the healing of all who live. To undertake that enterprise is to become, in truth, conscious cocreators in the making and the remaking of the world.

THE PURPOSE OF
THE SOCIETY'S OBJECTS

Published in *The Theosophist,* Volume 118, November 1996

R ecently a friend asked me to discuss with him my views on the present work of the Theosophical Society. A member for some years, he was still convinced of the value of the Society, its importance as an organization devoted to the dissemination of Theosophy, but he was concerned about a comment made by a prominent member to the effect that it could take centuries before the ideal of brotherhood would be realized. In my friend's view, this was a defeatist attitude. Further, he said, why should the ideal of brotherhood continue to be emphasized in our First Object if this ideal was virtually unattainable? As I had traveled so extensively, did I feel that brotherhood was a lost cause, an ideal never to be realized in our lifetime?

Some time before the above conversation took place, I had been queried by another member as to the purpose and intent of the Third Object. In this case, the question concerned what the Society was doing or had been doing to "investigate unexplained laws of nature." Was not such investigation the province of science, and since most members are not scientists, were not we a little presumptuous to think we could achieve this object? Furthermore, he continued, what about those "powers" latent in human beings?

Were we doing anything to "investigate" such powers, whatever they might be?

An examination of the questions asked by these two members on two widely separate occasions reveals the need for every member to ponder the purpose and meaning of all three of the Society's Objects. The centenary of their adoption in their present form provides an opportunity to undertake an exploration, in some depth, of precisely what is aimed at in the Objects as well as the extent to which they are realizable or attainable. An interesting aspect of such an exploration would be an historical survey of the development of the Objects, noting the several changes that occurred during the Society's formative years from 1875 to 1896. For example, the Society's aim as set forth in 1875 was comprised in the single sentence: "The objects of the Society are to collect and diffuse a knowledge of the laws which govern the universe." However, that statement should be read in the light of the preamble to the original bylaws or rules adopted at the time of the Society's founding; that preamble opens with the words "The Title of the Theosophical Society explains the objects and desires of its founders."

Without quoting the 1875 document (preamble and bylaws) in full, it may be noted that a thorough reading of it indicates three essential points that have a bearing on the Society's work. First and perhaps foremost, especially in the light of numerous other statements by H. P. Blavatsky and H. S. Olcott as well as in *The Mahatma Letters to A. P. Sinnett*, the ideal of brotherhood was emphasized from the beginning. In the preamble, the statement is made that, "In considering the qualifications of applicants for membership, it [the Society] knows neither race, sex, color, country nor creed."

The second feature that may be noted is the emphasis given in that preamble to the policy of freedom of thought. Among other statements, the following may be cited: The Society's "only axiom is the omnipotence of truth, its only creed a profession of unqualified devotion to its discovery and propaganda."

The third most notable point is that contained in the opening statement of the preamble, as quoted above. It is evident that the very name of the Society indicated its purpose, its aims, and its objectives. While no attempt was made in that 1875 document to define *Theosophical*, and no official definition of Theosophy has ever been imposed on the members, it is clear that there is "such a thing as Theosophy," to quote H. P. Blavatsky herself. That phrase is found in an answer she gave to the inquirer, in *The Key to Theosophy*: The Society, she said there, "was formed to assist in showing to men that such a thing as Theosophy exists and to help them to ascend towards it by studying and assimilating its eternal verities" (1972b, 32).

These three essential features, emphasized in the earliest document issued by the Society at its founding in 1875, may be said to have found explicit expression in the Three Objects as these were finally worded in 1896. It is obvious, for example, that the first principle—brotherhood—which in 1875 was noted as the basic consideration for membership, became finally the foremost pillar on which the Society rested. Not only was an acknowledgment of the ideal to be fundamental to any qualification for membership, but it was to be the aim toward which the members would aspire by themselves, becoming a nucleus of a universal brotherhood. One is almost inclined to suggest that the realization of such a universal ideal can scarcely be achieved by humanity at large, if even the members of the Society which holds to such an aim have difficulty forming a nucleus (which surely means a living center) of a genuine brotherhood! What is aimed at is certainly more than a mutual feeling of good will, although even such a feeling is often hard to achieve in the daily intercourse with all types and kinds of persons whose behavior, views, and appearances may all too often seem completely contrary to our own! How far, we may well ask, have we ourselves advanced toward the ideal? To what extent have we engaged in forming a true nucleus of brotherhood? Are our Lodges, groups, centers, examples of what such a nucleus should be? No better place exists to test our First Object than the local branch to which we belong, and yet how often have our Lodges faltered, stumbled, and even fallen on the obstacles created by mis-understandings among members, by intolerant views and dogmatic assertions propounded in the very name of brotherhood? If our Theosophical groups cannot be workshops in which we practice the skills of brotherhood (for the ideal is a skill as well as an art), then can we learn to develop the skills of harmonious relationship in the milieu of daily affairs? Does not the First Object lead us to examine our own conduct, our own reactions, our own relation-ships with others and with all forms of life, to see whether we have come even close to the realization of the true nature of brotherhood based on an absolute knowledge of the unitary nature of all existence?

Freedom of inquiry, the second principle enunciated at the Society's founding, is encapsulated in the Second Object, encourag-ing us to expand our horizons, broaden our sympathies, deepen our appreciation for the paths of others, by studying all the fields of human endeavor as represented by the three major categories of religion, philosophy, and science. Such study, undertaken not that we may become "walking encyclopedias" or scholastic giants, but rather that we may deepen our understanding of the numerous ways that lead to a knowledge of the One Reality, requires a genuine freedom of thought. The study must be without preconceived ideas, without prejudice or bias, and without blind belief in the superior-ity of one way over another, if it is to support the first principle of brotherhood. And there can be no other reason for such study, for that ideal is surely the overarching principle for which the Society was founded.

If, then, the fundamental principle of brotherhood, so often reiterated by the founders, H. P. Blavatsky and H. S. Olcott, and by their Mahatmic Teachers, is enshrined in the First Object, and if the principle of freedom of inquiry is implied in the Second Object, what relation exists between the name of the Society and the Third Object? For, as suggested above, the opening statement in the preamble to the 1875 Rules indicated that the Society's designation as *Theosophical* pointed to its purpose, its aim, and its objectives. Therefore, we may well ask whether there is indeed any relation to be found between the Third Object, which seems to link two quite disparate themes ("unexplained laws of nature" and latent human powers), and the term *Theosophical,* a term which, for the most part, has been left officially undefined? To answer that question demands a close examination of all that is implied in the Third Object in the light, first, of the ideal of brotherhood and, second, of the Society's name.

As already pointed out, there is no official definition of Theosophy, no definition which has ever been imposed on the Society's members, none to which they must pledge some form of allegiance. How often it has been said that our sole bond of union is our pursuit of truth; our single aim the realization of brotherhood, our essential purpose to awaken in ourselves and others the intuitive awareness of the unity of all existence? Could it be that by searching out those hitherto "unexplained laws," embedded both in the universe and in our own nature (since all that is within the macrocosm is or must be within the microcosm), we inevitably awaken our own latent powers, powers which are a direct reflection of the creative potencies by which a manifested universe (and all within it) is brought into existence? Could it be that the very laws by which this whole vast system comes into being are "unexplained" until we have revealed them in our lives, since we are truly cocreators with the One (since nothing exists outside that Ultimate One), coparticipants in the creative processes by which that One reveals Itself in the many? And could it be that in this lies the acme of our human potential, all the powers within us but reflections of the one universal power in its many permutations and manifestations throughout all the domains of existence, throughout all the kingdoms of nature?

On one occasion, to a question concerning the Third Object, the president, Mrs. Radha Burnier, responded:

> This object implies study not only of Nature in its outer manifestation but of the relationship of all things, for all law is a statement of relationships. Knowledge of the laws is power to accelerate progress . . . the understanding of ourselves is connected with the understanding of laws, and of the forces at work behind them. (Burnier 1990, 24)

The ultimate law, we may suggest, is the law of right relationship, which must obtain throughout the universe, maintaining order and revealing both meaning and purpose. No wording describes the beauty and power of that relationship better than brotherhood, the expression in the human kingdom of that love which a poet described as "the burning oneness binding everything."

And how else shall we know that law, and all "unexplained laws" which evolve from it, except by awakening within ourselves those hidden potentials of our nature which lead to a full and complete realization of our unity? The Neoplatonist, Iamblichus, said it well:

> There is a faculty of the human mind, which is superior to all which is born or begotten. Through it we are enabled to attain union with the superior intelligences, of being transported beyond the scenes and arrangements of this world, and of partaking of the higher life and peculiar powers of the heavenly Ones.

By this faculty we are made free from the dominations of Fate, and are made, so to speak, the arbiters of our own destinies.

In the first letter from his Adept correspondent, A. P. Sinnett was advised to consider the "deepest and most mysterious questions which can stir the human mind—the *deific* powers in man and the possibilities contained in nature." As those "deific powers" stir within us, as we awaken to the wonder and glory and mystery of our human-hood, with all its responsibilities as well as its vast potential for doing good, we come to recognize that the Objects of this Theosophical Society are all interlinked and interrelated toward the single purpose of bringing about the transformation of ourselves and thus of the world.

The Objects point us in the direction we—and one day all humanity—must walk, the direction of *being* brothers, of knowing our brotherhood not just as a theory, but as a reality, acting at every moment in harmony with ourselves, with others, and with all the life that surrounds us. Yes, an ideal perhaps not to be realized in one lifetime, perhaps not to be realized for centuries to come, but truly an ideal for which no effort can ever be lost, no failure to achieve can ever be final, no action toward its attainment ever too small or insignificant.

We have been given magnificent aims to set before ourselves. The purpose of the Objects is clear: to remind us constantly of why we are here, not just as members of this Society, but as men and women walking the ways of humankind toward the gods.

KARMA AND DHARMA

Published in *The Quest*, Volume 91, November 2003

In *The Mahatma Letters to A. P. Sinnett*, a letter dealing principally with answers to questions put by Sinnett concerning Devachan, the Mahatma K. H. writes:

> You can do nothing better than to study the two doctrines—of Karma and Nirvana—as profoundly as you can. Unless you are thoroughly well acquainted with the two tenets—the double key to the metaphysics of Abhidharma—you will always find yourself at sea in trying to comprehend the rest. We have several sorts of Karma and Nirvana in their various applications. (1993, Letter 68)

Such a statement deserves deep consideration, although there may be a tendency to dismiss it as simply abstruse Buddhist metaphysics, without a great deal of relevance to the more basic Theosophical principles to which we have become accustomed. Karma, yes, an essential concept inherent in the Theosophical worldview, necessary as a guide in our lives, but Nirvana? No, not really relevant. And if I dare to suggest, as indeed I propose to do, that the concept of nirvana is related to, if not identical with, that less familiar principle known as dharma, there may be considerable skepticism regarding my placement of these two ideas in a central position within the Theosophical framework.

Yet precisely because the human state is central to the entire metaphysic of Theosophy—for that metaphysic is rooted in the proposition that Reality is realizable and is possible only through consciousness, or, more precisely, self-consciousness—it is therefore in reference to the human condition that we must seek the fundamentals of the Theosophical worldview and the principles that can guide us today. Such a proposition indicates the coherence, the inner integrity, and the holistic nature of that worldview. This does not exclude paradox; indeed there is paradox and there is mystery, forever leading us onward in our quest for the realization of the Ultimate.

To make a beginning, let us recognize that we, all humankind along with all sentient beings, are engaged in a journey, a great adventure. Whether we perceive that journey as simply a progress, a pilgrimage, through the years that separate our birthing from our dying or, on a grander scale, through all the cycles that include the numerous incarnations from our unconscious beginnings to our conscious perfection, the pattern of the adventure is the same. And it is that pattern, that ordering, which we may discover and which, I suggest, constitutes one of the most exciting—if not the most challenging—concept inherent in the Theosophical worldview. For the pattern is one of beauty, of the perfect proportion of all things, the essential rightness of creation itself. And we participate in that; we are held by that; we move in accordance with that divinely appointed ordering; and ultimately we are one with that, the Truth of our being, the Supreme Order whose very heart is bliss and peace.

What is the heroic journey? Is it not to live each day, each hour, each moment in full and conscious awareness of the underlying order, that cosmic harmony, in which we are rooted? Is it not to live in accordance with the law of our own best being? To live always beyond ourselves and to act in such a manner that our every action mirrors in its spontaneous rightness the cosmic act of creation itself? The heroic journey, the great adventure on which we are embarked, is the journey of the soul through our humanity to the realm of the gods; it is the journey from the bondage of non-knowing to the nirvanic freedom of luminous wisdom; it is the adventure of the spirit involving both a descent into hell and the ascent into heaven, stages symbolized in all the mystery schools and re-experienced in our lives as the painful and the happy moments produced by our own thoughts, feelings, and actions. And the twin keys to this heroic journey, the journey in which each one of us is the hero of his or her own story, are those great ideas to which many names in many traditions have been given: karma and dharma. The law of karma is that "one eternal Law in nature," as H. P. Blavatsky defined it, that law which she said "always tends to adjust contraries and to produce final harmony," and dharma, from which conceptually karma cannot be separated, and which has been translated in so many ways, but which as righteousness, as duty, as that which upholds, sustains, and nourishes our very being, is indeed the essence of our being: These two, karma and dharma, are but aspects of that one cosmic principle known in the Vedas as *rta*.

The journey may be more simply expressed: It is the way we all must take, the way from non-knowing (avidya) to knowing (vidya), from non-seeing to seeing, from non-hearing to hearing, from karma to nirvana.

St. Paul spoke of the way when he wrote to the Galatians:

Stand fast in the liberty wherewith Christ hath made us free, and be not entangled again with the yoke of bondage . . . For, brethren, ye have been called unto liberty . . . Walk in the Spirit . . . the fruit of the Spirit is love, joy, peace, longsuffering, gentleness, goodness, faith, meekness, temperance: against such there is no law. (Gal. 5:1–23)

Words full of mystical meaning, indeed, when read in the light of the concepts we are here considering: To stand fast in liberty is to become one with one's dharma, to be established in that state in which one is identified with the Christ principle that animates us and therefore to be no longer subject to that outer law that has buffeted us about for so long because we have been ignorant of its nature. To walk the world in that knowledge is to know what St Paul called "the fruit of the spirit," that love, joy, peace, goodness, which is to realize nirvana, the extinction of the personal self, the bliss of the One Self, here and now. It is to know, as Nagarjuna, the great Buddhist sage, said, "Nirvana is samsara; samsara is nirvana; between the two there is no difference."

To come to the knowing, which is wisdom, and to answer what St. Paul termed the call to liberty, which is enlightenment or spiritual illumination, means simply, in the Theosophical context, to enter upon the way or path that leads to the realization of the essential unity of life. "Who can here declare what pathway leads on to the gods?" asked the Rig Veda seer. It is that pathway which we all must take, either in full awareness of the task before us or unconsciously driven onward by the inexorable laws that govern all manifested existence.

"Man was created for the sake of choice," declares a Hebrew proverb, and choice in the way of our going is surely the most priceless of our human rights, even when our choices appear to be wrong. For the wrongness lies only in the continued experience of disequilibrium, the sense of conflict and suffering, which we all too often attribute to karma. We fail to see that karma is merely the lawfulness of existence itself and therefore productive only of what is in harmony with the causes we ourselves set in motion.

H. P. Blavatsky has pointed out that "Karma is a word of many meanings," a statement echoed in the comment by the Mahatma K. H. concerning the "several sorts of Karma." Further commenting on this concept, HPB has stated that "it is owing to this law of spiritual development superseding the physical and purely intellectual, that

mankind will become freed from its false gods, and find itself finally—
Self-Redeemed" (1979, 2:420).

In *The Theosophical Glossary*, attributed to HPB, the term is equated with "ethical causation," and the further explication is given:

> Karma neither punishes nor rewards, it is simply *the one* Universal Law which guides unerringly and, so to say, blindly, all other laws productive of certain effects along the grooves of their respective causations. When Buddhism teaches that "Karma is that moral kernel (of any being) which alone survives death and continues in transmigration" or reincarnation, it simply means that there remains nought after each Personality but the causes produced by it; causes which are undying, i.e., which cannot be eliminated from the Universe until replaced by their legitimate effects, and wiped out by them, so to speak, and such causes—unless compensated during the life of the person who produced them with adequate effects, will follow the reincarnated Ego, and reach it in its subsequent reincarnation until a harmony between effects and causes is fully reestablished. (Blavatsky 1973, 174)

But karma is only one half of the key that unlocks the meaning of existence as we travel the pathway that leads on to the gods. It is not enough to eliminate the causes we ourselves have set in motion and from which we all too often seek escape simply by generating further and still worse effects; within the context of achieving the aim of the human quest, we have an obligation to undertake our dharmic responsibility to travel the pathway that leads onward to the redemption of ourselves and the world. For we are destined to be world-redeemers, as the Self-redeemed of the world.

So dharma is the other half of the key that unlocks the meaning and purpose of existence. As the contemporary Indian philosopher S. Radhakrishnan points out in his book *Indian Philosophy*, dharma is the most important concept in Indian thought. This is so, as Radhakrishnan states, not as a matter of chance but as the necessary consequence of the basic postulate of an Ultimate Reality that is both immanent and transcendent. Ultimately and ideally there is, as the Theosophical worldview postulates, no duality between Brahman and the universe; one is the mirror image of the other. Consequently our duty, as Radhakrishnan expresses it, is "to return from the plurality into the One" through our experiences with the plurality. As the law of morality, dharma is an invitation to perform just this task. It is the work of "becoming perfect" as the Christian scripture states; it is the task that the alchemists called the *opus contra naturam*, which is that work against the downward and outward flow of nature into diversity. Dharma then is the law of our best being, inspired by the one reality pervading and penetrating the entire universe, and to act according to dharma is desirable, fundamentally moral, and conducive to the fulfillment of our human state. Hence, too, dharma (from the Sanskrit root *dhr*, which means "to hold together, to support, to nourish") also means the characteristic nature of a thing, and the dharma of an individual is consequently the essential quality of a human being in terms of his or her moral obligations, since to be human is to be a moral or ethical entity. Krishna emphasized this fact to Arjuna in the Bhagavad Gita (18:48), when he enjoined him in no uncertain terms that he had to act, even though every action carries with it its own burden of consequences: "All undertakings indeed are clouded by defects as fire by smoke." There is always karma, yet "Better is one's own duty though destitute of merit than the well-executed duty of another. He who doeth the duty (dharma) laid down by his own nature incurreth not sin" (18:47).

Here is truly the royal secret communicated by Krishna to Arjuna, as it has been communicated by every teacher to his disciples from time immemorial. We had it already noted in the words of

St Paul, although in different phraseology: "Walk in the Spirit . . . against such there is no law."

How are we to achieve that condition in which karma and dharma are unified? In the yogic literature, the path is by means of *tapas*, the burning away or eliminating all that is nonessential; in Buddhism, the aspirant is asked to engage in *upaya*, skillful means, action that reflects both wisdom (*prajna*) and compassion (*karuna*); in the Gnostic tradition, the principle of self-discipline, the regulation of one's actions in accord with one's dharma, was known as *askesis*, or spiritual skill, a term from which we derive our English word "asceticism."

To understand fully the concept of dharma is as difficult as to understand fully the idea of karma, although the latter has often seemed much simpler because of our tendency to give it a very simplistic definition. As the Mahatma K. H. pointed out to Sinnett, "We have several sorts of Karma and Nirvana in their various applications . . ."; as already noted, I am suggesting that Nirvana in that context—the snuffing out of the personal, egoistic self—is nearly synonymous, or at least correlate, with the concept of dharma as the fulfillment of one's nature, a fulfillment in which the personal, egoistic desire-self is altogether dissolved. Dharma has been defined in a number of different ways in the various Sanskrit works, from the Vedas to the *Dharma-shastra* literature.

In terms of the individual, dharma may be said to refer to our moral obligations; in terms of society, dharma is often defined as social solidarity; while in the context of religion, dharma has been called beatitude, since that is said to characterize the essential nature of religion itself; in the context of law, dharma represents its essential property as justice. In every category, however, it represents what we may call the imperative necessity of the mundane order to reflect the cosmic order, while at the same time it also represents the potential for further growth and transformation since the dynamism of process is the characteristic feature of the cosmos.

Nowhere are these twin concepts of karma and dharma more beautifully described as characteristics of the original cosmic order than in those glorious hymns of ancient India, the Vedas, and most particularly the Rig Veda. A full examination of the Vedic concept of *rta*, or cosmic order, would take us far afield, but even a cursory summary may be useful in establishing the importance of recognizing that the two principles—karma and dharma—are not only intimately related but are essentially one as aspects of the fundamental structure of the universe in which we as human beings are active participants.

To understand the significance of the concept of *rta* in the Vedic tradition, we must turn briefly to the subject of cosmic origins as expounded in the Rig Veda. The *rishis* responsible for the great Vedic hymns thought of the origin of the universe as a projection into manifestation, through a process we can only call divine contemplation, of all that lies latent within the One, the Eternal That, an unfolding from within without, as *The Secret Doctrine* so aptly describes it. This emanative process moves through three different stages, implying three levels or world orders. The first may be termed the primordial or transcendental level, the original emergence from the One, manifesting the cosmic order, *rta*, as the blueprint for all successive emanations. It is the emergence of the gods, who are, as Jeanine Miller defines them in her work on the Vedas: "personified agents of *rta* or cosmic order or harmony whose ordinances shine through *rta*, that eternal foundation of all that exists . . . This *rta* implies that perfect harmony existing between the essence of being, *sat*, and its activity, i.e., between the inner and the outer, the latter being but the effect and in some sense, the mirror of the former" (Miller 1976).

The blueprint is thus established and the scene is prepared for that cosmic action which is in accordance with the inherent lawfulness (*rta*) of the entire process. As Miller states, "It implies also the spontaneous rightness observable in the majestic movement of the stars, the recurrence of the seasons, the unswerving alternation of day and night, the unerring rhythm of birth, growth, death of each form of life, that rhythm which is the very breath of the divine action."

So at the primordial level, *rta* expresses itself as the differentiating principle whereby the One becomes the two poles of manifestation, the two become the three, and the three the many. The constant transformation points to a law of becoming, of change and adjustment, to which all creation, all successive emanations will be subject, all being subservient to the one law of transformation or harmony (*rta*), that law which reveals the ordered course of the universal pattern. As the Rig Veda puts it: "By law (*rta*) the herds of the universe (i.e. the stars) have entered the cosmic orbit. Firmly fixed are the foundations of *rta* shining in beauty, manifold are its beauteous forms" (4:23).

In the natural process of emanation, then, the first level gives rise to the second, the intermediate level, where the gods themselves manifest and function. Here the universal law, *rta*, provides the dynamics for the unfolding in every realm of activity throughout the entire manifested system, each god or *deva* performing his task in perfect harmony: "one-minded, one-intentioned, unerringly move together to the one purposeful accomplishment" (ibid., 6:9).

Such is the beautiful description of the action of the intelligent forces in the universe; their solidarity, their essential righteousness, their concerted activity are the unique features of their manifestation, marking them as agents of the law of harmony, by which, through which, and in which they live and perform their various tasks:

One is the mighty godhood of the shining-ones. (Rig Veda 3:55)

Denizens of heaven, flame-tongued, thriving through the law, they abide brooding in the womb of law. (ibid., 10:65)

True observers of the law, faithful to the law, righteous leaders, bounteous to every man. (ibid., 5:67)

Law abiding, born in law, sublime fosterers of law . . . (ibid., 7:66)

Herdsmen of the supreme law, whose decrees are truth. (ibid., 10:63)

So the gods, intelligent agents of the law—not to be anthropomorphized at their loftiest levels and yet to be seen as the products of former systems who have won their immortality through past aeonic cycles—reveal *rta*, the cosmic order, embodying it in their very being, since they are established in that nirvanic state in which their nature is both compassion and truth, bliss and knowledge.

Finally then, as a natural emanation through the cosmic action of the gods, there arises the phenomenal world where the individual rules and by virtue of his or her freedom disrupts the divine equilibrium, shatters the original cosmic harmony underlying all things, and suffers the consequences (karma) in their progress along the pathway of return, that pathway that leads on to the gods, enlightenment, and illumination.

What is known as *rta* or cosmic order exhibits itself in the transcendental and intermediate realms as dharma, the law of becoming in accordance with the rightness of one's being, the inner obedience to that duty which marks one's place in the cosmic scheme; there, in those inner realms, a certain state that has been called "karma-less-ness" obtains, a state of nirvana since there is the extinction of all sense of separateness, of a personal self, in that "one-minded, one-intentioned" harmonious action which accords with truth (*satya*). Yet because of *rta*, cosmic order, there is that aspect of the law that we experience in this phenomenal universe, which we call karma, failing to recognize that the term itself simply means action, although too often, since our actions disrupt the harmony of the universal order, we attribute to karma the concept values of goodness and badness.

While we have grossly oversimplified the great Vedic tradition and have necessarily omitted from so brief a survey other and equally important aspects of the entire process of the emanation of a manifested universe (this in itself is the subject matter of the entire first volume of *The Secret Doctrine*), I suggest we begin to see the magnificence and splendor of the Theosophical vision in terms of its relevance for us who are embarked on the human phase of the journey that leads onward to . . . what shall we call that unknown goal toward which all creation moves? How shall we define a culmination still unknown to us, and yet which we dimly sense and in our profounder moments of insight know in some mysterious manner is both in the distant "there" and in the very present "here" of our existence?

To live in accord with the cosmic order, to travel onward in harmony with the law of our inmost being—these are the consequences of *rta* in terms of karma and dharma, twin keys to the heroic journey of our humanity. These are the self-imposed demands inherent in the phenomenal world because of the very nature of the transcendent realm of which the phenomenal world is an emanation.

As we turn to our journey in the realm of the phenomenal, in the worlds of manifestation, we may gain a new appreciation for the concepts of karma and dharma, perceiving in them both challenge and opportunity to move more quickly on our heroic way. For a certain heroism is called for, a bravery of the spirit to accept the challenge of the pathway that leads onward, a soul-courage to take up the opportunity that is our human birthright, the opportunity to win our immortality and join the gods, if I may put it thus, in their aeonic labors.

It is truly the great adventure of the spirit in which we are engaged, and the very word "adventure" is rich in meanings we have forgotten or overlooked. It is a word that appears frequently in the legends that arose in Europe in the twelfth and thirteenth centuries, legends telling of the quest for the Holy Grail. Some scholars, translating those legends from the medieval French, particularly Pauline Matarasso, have pointed out that the French word *aventure*, from the old French *aventiure* in Middle High German, both from the Latin *adventura*, translated into modern English as "adventure," raises problems both linguistic and interpretive, simply because it contains such a wealth of meaning that we have today no single word to comprehend. In essence, it meant both karma and dharma; and when, in the Grail stories, Perceval or Parzifal was told, "Go where adventure leads you," it is clear that the directive was intended as a command to the hero to act in accordance with the pattern established by his own past (what we would call karma) and also to fulfill his particular mission or destiny (what we would call his dharma). So, as Matarasso points out in her commentary of *The Quest of the Holy Grail,* the anonymous work attributed to the Cistercian monks:

> The adventure . . . is the challenge which causes man to measure himself against standards more than human . . . the adventure is above all God working and manifesting himself in the physical world. To accept an adventure is to accept an encounter with a force which is in the proper sense of the word supernatural, an encounter which is always perilous for the sinner or the man of little faith and much presumption.

She adds, "I think it is true to say that the author of *The Quest* uses the concept of the adventure as a symbol of providence just as precisely and consistently as he uses the Holy Grail as a symbol of mystical experience." In her translation of the legend, therefore, she has used a variety of words, commenting, "I feel . . . bound to stress that beneath the multiplicity of terms there runs through the story like an unbroken thread the idea of providential guidance which man can either accept, refuse, or simply fail to see."

One could illustrate this idea by numerous references to the Grail legends as they appeared in Europe during that turbulent period of the early Middle Ages, a period not very different from our own, when new values were arising and a new consciousness coming to birth. Joseph Campbell comments at some length on the use of the term "adventure" in the Grail legends in reference both to the new values coming to birth at that time in Europe and to the changing perspectives of our modern age. In his work *Creative Mythology* (the fourth volume in his series *Masks of God*), Campbell points out in his discussion of the term "adventure" in connection with the Grail legends that it had reference to the fact that "the casual, chance, fragmentary events of an apparently undistinguished life disclose the form and dimension of a classic epic of destiny when the cosmic mirror is applied, and our own scattered lives today, as well, are then seen, also, as anamorphoses."

The use of the term "anamorphosis," by the way, is most interesting, since the word (from the Greek, "to form again or anew") often refers to a distorted image, taking us back to the Vedic concept of this phenomenal realm as an image, too often distorted by our perception, of the transcendental sphere of the gods.

All of this is an interesting study in itself, and of course it is closely related to a deeper study of karma as a central concept in understanding human destiny.

However, what I have sought to emphasize is that by following the advice of the Master K.H. as to the importance of a study of "Karma and Nirvana," we may derive a new understanding of the manner in which these principles may serve to guide us today. We may come to recognize that in meeting all that is appropriate to us as a result of our past—that which we call our karma—and in accepting the challenge of our inevitable destiny, the rightness of our self-becoming nature—that which we call our dharma—we will have made clear the pathway that leads on to the gods. This is the nirvanic pathway, if you like, for it is essentially the way of bliss in which the separate self is extinguished in favor of that greater light of the Universal Self.

From the Vedic seers and rishis to St. Paul onward to the Gnostics, the alchemists, and those who penned the Grail legends, the story has been told of the human—the heroic—journey. The patterns of events in our lives, when we have eyes to see the patterning, reveal that, as Joseph Campbell puts it, "Beneath the surface effects of this world sit . . . the gods." For here we may learn to mirror that cosmic harmony that holds the stars in their orbits and reveals itself in the rhythms of tides and seasons.

In *The Voice of the Silence*, reference is made to a stage when "once thy foot hath pressed the bed of the Nirvanic stream." Then is asked the question: "What see'st thou before thine eye, O aspirant to god-like Wisdom?" And the traveler replies: "I see the PATH; its foot in mire, its summits lost in glorious light Nirvanic. And now I see the ever narrowing Portals on the hard, the thorny way to Jnana."

Hard and thorny it may appear to be, the road to jnana, knowing, to Gnosis or Sophia-Wisdom, but our destiny is no other than to walk onward, for:

The way to final freedom is within thy SELF.
That way begins and ends outside of Self.

SELF-TRANSFORMATION

THE NEED
FOR REGENERATION

Published in *The Theosophist*, Volume 89, March 1968 under the title "The Regeneration of Man"

This may seem a strange time in which to engage in some long-term weather forecasting for humanity and even to suggest that it is possible for us to alter our own human temperatures, for it would appear doubtful whether we can even weather the next storm. Violence seems to be the natural order of things, and every country of the world is experiencing an upheaval of one kind or another; disturbances that are political, racial, social or economic in nature. Today, *right* has come to be spelled *r-i-o-t* and protest demonstrations have taken the place of discussion and dialogue.

In view of our present capability to destroy not only ourselves but the very earth upon which we walk, we may be inclined to shrug off, as the words of an impractical dreamer and idealist, the musings of the American jurist, Oliver Wendell Holmes, who once wrote, "I think it not improbable that man, like the grub that prepares a chamber for the winged thing it never has seen but is to be—that man may have cosmic destinies that he does not understand." Today, in the Western world at least, those cosmic destinies are more likely to be interpreted as "life, liberty and the pursuit of hallucinations."

Yet a case can be made for the view that we achieve some measure of understanding of ourselves and our world only in facing crises. The historian Arnold Toynbee suggested that only by meeting challenges do individuals raise themselves to a new level of creativeness. Surely the challenges today are of such a nature as must compel us to seek new stages of creative exploration if we are to resolve the conflicts in which humanity is engaged. The word "crisis," after all, comes from a Greek word which means literally "point of decision," and one can hardly escape the implications of the decisions with which we are daily confronted. While in some instances we may attempt to escape from the responsibility of decision, there are all too many instances where we cannot escape.

Fundamentally, the response to any crisis as a point of decision in our lives is determined by our view of ourselves, our view of who we are in our essential nature. After all, it is we who are examining the world, not the world that is examining us, and in our humanly possible process of thinking, it is *we* who are constantly making determinations that affect both ourselves and the world about us. Therefore, we must start with ourselves and our vision of ourselves.

The experience of our time may lead us to accept a vision of the human—if "vision" is the correct term for such a conception—in which madness, emotional degradation, illicit "love" and drug addiction are truer than sanity and emotional harmony, health, and love itself. Today our inhumanity to each other has increased to perilous levels, and this would seem to be fostered not only by the events on the battlefields of distant lands but by the pseudo-events to which we are daily subjected on our television screens. Dr. Erich Fromm has well described our present situation, including our present peril: "A man sits in front of a bad television program and does not know that he is bored; he reads of war casualties in the newspaper and does not recall the teachings of religion; he learns the dangers of nuclear holocaust and does not feel fear; he joins the rat race of commerce, where personal worth is measured in terms of market values, and is not aware of his anxiety."

Even as theologians debate the death of God, we are more directly confronted with the possibility that human is dead, transformed into a thing, into a mechanism producing and consuming and idolizing other things. The anti-Hero has become the hero of the age. The cult of instant enlightenment has been matched only by the risk of instant conflagration. Here indeed is the crisis, a "crisis of confidence" as it has been called, for we have lost the age-old conception of what it means to be human which for so long spurred on our achievements in the arts and sciences. We no longer trust ourselves, which means we trust no one else.

Yet there is no one else to trust. As the spokesman of nihilistic existentialism, Jean Paul Sartre once put it: "Man can count on no one but himself. He is alone, abandoned on earth in the midst of his infinite responsibilities, without help. With no other aim than the one he sets himself, with no other destiny than the one he forges for himself on this earth." There is both despair and hope in such a vision: despair when human beings are viewed as shadowy figures in the half light of madness, degradation and death; hope, when people are seen as something more, noble figures of dream and aspiration, whose stature reaches to the stars. Prophecy may be a fatuous business, but it hardly requires prophecy to foresee that people in coming ages may look back on this century as among the most splendid and most terrible in the annals of the human race. For ours is truly a great and a tragic time, when intrepid individuals have gone farther outward into the unknown and farther inward into the unknowable than in all the centuries before. It is a time heroic as few ages have been heroic; trusting ourselves, we have orbited ourselves into outer space, even as we have mistrusted our neighbors and engaged in vast wars and horrible cruelties.

Given a wider vision of ourselves—a vision of our essential nature which comprehends all our possibilities—the future can be even more splendid with achievement. Our age, of course, is not really unlike any other in predicting that we have already achieved as much as possible, have attained as much as we can ever know. After the Copernican revolution, it appeared as if humanity had been permanently belittled, reduced to a traveling position on a relatively insignificant planet far from the center of things, and the astronomy of the last four centuries has made our earthly habitation more and more trivial in terms of the vastness of the cosmos. The evolutionary theory propounded in the nineteenth-century showed our derivation from humbler forms of life, our basic dependence upon techniques of survival not essentially different from those of other living things, and so served to cast further doubt on any special position of importance the human might occupy in this universe. Edward Gibbon in his famous *Decline and Fall of the Roman Empire* assured this age that man had, at last, fought his way out of superstition and confusion, and had achieved a rational perspective on himself and the world, so that there was no longer any need for revolutions or changes in human society. And Gibbon, we may remember, wrote just before the French and American revolutions. Science, whether it be biological, psychological, or sociological, has always tended to see man in terms of what he is, seldom in terms of the untapped potentials within him.

So it is that today we seem to face the formlessness of our present life only in terms of a limited view of ourselves—a view that permits of no further development beyond our present psychological structure. That formlessness appears under three obvious aspects: first, an environmental chaos, which includes a waste of human and material resources; second, a social chaos, which includes a lack of common ideas, common feelings and common purposes; and finally, an inner chaos, which includes our individual inability to live in harmony with ourselves. Three basic tasks are before us, therefore, and it is these that constitute the necessity for a regeneration of humanity. We must build bridges between humanity and Nature, between one person and another, and between our biological-psychological nature and our deeper Selves, for ultimately it is only as each individual unifies themselves within that they can aid in unifying the world, creating a new social structure that will, as a consequence, construct a new physical environment. For only the individual who can work with himself can work with other people. The building of these bridges, the reintegration of all aspects of our life, is the great contemporary challenge, and in this work the full power of creative vision coupled with the development of our inner sensibilities must have a central role. The full potentialities of our humanness must be called into play, but those potentialities must be seen not merely as incompletenesses, but radically new developments possible because of our very nature as human beings. The possibilities of growth within us bear the relation of acorn to oak tree, of caterpillar to butterfly, or of ovum to adult. So in thinking of these potentialities, we must keep in mind a principle well known among biologists: no germ has an absolutely predestined future, for its future always depends upon the conditions of growth and realization afforded it, and no conditions of growth and realization produce the same consequences with different germs. We confront, both in Nature and in ourselves, an infinite number of realizations of potentialities.

So the one great reality that must never be forgotten is that there is always more. There is the rim of the sea beyond which one pushes, and there is land beyond. When the surface of the globe has been fully explored, when the known sidereal universe is scanned, there is the question of other universes. But often, as we shall see, the new development must be in a radically new direction—a direction perhaps inconceivable from our present vantage point.

Dr. Gardner Murphy, in his excellent study of *Human Potentialities*, posits three kinds of human nature (1958, 15–25). The first is essentially the product of the evolutionary process, not necessarily a fixed biological human nature, but a biological framework which serves as a pattern or mold for further developments. The interaction of this human nature with the world or the environment about us results in a simple stimulus and response mechanism; my body sits upon a chair and an impression is made, which may be termed a response to the stimulus of the chair. That response soon becomes interpreted, however, so that we may say: "This chair is uncomfortable," though we may note, in passing, that it is not really the chair which is uncomfortable, but our relation to the chair that produces some discomfort; in other words, it is we, not the chair, that is uncomfortable. Therefore, since the individual is more than our biological heritage, there comes into play a second human nature, filled with the interpretations of our responses to the stimuli of the external world, a human nature which Dr. Murphy refers to as the cultural mold, for it involves the development of ways of feeling and thinking. The world of language, of physical invention, of logical and mathematical reasoning, of religion and ethics, are all examples of worlds of cultural derivation, which, being shared with others, become standardized and transmitted, essentially intact, from generation to generation. This nature can act on, modify, and even change biological considerations. The emergence of this second human nature may be visualized as the creation of a life-space or a life-field in which the interaction between what we term our personality and the world about us takes place. It is, of course, never the whole of the personality that is engaged in the contact with our environment, but only various aspects of it which grapple with aspects of the environment, and consequently the environment and the personality are both, in a sense, fragmented. Often as a result of this fragmentation, we experience our separateness, our alienation, and our isolation.

Unfortunately, however, a certain rigidity develops in the inter-action at the cultural level, a certain arbitrary "self-evident" quality that results from the transmission of modes of behavior, of thought, or of feeling. This is the source of the great inertia, the great rigidity and refractoriness to change that frequently exists at the cultural and social levels of human existence. Hence, when there is rebellion, as there is in the world today, particularly among our young people, it appears violent, wild, primitive, and we do all we can to bring it back under control, making it conform to what have been accepted as the proper modes of behavior, of ethics and morals.

But, Dr. Murphy suggests, there is a third human nature, which can be called into play and which represents the possibility of a new development by which we can heal ourselves and thus heal the world. Before examining this third human nature, however, we may digress briefly to note the correspondences between the three human natures as Dr. Murphy defines them and the Theosophical conception of the human being as portrayed in that most remark-able book, *The Secret Doctrine* by H. P. Blavatsky. For the Theo-sophical student has a vision of the human being as a union of a great complexity of forces, from the most subtle or spiritual energies to the most dense or material elements, and this union or combina-tion is effected by mind, *manas,* a term that comprehends much more than the English word "mind," for it includes the principle of insight, of discrimination, as well as of pure thought itself. We are, then, far more than a physical or material form; we are even more than simply spiritual being; we are, rather, a unique embodiment, a unique expression, of both spirit *and* matter, harmonized by the presence of manas. So, in understanding the human being, HPB suggested that we must take into account a triple evolutionary pro-cess, what Dr. Annie Besant referred to as man's triple pedigree.

There is, corresponding to Dr. Murphy's first human nature, the physical or biological pedigree: here is the simple life energy of the physical-etheric entity. There is, next, corresponding to the cultural mold, the intellectual evolution, the manasic unfolding, where indeed patterns do tend to become rigid, dogmatic, static, inflexible, although the mind also holds the key to our further development as man in the release of potentialities from a deeper center, which is our third human nature, the monadic or spiritual pedigree.

For there comes a time when we are aware of something more—something beyond the stimulus-response patterns of the biological nature and beyond also the psychological reactions in the life-field we have created about us in the cultural mold of our habitual existence. That something more may come, first, as a small voice, often a dissident voice, which may at times erode and even ultimately destroy vast rigid blocks of cultural tradition. It is the kind of voice that spoke through Jesus the Christ and Gautama the Buddha, as well as through every great world teacher, and which has always quite literally revolutionized the cultural milieu of the time. Such a voice comes first as a creative thrust towards understanding, a creative thrust inwards which calls forth a response from a new level, a level of our being previously untouched and hence unexperienced, but which, once experienced, becomes the new center of action, so that we are no longer caught in the reactionary field of the personality and its limited psychological patterns, but are free to act from that point of decision which is the Immortal Self. As a result of a new thrust inwards, which is really the only direction left open to us today, we are able to open up a new channel of creative energy, discovering new potentials, which enable us to act directly upon the world since we are no longer subject to the reactionary patterns of the past, which have bound us to the karmic wheel of action and reaction. This is, quite literally, a movement in a new direction. The essence of this way of thinking is that the human nature of the future cannot, then, be predicted by a sheer extension of the trends of the present. I suggest that this "visionary" way of thinking is indeed the only way of thinking left open to us.

An excellent and most useful analogy is available to us in the transformations undergone by certain animals in the course of their lives. From time immemorial the metamorphosis of the caterpillar into a butterfly has served as a metaphor for the intimations of a higher being within ourselves. For the same creature, in the quiescent pupa, the nymph or chrysalis, has provided a beautiful image of contemplation, of serene expectation of things to come, of the promise of resurrection and regeneration. It is interesting to note that biologists today recognize that in insects with complete metamorphosis, the egg contains the rudiments of all the organs that distinguish the three stages of larva, pupa and mature form, and, in addition, all the equipment necessary for the processes leading from one stage to the next. In fact, three radically different forms are prefigured in the egg of the butterfly. In the caterpillar stage, certain organs function fully, while certain others that will develop in the mature stage of the butterfly are no more than little groups of cells that are called "imaginal discs." Experiment has revealed a complex mechanism by which the modifications of the various forms and the transformation from one stage to another are strictly regulated. The study of the processes of development indicate that the infinitesimal quantity of living substances constituting the egg creates these patterns and guides and regulates the events which ultimately result in the ordered sequence of the animal's future growth. However, most biologists agree that the discovery of this mechanism does not reduce the egg to a mosaic of patterns, functioning together like parts of a machine, but that it leads to a view of the mechanism of growth as a system "developing itself," a process embodying the whole specific nature of the living creature. Creative potentials of growth and realization are present even in the imaginal discs! While science still cannot account for the change of mood that must take place in a caterpillar whereby after a long, monotonous period of feeding on some plant (and frequently only one particular plant) the creature suddenly looks around for an entirely different place favorable for pupation, nor what, finally, leads the creature to cast off the pupal covering, spread its wings, and totally alter its mode of life to become a butterfly. A number of experiments have shown that the brain of the insect exerts an indispensable influence on the entire process of metamorphosis. It is known that a caterpillar can be kept alive for a considerable time without a brain, but no metamorphosis will occur. It appears that at a certain moment a particular activity of the brain sets in, producing in the organism as a whole a state of readiness for transformation.

This mysterious and beautiful process of metamorphosis may find its correspondence in our own growth, for within us, from the very beginning of our entry upon the human stage, exist all the potentials of our future splendor, our ultimate achievement. What change of mood must occur within us that prompts us to turn in a new direction, what inner processes must occur to produce that state of readiness for transformation that will lead us from what David Riesman has called the "linear" way of thinking—taking one gentle step at a time—to that creative thrust upwards or inwards which will release the creative energies of the Immortal Self, enabling us to alter our present mode of existence and to soar free in the dimensionless realm of the spirit? Here we are asked to consider the possibility that we are part of the sweep of the cosmos and that our fulfillment is in a sense dependent on our realization of deeper contacts with cosmic structure than we ordinarily allow ourselves. As we open this new channel inwards, become aware of the possible self that lies beyond the present actual self, we effect a breakthrough so dramatic as to change ourselves and our world, creating a new relationship within ourselves that must result in a new and dynamic relationship between ourselves and others, and between ourselves and the world.

Someone recently has called those who have affected such a breakthrough into the source of the Self the "real swingers" of our age, including among them such individuals as Jiddu Krishnamurti, Teilhard de Chardin, and Michael Polanyi. It has been suggested that "the openness to transcendental possibilities is undoubtedly one of the most decisive characteristics of the real swinger. For whatever name it goes by, it enables him to think and act radically." Such thought and action is not to be confused with the rebellious and violent behavior that flaunts tradition by creating new conformities. It is indeed one thing to react contemptuously to the corruption of the world, but quite another to reach constructively for the vision and technique which will transform that which is corrupt into something whole again.

Within each one of us hides the real swinger, the Immortal Self. It may take courage, endurance, and patience to call forth that element in us, but today we have no other choice, for the crucial issue of our time is the emergence of this swinging Self. We must now take our destinies in hand and permit the emergence of those monadic energies which alone can transform manas from its attachment and association with desire (kama) in the relentless circle of action and reaction to its deeper linkage with love (buddhi), releasing ourselves from the caterpillar life of animal existence that we may embark upon our truly human career. So our regeneration becomes the transformation of the world, for regeneration always means a spiritual rebirth, a rebirth from the center, a creative renewal in terms of what is possible because it exists within us, and such regeneration alone can effect the world's healing.

Dr. Erich Fromm has said that he believes, "the One World which is emerging can come into existence only if a New Man comes into being—a man who has emerged from the archaic ties of blood and soil, and who feels himself to be . . . a citizen of the world whose loyalty is to the human race and to life, rather than to any exclusive part of it" (1962, 178). Thus indeed there is "help for man only in man" as an old saying has it, but not in the being of psychological reactions. There is help for us only in the Immortal Self, that in us which is forever recreating us and so recreating the world. A great Adept has written: "Since there is hope for man only in man, I would not let one cry whom I could save."

For all practical purposes, living in such a manner means developing the child heart and learning to love all things beautiful; it means becoming more honest and simple and true, not impatient with the faults of others or irritated with their weaknesses. It means sensing the sweet side of life and getting to know each other better. It means we bother less about whether we are impersonal or not, for we live from a deeper center which is the Self, aware always of one's self as part of the great hierarchy of life. Most of all, it means expanding the sense of identity from the narrow circle in which we move to include every other member of the human race in the full realization of universal brotherhood.

THE QUEST
FOR MEANING

Published in *The Theosophist,* Volume 102, March 1981

No cry is more plaintive or more persistent, no cry more heart-rending or difficult to answer than the simple plea, "Why?" Even as children beginning the exploration of the world about us we seek to know why things are as they are: *Why is water wet? Why does fire burn? Why do trees grow upwards and not down?* An endless series of questions—each one beginning with "Why?"—marks our entry into awareness of ourselves and our world of people, events, and things.

Growth from childhood into maturity only changes the object of our inquiry; the question remains essentially the same. We demand meaning, not simply knowledge of how things operate or what things are; and this imperative demand for meaning pushes us relentlessly forward to explore the unknown territory of life itself. For all the "whys" we have asked—*Why did this happen to me? Why did my friend have to die? Why is there so much injustice in the world?*—all the "whys" we can ever ask, are finally resolved into one imperious question: "What is the meaning of life?"

That question—forged in the fires of suffering and heartache, of pains and struggles, shaped by our expectations, aspirations, and dreams—leads us forth on a most singular adventure; an adventure towards wisdom and enlightenment toward the kind of experience that is genuinely numinous in its transformative character because it enables us at the end of our quest to say, "I *know*."

The journey of life is essentially the quest for meaning, and the experience of meaning seems granted to us only in becoming conscious of new knowledge. So it is that the great metaphysical task lies in a continual expansion of consciousness, and our destiny, as individuals, is to push outwards the boundaries of self-awareness even when the process involves pain and suffering or demands a ruthless and honest confrontation with ourselves. According to Carl Jung, "Because of the self's drive toward realization, life appears as a task of the highest order, and therein lies the possibility of interpreting its meaning, which does not exclude the possibility of defeat." For even when we momentarily fail in the quest—and failure is only temporary so long as we do not cease the quest—our very defeat marks a further advance on the road to full self-awareness and self-realization.

For Jung, the meaning of life lay in the realization of the Self, by which he meant the realization of the divine in man. Perhaps that may be the best—or at least the easiest—way in which to express the end of the quest, for it sums up all the religious traditions while at the same time pointing to the fact that the journey and the goal lie in "the here and now" of everyday existence.

THE HEROIC JOURNEY

In the words of *The Secret Doctrine*, the quest for meaning is "the martyrdom of self-conscious existence," in which we must, by our own efforts, win our immortality, achieving the goal of self-realization while in incarnation. This is no easy task and, consequently, it has always been depicted in myth and legend, in scripture and in sacred literature, as a heroic journey in which every person is the hero of their own story, however unheroic the individual may appear to himself/herself or to others.

The retellings of the ancient tale of the human quest for meaning are so numerous that one can turn to any culture or tradition and find some version of the epic. Yet we continue to search, and today the search has seemed to take on a certain desperation, for we feel that the world, as we have known it, is rapidly crumbling. As a consequence of our desperation, we feel there must be short cuts to our goal, that almost anyone who promises to endow existence with meaning must be on the right track and that all we need to do is to follow blindly. Unfortunately, the psychic and spiritual wrecks that strew the paths thus taken do not always seem sufficient warning to the newer questioner. Perhaps it would be well to heed the words of the well-known mountain climber, Edward Whymper:

> Climb if you will, but remember that courage and strength are naught without prudence, and that a momentary negligence may destroy the happiness of a lifetime. Do nothing in haste: look well to each step; and from the beginning think what may be the end.

Every chronicle depicting the age-old search gives the same advice, and nowhere in the Western tradition has the lesson been presented with greater urgency or more convincing example than in the numerous retellings of the quest for the Holy Grail. The power and beauty of the Grail legends, intertwined as many of them are with the Arthurian stories, still stir the heart and mind of many whose normal, mundane lives appear dreary and fruitless.

QUEST FOR THE GRAIL

Somewhere, we feel, Camelot and Avalon must exist. Some day, we hope, all humanity will sit together at the Round Table, in peace and harmony of purpose. These very words conjure up dreams of a time and a place when a Golden Age will dawn again, break through the hard empirical crust of our vaunted rational minds to awaken within us the possibility of another kind of existence, a life lived more fully, more meaningfully, more richly. We are drawn outwards, as was Parsifal, from the forest of our unknowing to seek the "King who can make knights," and to find the Castle of the Grail.

For the Grail itself symbolizes meaning. It is that vessel which is the container of wisdom, for which every individual seeks throughout the world. The quest for meaning, then, is the search for the Grail. The "King who can make knights," whom Parsifal first set out to find, is that Immortal Atman—the One Self—as well as the Great Initiator who, once seen, forever after claims our allegiance. So every person begins the journey as did Parsifal—the simple fool, naive, unknowing, pure. Along the way we meet with every temptation disguised as dragon, giant, demon, and witch, or as fire, water, earth, and air. We are befriended by lovely maidens or wise old men. We experience terrors of the night of despair, and at dawn we glimpse anew the vision of our own certain triumph. At the end of the journey we enter the heavenly city, the Castle of the Grail. There we perceive the unveiled light, the holy wisdom, and thus becomes an enlightened one, a savior of the world.

In the Galahad version of the Grail legend, one hundred and fifty knights undertook the quest, but only three were blessed with Galahad's continued presence. Galahad alone—the perfect knight, the truly initiated one—is judged worthy to see the mysteries within the holy vessel and to look on the ineffable. Students of Theosophical literature will recognize here a multiplicity of symbols: Galahad and the three who accompany him to the journey's end are perhaps the four *Kumaras*, bringing light, intelligence, and wisdom to a new cycle in the evolutionary process. Galahad may be seen as the avatar promised in so many traditions as coming when there is "decay of righteousness" and when the world faces a new crisis of the spirit. Galahad and his companions are those who overcome every trial and difficulty to join the ranks of those "just men made perfect" who are the Brotherhood of Adepts, the Masters of Wisdom and Compassion.

ARTHURIAN SYMBOLS

Basic to the story of the Grail quest is the magnificent concept that there exists a mystery-race of King Adepts who take incarnation periodically in order to aid mankind in its long journey toward the sacred place where meaning is discovered. So it is said that, just as every Mason learns to direct his steps from West to East, the Adept-Kings of that mysterious Grail race journeyed eastward with the Grail. But, from time to time, one or another of that mystery-race may journey westward with the Grail of Wisdom to awaken in humankind a knowledge of their forgotten birthright. Such, indeed, was the case when the Theosophical Society was founded, and through it is given the Ageless Wisdom, which alone imparts meaning to existence. It testifies to the fact that there is a Path to the Castle of the Grail and that the stages on the way are as clearly marked today as they ever were. It also sounds the warning that the traveling demands nothing less than all we have and are. The brave in heart, willing to walk that way, must say as did Parsifal, "Go I will, cost what it may."

Let us, then, examine this eternal quest, using some features of the Grail legends to serve as guides along the way. Every archetypal symbol of these legends lies within us. The Waste Land is the field of personal incarnation when the "King" or Atman is "wounded" due to our non-recognition of his existence. The Sword is a symbol of *manas*; the Lance, a symbol of an intuitive, direct perception. These are all elements of our own nature, symbolic of faculties to be awakened, or aspects of ourselves to be experienced and made conscious. Each participant in the drama of the Grail quest, whether called Parsifal or Merlin, Guinevere or Gawain, is within us now, for, as the American poet Walt Whitman once wrote, we "contain multitudes." As we read the legend we may see ourselves as Bors the plodder, subject to the temptations of the intellect, faced with a moral dilemma—the choice between conflicting duties—and yet able to make a reasoned decision to continue on the quest. Or we may find in ourselves the figure of Lancelot, needing continuous help, stumbling again and again on the way through the valley of humiliation, the dead weight of our past dragging us down, and yet ever full of good intentions to reform.

Or we may be Gawain, brave, magnanimous, staunchest of friends, the first to leap to his feet when the quest is announced, but somehow failing to understand its nature, taking counsel of wise men and, at the same time, excusing his inability to follow the advice he is given. And within us, too, is Galahad, chaste and pure in aspiration, following the single path to the vision of the Grail, ever tender in his relations with others, perfect in virtue, patient with the failings of his companions, and with an aura that draws all to him, inspiring each to be his best as he moves toward his goal.

So it is for each one to decide whether to hasten the quest, seeking meaning in the Grail of Wisdom, or whether, ignorant of our true purpose, we choose to play about in the magic garden of Klingsor, content with the enchantments of the illusory and psychic realms. The legend of the Grail quest reminds us that we alone can save the world, and that only in saving others do we save ourselves. For the "Heavenly Man," as H. P. Blavatsky termed the archetypal pattern for humanity, alone imparts meaningfulness to the world. Or we may say that meaning is exhibited only through us as we become the self-conscious beings we are meant to be. Wagner, in the finale of his magnificent retelling of the ancient legend of Parsifal, phrased it:

Miracle of highest grace
Redemption for the Redeemer.

ONE TRUE ADVENTURE

Today, as in all periods of history, we are called to awaken from our sleep of non-knowing, cease dreaming psychic visions, and set forth upon the quest of our own humanity, the one true adventure that leads each of us to become, in due time, a Grail-King. We then become one of the race of King-Adepts who are truly the saviors and guardians of the world, an Inner Brotherhood whose work continues from age to age silently building the fane of imperishable thought. This is the meaning of our existence; this the Holy Grail on whose quest we venture forth.

To set out on this immortal adventure demands, indeed, a certain bravery of the soul, a courage which is willing to face every circumstance with equanimity. As Carl Jung once said, "he is no hero who never met the dragon, or who, if once he saw it, declared afterwards that he saw nothing." Wagner's music-drama, *Parsifal*, opens with the words: "Brave, and slowly wise: thus I hail my hero." In our very bravery, we must be content to grow "slowly wise" and yet, like Parsifal, be willing to leave the security of our mother's home in the forest.

So rich in symbolism is the story that we cannot examine all its elements. We may note that when Parsifal sets forth, he does not even know his own name. We, too, at the beginning of our journey, are unaware of the true name of the Self. We are called outwards from a primitive state of consciousness in which we have lived close to the instinctual life symbolized by the plant and animal life of the forest. The restricted horizon of a forest indicates also that we have lived in a condition of limitation from which we must now break free. The forest also represents those collective social values that have dominated our existence and from which we must now venture forth to discover our individual worth as free-thinking, free-choosing beings. Parsifal, like Arjuna, is a symbol of modern man before whom is laid the colossal task of becoming human; the task of choice, based on wisdom, the need to know our own name and to realize our totality.

One of the words frequently met in describing the journey is the apparently simple word *adventure*. Usually this term is used to denote an exciting and somewhat dangerous undertaking. It is interesting to observe, however, that in several versions of the Grail legend the term appears to represent a key factor in the quest itself. In the Parsifal version, for example, the hero is told, "Go where adventure leads you," while in other versions nearly every chapter begins with a statement that now the "adventure" of one or another of the seekers will be presented. Gawain—one of the boldest of the knights to take up the quest, but whose ineptitude for the spiritual life leads him to futile bloodshed because of his failure to heed the advice of wise men he meets—remains perpetually astonished at his own inability to meet with any worthwhile adventures.

THE STARTING POINT

Actually the term *adventure*, as used in the Grail legends, derives from the French, and indicates that our search must proceed in accordance with two fundamental principles well known in Eastern philosophy: dharma and karma. In the Grail legends, to accept an adventure meant simply the acceptance of a challenge which, resulting from one's own past, was inherent in one's own nature. So to "go where adventure leads" symbolized the willingness to obey the inner directive to act in accordance with the pattern established by one's own past, and also to fulfill one's true mission, or dharma. In this respect, the legend records the difficulties encountered when one individual attempts to follow the adventure of another, reminding us sharply that, as the Bhagavad Gita states, "Better one's own duty, though destitute of merit, than the duty of another, well discharged!" This is not always an easy lesson to learn, yet in the quest for meaning we can only proceed in accordance with our own karma-dharma complex, following our own adventure.

This also means that we must start where we are—a fact beautifully symbolized in all the Grail legends. When Galahad appears at the court of King Arthur, he addresses the Knights of the Round Table: "I came because I must, for this is to be the starting-point for all who would join fellowship in the Quest of the Holy Grail." So speaks the eternal Self to the personality: the starting point is here in physical incarnation, equipped with what we have, however inadequately prepared to face the rigors of the search. And if we think the road will be an easy one and the goal one to be swiftly achieved, we may well remember Arthur's words: "I am well aware that of those who leave my court when the hour comes, all will not return: on the contrary, many will fail in this Quest, and success will not come so swiftly as you think."

The Voice of the Silence counsels the aspirant: "Have patience, candidate, as one who fears no failure, courts no success."

Those who heard the call of Galahad, (whose name, it has been said, is one of the mystical designations of Christ) rose from the Round Table, symbol of the world and its collective consciousness, and "each one went the way upon which he had decided, and they set out into the forest at one point and another, there where they saw it to be thickest."

The road is a lonely one, and it is forged through the thickets of the personality, which must be cleared away if the "vision splendid" is to be attained. Commenting on the commencement of the journey, the eminent student of comparative mythology, Joseph Campbell, has written: "Each, entering of his own volition, leaving behind the known good company of Arthur's towered court, would experience the unknown pathless forest in his own heroic way . . . Today, the walls and towers of the culture-world that then were in the building are dissolving; and whereas heroes then set forth of their own will from the known to the unknown, we, today, willy-nilly, *must* enter the forest . . . and, like it or not, the pathless way is the only way now before us."

WANDERING FROM THE PATH

For those who can, as Campbell has put it, "contrive to live within the fold of a traditional mythology of some kind," the established systems of thought in religion and culture are quite sufficient. The search for meaning is not yet for them, since they are content with second-hand knowledge handed down by priest or guru. But there are others (and we ourselves may be of their company) for whom the protective tradition is no longer adequate to meet an expanding awareness, and who must, therefore, walk out—again to use Campbell's words—into "the unchartered forest night, where the terrible wind of God blows directly on the questing undefended soul." The tangled ways may, at times, confuse and bewilder, and we may often go astray down blind alleys of our own false searching, beguiled by sense experience, enamored by psychic displays that we mistake for the genuinely mystical moment of knowing. But we must advance, saying with Parsifal, "Go I will, cost what it may."

The search—the quest for meaning—lies before us, that adventure which is compounded of both karma and dharma. The German philosopher Schopenhauer perceived this very clearly when he wrote: "Everyone, during the course of his lifetime, becomes aware of certain events that, on the one hand, bear the mark of a moral or inner necessity, because of their especially decisive importance to him and yet, on the other hand, have clearly the character of outward, wholly accidental, chance. The frequent occurrence of such events may lead gradually to the notion, which often becomes a conviction, that the life course of the individual, confused as it may seem, is an essential whole, having within itself a certain self-consistent, definite direction, and a certain instructive meaning—no less than the best thought-out of epics."

It is for this reason (because in one sense our lives themselves are hero-stories with their successes and failures), that we can find in legend and myth the paradigms of our own human experiences in a depth dimension. Just as the legends recount the perils on the way (usually in exaggerated form), so we may find in our daily lives the semblance of those conflicts, difficulties, and problems, even when we do not recognize the same elements within them. A fact that emerges from all this is that the peril or problem in every instance is precisely in accordance with the nature of the hero. Similarly, each difficulty we face is commensurate with our own destiny, both as a result of past actions (karma) and in preparation for our future work (dharma). If we examine closely any one of the great adventures of the Grail heroes we will see, magnified as on a cinema screen, some small adventure of our own.

Perhaps no hero in those stories represents us better than the aspiring, well-meaning Lancelot, confronted again and again by a certain paralysis of will. Loving overmuch his sovereign's queen, representing his desire for physical and psychic experience, Lancelot yet repeatedly resolves to reform himself. Full of self-reproach when he is shown, as in a dream, the effects of his actions, he laments: "I have gone to my death down that wide road which at the outset seems so smooth and honeyed and is the portal and the path of sin. The devil showed me the sweets and the honey, but he hid from my eyes the everlasting woe that lies in store for him who treads that road to its end."

FAILURE ON THE WAY

Lancelot who, again and again, finds himself back in the forest from which he had thought to emerge, thrown back into a condition in which he excuses his failures as actions that are no different from other men's, is still given aid on the way. He knows all too well his own weaknesses. As the legend records: "For there, where he had thought to find all joy and honor and worldly acclaim, in the adventures of the Holy Grail, he had reaped only failure and its bitter gall." In his extremity he cries out, as each of us may well do when we honestly confront our natures: "Ah, God, my sin and the wickedness of my life now stand revealed. Now I see that above all else my weakness has been my undoing. For when I should have mended my ways, then did the enemy destroy me, blinding me so effectually that I could not discern the things of God. Nor should I marvel that I am purblind . . . for, more than any other, I have given myself to lust and to the depravity of this world."

The language may be exaggerated in its self-reproach, but we may see, as in a mirror, our own failures and weaknesses as we are drawn by desire, prejudice, passion, and even simple expedience, into a way of life that is not wholly consonant with our ideals.

Yet we are never left without assistance, for humanity has always had its Teachers, and there is still that race of King-Adepts who are the guardians of the Grail, the Eternal Wisdom. To Lancelot, one of that race disguised as a hermit spoke: "Just as you may see a man wander at times from his path when he falls asleep and retrace his steps at once on waking, so also is it with the sinner who falls asleep . . . and veers from the right path; he too returns to his path."

We must, indeed, come awake and give our attention to the journey we have undertaken. As the hermit reminds Lancelot: "Should your heart not be entire, I do not recommend you to pursue this Quest . . . for this is no Quest for earthly things, but those of heaven."

Such advice is reminiscent of the words of another Master Teacher, that we must come out of our world into theirs, that we must be single of vision, aspiring with a wholeness of heart and mind, willing to leave the broad plains of ordinary existence to ascend the mountain of the spirit where the vision of the Grail is granted the hero soul.

In the Parsifal version of the Grail legend, one further step is required: the hero must return from the mysterious adventure, for now he has the power to bestow boons on his fellow-men. The ultimate boon is said to be the inauguration of a new age of the human-spirit, an era sustained by self-responsible individuals acting not in accordance with collective values but in terms of ever-expanding conscious realization of that moral imperative which Plato termed the Good. Such a step reminds us that we have a responsibility not only for ourselves but for the world. If we have been vouchsafed the vision splendid, we have an obligation to become bearers of that vision, transmitters of the wisdom, to all who are still struggling on the upward path. We must awaken those who still slumber, assist those who are only coming awake, extend the hand of sympathy and courage to all who falter, as we ourselves once did.

For us, as for Lancelot, it is a slow ascent, and we often become impatient with the process. We come to many a fork in the road and, sometimes taking the wrong turning, we must retrace our steps and set out again with renewed courage. "Cost what it may," the quest for meaning must be undertaken. The twentieth-century poet T. S. Eliot expressed the attitude that must characterize us:

> For most of us, this is the aim
> Never here to be realized;
> Who are only undefeated
> Because we have gone on trying.

The word "try" recurs frequently in letters to the president-founder of the Theosophical Society, H. S. Olcott, letters which bear the signatures of Adept Teachers who took an interest in the founding of this movement. And in the words of that memorable classic, *The Voice of the Silence*, given us by HPB: "If thou has tried and failed, O dauntless fighter, yet lose not courage; fight on and to the charge return again, and yet again . . . Remember, thou that fightest for man's liberation, each failure is success, and each sincere attempt wins its reward in time."

No Turning Back

Once we have embarked on the quest for meaning, there can be no turning back. The Grail legends represent that quest as a call, the eternal summons of the Self to the self, of the monad to the individuality, of the individuality to the personality, of immortal soul (so often disguised as a maiden in distress) to the incarnate individual (the knight in all his armor). It is a call to the heights, as well as a call to the depths, within us. The King, whether Arthur presiding over his Round Table or the Fisher King or the Maimed King, is that Immortal Self—the one Atman—who sends forth his knights errant (representations of himself in the fields of manifestation) into the forests of incarnate experience to seek the Gnosis, the Grail, which is meaning in its fullness. The summons to the great adventure comes to each of us and there is then that solitary journey to fulfillment, that lonely, dangerous quest, which is the only way to an individual life. There is but One Path to be taken which alone leads to the realm of the Adept Teachers of humankind.

Treasure Hard to Attain

Our task today is the same as it has always been—the task prefigured in myth and legend, in scripture and in the lives of the world's saints and saviors, humanity's noblest men and women. The Gnostic Sophia, whether called *Kundry* or *Orgeluse* or by some other name, spellbound by illusion, entrapped in the magic garden of the world's unknowing, must be set free to work in the world as the wisdom which can carry humanity into a new era of sanity, an age of brotherhood and peace. As always, it is through *amor*, divine, eternal love and compassion, that *Sophia* is freed, joined with the eternal godhead, *Theos*, to become that *Theosophia* of which modern Theosophy is representative in the world today. As one of the ancient Upanishads puts it: "The Atman can only be known by the Atman, by him who has chosen the Atman."

The Grail is not to be identified with some vessel known to history nor is it to be seen as a purely Western symbol. It is but another name for that "treasure hard to attain" which is Theosophy itself, the forgotten truth whose very nature defies delimitation and whose full definition can only be exhibited in a life that is wholly given in service because one has encountered, in their full numinosity, the abiding principles of the Wisdom. It is the cup from which one must drink deeply in order to be restored to one's true nature, for it contains the Wisdom which alone imparts ultimate meaning to life and which must be assimilated and made our own if it is to become meaningful in existence.

Although the philosopher Nietzsche would have denied the spiritual implication of his own words, he may have expressed it best when he wrote in *Also Sprach Zarathustra*: "That the Great Man should be able to appear and dwell among you again, again, and again, *that* is the sense of all your efforts here on earth. That there should ever and again be men among you able to elevate you to your heights: that is the prize for which you strive. For it is only through the occasional coming to light of such human beings that your own existence can be justified . . . And if you are not yourself a great exception, well then be a small one at least, and so you will foster on earth that holy fire from which genius may arise."

The "holy fire" is that which enkindles among all peoples that genuine brotherhood which is truly the "genius" of humanity.

Transformation— The Solution

Inaugural address at the 1982 Indo-Pacific Federation Conference. Published in *The Theosophist*, Volume 105, January 1984

During the recent Centenary Convention at Adyar, attention was drawn to the statement in *The Mahatma Letters* that the work of the Theosophical Society is to bring about a regenerative brotherhood. This is not simply the acceptance of that which already exists but the realization that there is such a thing as a universal brotherhood in which a constant renewal or regeneration is taking place.

I was struck by a statement of Albert Einstein in a letter that he wrote soon after the launching of the "Atomic Age": "The unleashed power of the atom has changed everything except our ways of thinking." Today, we are faced with a threat so overwhelming that every member of the human race, Theosophist or not, should be deeply concerned. The distance between peaceful progress and catastrophe is, as Indira Gandhi, the late Prime Minister of India, warns: "simply the distance between two adjacent buttons, the right one and the wrong." "We shall require," continued Einstein, "a substantially new manner of thinking if mankind is to survive."

The Theosophical Society was born in the nineteenth-century in order to begin a process, which is still continuing. Its work is far from done. There are those who believe that it is out of date. The glittering array of new saviors and teachers, new messiahs and gurus, to whom they flock is all too absorbing. But the work of the Society is still as it has always been, to transform the world within, to initiate a "new manner of thinking" as Einstein calls it.

I have chosen Einstein's words, not only because they are significant in themselves, but because he was a preeminent scientist, and science, in our time, has become increasingly the major mode of knowing. But there are tremendous changes in scientific thinking—not, perhaps, by all scientists but by many who are in the forefront, particularly in the field of physics, to some extent in biology, and certainly in psychology. Secondly, and perhaps even more importantly, Einstein was not only a scientist but also a human being deeply concerned for humanity's welfare. It is this combination of disciplined knowing and a recognition of fundamental principles with a caring for life, in whatever form it appears, that enables us to find our way through the tangled course of our present uncertainty.

It seems apparent, then, that we must awaken to a manner of thinking that comprehends the unitary nature of the world and of humanity—of life itself. We no longer live in a world in which the human and nature are separate. It is now suggested by physicists that the very act of observation at the subatomic level influences, in some manner, that which is observed. We live in a participatory universe. We are not separate from it; the universe is no longer "out there." This is not very different from the statement made by J. Krishnamurti: "The observer and the observed are one." We cannot separate the two. We cannot observe the world without, in some sense, altering it. Consequently, we must be alert to the fact that the way we see the world is the way we project on the world that which is within us.

We must ask the serious questions: "Are we ready to move in a radically new direction? Are we, as individuals, prepared to undergo in ourselves that kind of transformation which will bring about a genuine transformation in the world—a transformation that will inevitably bring about a new vision?" Today, all other modes of thought are outmoded; all other ways of thinking are unthinkable.

To explore such questions implies also a willingness to probe deep into our own natures. To understand ourselves is to understand the world of which we are so intimate a part. By our very nature we are world-creating, but we have become world-destroying—a fact that the ecological movement is making apparent. We observe a world outside ourselves and seek to manipulate it to our own ends. We assume that its resources are inexhaustible and that they are there for our sole benefit, that the seas and the earth may be used as dumping grounds for the waste that we produce on such an appalling scale.

We have now come to recognize that we need a transformed mode of thinking in which it is no longer the human and the world, or the human against the world—a view so long prevalent particularly in Western culture and, unfortunately, being increasingly accepted in the Eastern world as well. The technology imported by many Asian countries is designed to help mankind manipulate the world for our own selfish ends. Martin Buber, the Jewish theologian, describes an "I-Thou relationship" in which the world is the "Thou" and the "I" is also the "Thou." Everything is precious and must be cared for. There should be a concern for all life including the life of the planet itself.

The universe is interrelated and interdependent, rooted, as the Theosophical worldview has always maintained, in an Ultimate Reality that both transcends and participates in all that exists. "With one portion of myself I pervade the world," says Sri Krishna in the Bhagavad Gita, "and yet I remain." It is a mysterious paradox that the universe is relational because of an Ultimate Reality that permeates all existence and yet remains forever transcendent.

Now we must not only seek to extend the boundaries of our present knowledge, but by an expansion of consciousness, to embrace the universe itself. This is the genuine knowing in which we become one with that which we seek to know. "A mind that embraces the universe," to use a phrase found in *The Secret Doctrine*, points to the presence within the universe of a consciousness established in wisdom. Such an expanding mind is the truly Theosophical mind.

The Theosophical mind is that consciousness which embraces all life, and it is a growing mind—not one set in tradition. Our minds tend to move in certain well-worn grooves, so that our beliefs become fixed. We are so convinced of the rightness of our own points of view that we cannot change our beliefs and attitudes. We look at each other out of the past, as we *were*; we never see each other as we *are*.

We are told that since it takes a vast amount of time for the light from distant stars to reach us, when we look at the heavens we are looking at things as they were millions of years ago. There is also a measurable amount of time between my looking at you and my recognition of you. In that infinitesimal moment you can change utterly, because transformation is not a matter of measurable time. In that timeless realm, being is always be-ness. So we can begin to realize that, even in looking at each other, we may do a disservice to each other—indeed to the world about us—if we say, "This is how things are." The mind that is transformed—the Theosophical mind—realizes that knowing is a process just as life itself is, and that as process, knowing can grow to embrace more and more of understanding.

So we begin asking ourselves questions: What are the boundaries of our knowing? How do we define ourselves? Is transformation a goal? Or is it a process that is constantly taking place within us, emerging from a fresh and regenerative mind with a way of looking that is constantly new? There are no final or easy answers. Part of our work is to learn to live with questions and paradoxes. For life cannot be simplified into black and white. There are shades in between. Can we not learn to accept the "shadings" so that two things can be true at one and the same time even though they are apparently opposites? Fortunately, we have within us the ability to comprehend all colorations. Physicists had to accept the fact that light is both wave and particle and coined the word "wavicle" to describe its nature.

Often we seek answers without even knowing the questions. We are content with the customary answers given to us from outside. "It has always been done this way," one hears even in Theosophical lodges. The very definition of the term "Theosophical" should preclude any such lazy way out as "we have always done it that way." New situations demand a transformed mind. We look for answers from those invested with a certain authority but, ultimately, their answers never suffice. The new mode of thinking that is now required demands of us the ability to live with questions, to realize that life itself is constantly challenging us—that instead of "true" or "false" alternatives there are multiple choices. This last is perhaps the most difficult of all for us to deal with.

How, then, do we define ourselves? Our original face has been marred by a number of metaphysical crises that have occurred in the West and inevitably have had their effect on the entire world.

Historically, these crises may be seen in a variety of ways. First, there was the attempt by religious authority to dominate secular life or to separate theological answers from secular life, thus cutting human beings off from direct access to their own transcendence. In a well-known letter from one of HPB's Teachers, one of the Adepts suggested that nine-tenths of the evils of the world stem from religion. It was a metaphysical crisis that led, a century or two ago, to the objectivism of the scientific method and the Cartesian dichotomy with its philosophic implications, giving official status to a dualistic position which reduced the individual to a mere epiphenomenon of nature, and the separation of the profane world from the sacred. Finally, in the nineteenth-century, at the time of the birth of the Theosophical Society, the major metaphysical crisis was the locking of horns between a scientific determinism and a religious dogmatism which left human beings cut off from their roots, the playthings of blind faith, unable to control their own destiny.

It was into that philosophic milieu that the Society was born to reaffirm an ageless wisdom tradition grounded in a unitary view of reality. In one sense, it was at least a hundred years ahead of its time. It has, in some ways, leavened the mind of the times to bring about, perhaps in subtle ways, a change in the consciousness of the world. We must still be at the forefront of that further regenerative process of changing consciousness by changing our own consciousness.

The restoration of our original face can come about only through a restoration of that worldview which perceives a unity in which the human and the world are but different modes of functioning. It is a worldview in which the symbolic unity reverberates in every human consciousness as its diverse experiences for it is one consciousness functioning in a diversity of modes and experiencing the world in a multiplicity of ways. The multiplicity that we perceive both within and outside ourselves is rooted in a principle of unity, which can comprehend all contradictions. We have to define ourselves, then, both by the uniqueness of our perception and the multiplicity of our experience as rooted in a yet more fundamental reality, growing outwards in consciousness, in exploration of the boundaries of knowing. In this sense we are both being and becoming—that which is and that which is forever in process.

The metaphor of a journey can be especially meaningful when considering the human condition. The two constants in mythology appear to be an obligatory journey and a choice of ways. Every journey contains its own potential for transformation, for the very structure of consciousness is altered by our "walkabouts" in the world. Our journeys may subject us, now and again, to "culture shocks." The structure of consciousness itself, whether we realize it or not, may repress or reject them, but that very rejection and resistance alter the structure of consciousness. Our wanderings—those numerous inner and outer journeys we take in the course of a lifetime—always alter consciousness. We may not always be aware of the transformations that take place, but there is a continual becoming which is apparent when we look backward from whatever vantage point we may now have reached. However we view existence, whatever our reaction to events, the sense of change, and even of choice, appears primary to consciousness whether we resist or welcome it. The inevitability of this movement shadows all our days.

We learn of death and recognize its certainty even though the hour of its coming is one of the major uncertainties with which we must live. We know with an inner knowing that defies description that every death is the prelude to a new birth, even as the mini-deaths we experience every night in sleep are preludes to a new dawn of awareness in the morning. Death and birth, sleep and waking, are parts of an endless cycle in which consciousness is forever expanding. Existence is a spiral growth in which change becomes meaningful as we move towards constant transformation.

Change, of course, is not always transformation, but there cannot be transformation without a change in condition. Perhaps the one essential that should grip us is what might be called a passion for the possible. As we move toward a new mode of thinking which will embrace the universe, in our inmost selves we are that consciousness, because consciousness, as has been said, is forever a singular of which the plural is unknown. We have to discover within ourselves, each for himself, the limits or the limitlessness of the boundaries of our knowing. It is always a movement from within outwards in accordance with "the spiritual evolution of the inner mortal man that forms the fundamental tenet in the occult sciences." In the context, therefore, of that principle, transformation is not merely the formation of a new structure but the emergence of a new being.

The eminent Christian theologian, Dr. Paul Tillich, wrote of the essentially religious demand within every person for the coming to birth of a new being. He pointed out in a number of his books that our ultimate concern must be our passion for the new creation that flowers towards freedom, joy and healing. No longer do we see the universe as subject to the law of death out of birth, but to a higher law—the law of life, which embraces birth and death alike. The universe therefore is not what it was, for nature has received another meaning: history is transformed; and you and I are no longer (or should not be) what we were before.

Where there is a new being there is genuine resurrection, regeneration and transformation. It is because we have never believed in ourselves or known ourselves that we say, "I can do nothing." If we believe with that passion for the possible that consciousness is constantly being transformed, each one of us can transform the world.

This was the experience of Gautama. As an aspirant to know the cause of suffering, Gautama arrived at this not simply by collecting the facts of existence, but by moving within his consciousness in supreme contemplation of the ultimate realities underlying all existence. Not in a moment of time but in that timeless realm of reality he "came awake," became the Buddha.

We must cease being sleepwalkers, moving about in a comatose state and, like the Buddha, "come awake." We must open our eyes and see what is there before us; we must re-cognize the world. This is resurrection—the rising again of the primordial Self, the root of our very being, which has been for so long disfigured by our identification with the transient vestures through which it functions. Like the traditional resurrection, it is an awakening from the dead, or the deathlike state in which we have been content to rest.

Such an awakening is both radical and wrenching. It is a rebirth, felt as a sudden outflow of inner energy, of freedom in which there is the sense of things being "never again the same." So it has been called a miracle and, indeed, it is the supreme miracle present in life itself. Such an awakening calls for both *faith* and *courage*, both of which are essential elements in the transformation process.

Faith means being grasped by a power greater than ourselves—a power that shakes us, transforms, and heals us. It is a surrender to the Primordial Self—a surrender known in the yogic tradition as *Ishvara pranidhana*. It arises out of a complete absorption in that which we essentially are. It is the universal and essential self-affirmation of our being. Plato related courage to the element within the Soul which forever strives towards the good, the true and the beautiful.

Out of our passion for the possible, with faith and courage, we move on our journey in a constantly transformed and transforming condition towards a consciousness that embraces the unitary nature of ourselves and the world. It is a journey into an awakening, ever fresh and new, of an altogether "other" experience.

The most important image that anyone of us can ever have—and that determines our entire existence—is the image of the Self. If it is a vision confined to the vestures worn at one particular time or in one particular place, then we have to find the courage to break through that limited view. If it is a vision that there is but one Self of which I am but an expression, then there is the possibility that, at every moment, I may change the world by changing myself. It is a transformation process, which happens not once but continuously.

Today there is a movement towards a recovery of creativity and a consequent willingness to forego rigid attachments to intellectual systems in favor of the experience towards which those formulations point. It may perhaps be expressed as a movement from structural concerns to a mystical experience. This is exemplified in Fritjof Capra's *The Tao of Physics*. There is indeed that almost near union of the physicist's observation in which he knows that his observation is subtly changing the sub-atomic structure which he seeks to measure. He realizes that he cannot measure the position and the velocity of a particle at the same time, for measurement of one precludes measurement of the other.

This is moving towards a genuine mystical experience, which as Fritjof Capra puts it, is "the Taoistic experience." It is a constant movement between the Yin and the Yang, which is always present in the world. It is a willingness to forego rigid attachment to the formulations of systems. The effort, in other words, is to synthesize knowledge within consciousness in a manner that will result in a genuine transformation and the arising of the new mode of thinking of which Einstein wrote. It is a mode that is really not so much new as *newly discovered* by each one of us in and for ourselves.

Creative periods in history often seem to coincide with times of crisis and danger. At such turbulent times, we look for the emergence of the unique person who will embody the creative or transformative process. Today is such a time. A nuclear threat hangs over the whole planet, ecological disasters are destroying it slowly and inexorably. There is an increase in violence and crime, a lack of morality, a breakdown of ethics. We can point to the disasters of the day and thus be stuck in the past, or we can have the vision that perceives a new being emerging from our age of turbulence.

I think of that moment in American history when, out of the chaos of a congressional session, a Constitution finally emerged. One of the wise men of that time, Benjamin Franklin, rose to his feet and pointed to a carving on the back of the chair on which had sat George Washington, president of the Constitutional Convention. It depicted the sun low on the horizon. It is reported that Franklin said, "Through all of the turbulence and the difficulties of this Convention, in forging a bond of unity, there were times when I looked at that symbol and saw it as a setting sun. But we have come through these difficulties, this turbulence and dissension, and we have forged a document which symbolizes our unity, and I know now that it is a symbol of the rising sun."

Transformation is a process, not simply a goal. Whether the sun rises or sets is dependent on where we stand. If we see only the sun setting on a past mode of thinking, on a civilization and a culture that we have held dear, we must turn to the East, traditionally the place of light, and face the rising sun. Then, when we have turned ourselves squarely in that direction, we shall know transformation, awakening, resurrection, regeneration—the recovery of our original Self, which is the One Self in all life.

THE IMPORTANCE OF QUESTIONING

Published in *The Theosophist*, Volume 105, March 1984 under
the title "Answers to Questions"

It has been asked how "repentance of sin" is related to human transformation. In several places in the New Testament the word translated as "sin" carries the meaning of failure to hit the mark or the target. When we miss the target, there follows an effort to train our eye. And we question ourselves: What are we to concentrate on? Are we to concentrate on the drawing of the bow? On the arrow? Or must we fix our sight on the bull's-eye itself? If we miss the target, do we say, "Oh dear, I shall never be an archer; I shall never be able to shoot straight"? We can give up in defeat and say, "This is not for me; I can never do it!" Or do we say, "Obviously, I was not giving it my full attention. I shall try again."

It seems to me that if we can see "sin" in this manner, "repentance" will be to simply try again. "Re-pent" is to "think again." It is to act in a new way, with clarity of vision. And this is part of the process of human transformation. Failure in itself is not so very bad; it can, in fact, be good for us. It is better to be a glorious failure than a mediocre success because anybody can be successful at something he already knows how to do, but we are called upon to move beyond ourselves. As Browning put it, "a man's reach should exceed his grasp, or what's a heaven for?"

The process of transformation begins with the consciousness that awakening or enlightenment is possible. This is not to be achieved at our first attempt. The Buddha, being a human being like the rest of us, did not achieve Buddhahood at the moment of his awareness of its possibility. The process "takes time." Time was once seen simply as linear, but today we recognize other modes of time such as biological and psychological time. We know, too, that there is mythic time—the "once upon a time" with which every good fairy story begins. It is not a historical date but a time-ness that is ever present.

So, we shoot the arrow. If it fails to hit the mark, we retrieve it and view the target again. The acceptance that one has missed the target—that one has, for the moment, failed—is part of the trans-formative process. Let us not be afraid of failure. If we have never failed, it only means that we have never tried to do anything. We fail because we are trying to achieve something that is beyond our-selves. Let us pick up the arrow and shoot again.

It has been stated that much of the evil in the world stems from religious dogmatism. Popular Christian belief considers the Bible to be the Word of God, the infallible source of spiritual belief and knowledge. H. P. Blavatsky, in *The Secret Doctrine*, questions reli-gious dogmas based on the Bible. Should the Theosophical Society continue her struggle against dogma as part of its work for human transformation? Today, theological dogmatism is arrayed against scientific determinism. Where does Theosophy stand on this issue?

Before considering religious dogmatism—whether it is the Christian belief in the Bible or the Hindu in the Vedas as the final word of the Divine, or any other religious orthodoxy, we must examine what we mean by the word *religion*. It is said that the Theo-sophical Society is to be the cornerstone of the future religion of humanity. This indicates that religion in itself is not wrong; indeed, I think that we should foster true religious feeling. Most of the great religious teachers pursued a path to understanding and did not set out to found a new religion. They were in search of answers to serious questions. They probed into the root of these questions and out of their enquiries their followers developed dogmas and creeds that they said must be adhered to.

There is the story of a cat that kept on mewing and moving restlessly about in an ashram. This disturbed the meditation of one of the monks, and so he tied the cat to the bedpost to keep it quiet. By and by, the monk achieved interior enlightenment. His followers assumed that all they needed to do to reach the same spiritual state was to get a cat and tie it to a bedpost! This is what has happened in most religions; only their "cats" are dogmas and creeds. If you tie a cat to the leg of your bed you no longer have what Socrates called the "examined life," or an alert and open mind that asks questions.

Modern scholarship has greatly expanded our knowledge of the Christian Bible. It is made up of books written by human beings, some of whom were enlightened sages, others were visionaries, others were the journalists of the day who wrote about contemporary events or about the acts of a great person, or who simply recorded what they saw. Others were initiates who presented the mystery teachings in symbol and allegory.

These books were selected out of many others by certain elders of the Church who then constituted them into Holy Scripture. We know from modern discovery—the Dead Sea Scrolls, for example, or more recent translations of certain Gnostic texts—that there were many other versions, interpretations, and statements of the wisdom-tradition. We also know a great deal more about the exact meaning of the Hebrew from which the Old Testament was translated, and of New Testament Greek, thanks to the advances in the field of linguistics and to the study of comparative language.

It was only in the last century that many of these linguistic and etymological discoveries were made and, today, scholars tell us that there must have been a language pre-dating the Indo-European. HPB refers to this language as *Senzar*. This may have been the root language that gave rise to the Indo-European languages. Of course, there are other families of languages in the world besides the Indo-European—Finnish-Hungarian, for example.

The advance of scholarship, then, gives new meaning to the words of the Bible and so we have the American Revised Standard Version as well as other translations. In addition, there is a good deal of information dating from the early period of Christian history and of other religions also.

HPB says that a Theosophist is one who engages in independent inquiry. Are we genuine inquirers who are seeking to understand? Or have we merely a set of ready-made answers?

The world that we live in today is not the world of HPB more than a hundred years ago. Theological dogmatism and scientific determinism belong to the century in which the Theosophical Society was founded. Today there is the battle between those who accept the theory of evolution and those who promote what is called intelligent design. Not everything that HPB wrote, or that appears in the Mahatma Letters, is necessarily correct. We must be alert to the conditions of today. The principles are the same, but why should we apply them in the same old ways? They must be newly applied by original thinkers. "Science is our best ally," declares one of the Mahatma Letters. Although there has been much progress in the realm of scientific thought this does not mean that every scientist has abandoned determinism or behaviorism. But the scientist is forever probing, and it is this spirit of research that is really true science. The human being was not meant to be mindless. The very word *man* is derived from the Sanskrit word *manas* implying "to know, to have a consciousness that embraces, that is ever expanding, that is constantly alert." Some religious leaders, for example Martin Buber, are among the great thinkers of our time. Is the Society equally alert to the human condition of today?

We are sometimes asked what the Theosophical Society has done for world peace. Perhaps we underestimate the Society. We sometimes forget that it has already had a considerable influence on world thought. Einstein, for example, is said to have read *The Secret Doctrine*, not to gain scientific knowledge but, as he is reported to have said, to stimulate his thinking. Robert Andrews Millikan, who discovered cosmic rays, once declared that it was *The Secret Doctrine* that impelled him towards the discoveries that led to his Nobel Prize. Not because it gave the answers but, again, because it provoked thought. And if we believe that thoughts are energies, the Society can still exert its influence in the world.

H. P. Blavatsky, a woman from the nineteenth-century, is still being talked about, either praised or blamed—mostly blamed. Annie Besant is still a living presence, at least in India. Why should people still be interested in these women? What is the force that is still felt in the presence of people like these?

In the same way, Theosophical philosophy, with its vision of a unitary reality, of an ordered system, of a meaningful and purposeful universe, still has its impact and will continue to command attention if we give it new life and vitality. That is, of course, if we have experienced it for ourselves—if it is meaningful to us. We can, each one of us, exert an influence; let us not underestimate what the individual can do.

THE MYSTIC VISION AND HUMAN TRANSFORMATION

Published in *The Theosophist*, Volume 115, May 1994

In a lecture given in London more than eighty years ago, Dr Annie Besant spoke of a "wave of mysticism passing over the world." Such a wave seems to be apparent today, as so many people express a hunger, an inner yearning, for a genuine spiritual experience. Not satisfied with the answers which either science or religion has to offer, many have sought out teachers, gurus, psychics of varying degrees of reliability, anyone who seems to promise fulfillment of an inner need. At the same time, science today seems to be pointing beyond itself, or at least beyond its materialistic boundaries, to what we might call a "meta-science" which admits the possibility that consciousness may be primary. And in many religious traditions, there has been a re-awakening to the esoteric wisdom hidden within the outer forms, an esoteric wisdom which by its very nature participates in the mystical.

The philosopher of religion, Hans Jonas, has suggested that there exists a historical sequence of development that leads from objectification, as he calls it, to interiorization. He refers specifically to the movement from religious knowledge or theory to the subjective inhabiting of the framework, which such theory provides. In his view, one generation's conceptual structure becomes the next generation's guide to inner transformation. This is to say that our ideas, our beliefs, all that constitutes our basic world-view, must become known experience in such a manner as to bring about a radical change in our lives.

Such a sequential development, however, is not only a development from generation to generation, but must occur within us in a kind of continual pattern of assimilation. Every great teacher, for example, has recognized the need to translate objective theory into practical experience. Theosophy itself, we may say, is not only a magnificent internally consistent, coherent, and all-embracing philosophy, founded on such basic principles as unity, periodicity, lawfulness, etc., principles which can be elucidated in books and study courses; it is also a way of life, a mode of being, a transformative path. No single definition of Theosophy will ever suffice to encompass the totality of wisdom the very term represents. To put the matter another way, we may suggest that from being a noun, Theosophy as the one Wisdom-Religion, as H. P. Blavatsky called it, must become a verb, a process which we are or should be continually experiencing.

A recently published book, *The Search for the Pearl,* focuses on what the sub-title of the work calls "A Personal Exploration of Science and Mysticism." The author, Dr. Gillian Ross, holds degrees in anthropology and behavioral science, but relinquished an academic career to work with holistic philosophies and practices, including yoga and meditation. As she writes in her introduction, "This book is about our loss of the Tao and the path to its rediscovery."

Essentially the experience that we may call mystical is the experience of our interconnectedness. Above all, as Dr. Ross discovered in her exploration, the mystic vision is an "experience of the heart," and as such, to quote Dr. Ross further, "Mysticism and compassion are inseparable." The vision that transforms becomes transformative. Because we are the world, to put the matter simply, the vision that transforms us transforms the world. In our interconnectedness, the consciousness of each must reflect itself in the consciousness of all. Human transformation arises out of the transformation of individuals.

Speaking on "The Meaning and Method of Mysticism," since published in her little book entitled *Mysticism*, Dr. Besant said that we do not know the world. "We only know," she pointed out, "the response of consciousness to impressions made upon us from what we presume to be an external world." One cannot help but think how Annie Besant would have rejoiced with the developments in scientific and religious thought today that are expressing the same idea, even if in different language. The "response of consciousness," to which Dr. Besant referred, is determined by the level at which consciousness is functioning. There are, as she pointed out and we can verify for ourselves, the impressions that come from the senses. Further, there are those impressions which arouse feeling, while another set of impressions give rise to thoughts and ideas. The union of all these impressions—sensuous, emotional, mental—spell the "world" for us.

But is this all there is to the world? Do we not all have experiences that speak to us of something greater than the sum of these various impressions? Annie Besant described it in these words:

> A presence which in our quietest, our noblest, our purest moments, is more perceptible than in the rush and turmoil of the world . . . something so great that it enfolds our whole nature; something so profound that we know that nothing in our own nature is alien from it. (1914, 6)

One of the problems that inevitably arises is that of differentiating authentic mystical experiences from subjective and imaginary fantasies. Such a problem is due, at least in part, to the confusion of visionary content with mystical awareness. Visionary experiences may and often do point toward the mystical experience, but they do not necessarily do so. Authentic mystical experience implies a complete transcendence of any sense of a separate self and therefore an awakening to an awareness of non-duality. No one can deny the transformative nature of such awareness. At the same time, such an awareness—the awareness of non-duality or true unity—becomes grounded in the rational.

Dr. Erich Neuman, one of the foremost successors to Dr. Carl Jung, once proposed that the human being is essentially *homo mysticus*, which is simply to say that the ground of our being is in that inexpressible reality which has been termed, in Theosophical literature, the Atman. The mystical experience or vision is none other than the realization that Atman is Brahman, or in Upanishadic terms, *tat tvam asi*, That thou art.

While the experience, then, is immediate and by its very nature unitive there may be defined both a progression and the unique characteristics which are present at every stage in the developmental process. As Dr. Neuman suggested, the true development of consciousness occurs through archetypal encounters, which give a mystical stamp to the inner development of every person. Further, he proposed, it is possible to see the major phases of the life cycle in terms of the growth of mystical consciousness. The characteristics of the mystical vision or experience are the same at each stage, while at the same time there is a development of consciousness within the life pattern of each incarnation. Three major stages may be identified as early or source mysticism, associated with childhood, a zenith mysticism identified with maturity, and a last stage or death mysticism characteristic of the individual who has truly "died" to the separated self, the one we often describe as liberated.

While these stages may be viewed as sequential, in the development of consciousness they may also be seen as simultaneously present. From the sequential point of view, source mysticism extends back into that unknown sphere or the realm of the unconscious before the emergence of any sense of a separate "I." Zenith mysticism is experienced in those transcendent moments when the "I" is not present, while death or immortality mysticism is the realization of the One without a second and is indeed the experience of the extinguishing of any sense of a separate self. Perceived as simultaneously present within us, these stages constitute the totality of our experiences of pure Being.

The mark of authenticity of the mystic vision, however, lies neither in some clearly demarcated progression in the growth of consciousness nor in some collective listing of characteristics of the mystical experience, but rather in the transformative impact which even a partial experience of the unitive state has upon our ordinary lives. All too often, visionary experiences end up being used in the service of ego-centered goals. The mystic vision not only results in an inner sense of renewal and peace, but even more profoundly in an outpouring of love and compassion for the suffering of the world. Quite simply, the authentic mystical experience tends to manifest in ordinary life as ethical behavior founded on a genuine realization, far more substantial than theory, that all life is one.

Annie Besant, in concluding her lecture on "The Meaning and Method of Mysticism," referred to this essential transformative nature of the experience:

That is the splendor of the mystic life, this power of service which only this inner form of realization can possibly give to any one of us . . . We are climbing towards it as we begin to understand something of its possibilities as we live a little of the truth we know . . . If you would become a mystic . . . never pretend to believe a truth which you are not willing to act out in the world . . . for truth is only truth when you have learned to live it. (1914, 28–29)

The mystic vision, then, may be said to constitute an in-break of the creative-sacred into our lives, in our immediate, existential situation in such a manner as to cause an out-break of genuine and unconditional love for all beings. One writer has stated that the individual who has had such an experience, the authentic mystic vision of unity, must respond to a new calling, the truly human vocation, "to serve the fullness of time and the brotherhood of humanity in the historical creation of an optimal way of life" which is a way of peace and happiness for all. From such a point of view, the mystic is the redeemer, self-redeemed and so the redeemer of the world. Or, as Hugh l'Anson Fausset, in his beautiful little work, *The Lost Dimension*, has expressed it, "To be human is to bring the Kingdom of Light down to earth and to raise up earth to heaven."

Mysticism for the mystic, however, is not an occasional experience. It is a life surrendered to the mystery behind the ordinary. In that surrender, the ordinary becomes miraculous. As the well-known Zen Buddhist saying has it: "Before enlightenment, trees are trees and mountains are mountains. After enlightenment, trees are still trees and mountains are still mountains." For convenience, we speak of a progress or path, but in actuality there is neither progress nor path. There is, if we may characterize it in any way at all, an ongoing and continual surrendering of intellectual knowledge to heart-wisdom, a continual awareness in the midst of daily existence of that mystery which animates the entire cosmos and which makes us all of one family.

I am reminded of the statement by the Buddhist scholar Robert Gimello:

The mysticism of any particular mystic is really the whole pattern of his life. The rare and wonderful "peaks" of experience are part of that pattern, but only a part, and their real value lies only in their relation to the other parts, to his thought, his moral values, his conduct towards others, his character and personality, etc. (Katz 1983)

It is precisely in the relation of every part of our lives to the total pattern of our existence—our thoughts, feelings, actions, our moral and ethical values, our conduct toward others including animals, the environment, all the relationships we can think of—the relation of these to the total pattern of our being, that the authenticity of the vision reveals itself. Or, as the pseudo-Dionysius is said to have stated, "We must not only learn the truth, we must suffer it." We may paraphrase this to mean that we must not only have the vision of unity, we must carry that awareness into every aspect of our lives, because the totality of our lives—our entire life pattern—has been transformed by the unitive experience.

Not only *what* we see in the world, however, but *how* we see it determines how we will act toward all things. Using H. P. Blavatsky's definition of the world as the individual "living in his personal nature," we begin to understand why the mystical vision authenticates itself by the transformation that occurs in that "personal nature." Both the world that is the self and the world that we have thought of as not-self are transformed because we now see the underlying unity of existence. We know ourselves as part of a greater whole in which the personal self no longer clamors for attention. The whole manner of our seeing, how we look at the world, is changed. That seeing, that looking, is itself the very perception of the truth of things. But truth, as Annie Besant said, "is only truth when you have learned to live it."

Our human destiny, it may be said, is to know. To know fully and wholly, not simply to theorize, to have opinions, to conjecture, to believe, but really to know is to be the mystic. To know is to encounter reality at every moment of time, in every place in space. Out of that encounter, which is truly the mystic experience, arises naturally a new way of living, a way of living that is both simple and beautiful, a way that is one of commitment to the cosmos, to our fellow human beings, to life itself, a commitment of the personal self to the One Self seated in the heart of all beings. One's action is one's presence in the world and one's presence in the world is action in accord with the ethic of love, compassion, and harmony. Out of our encounter with reality, with the vision of oneness, we fulfill the challenge given by Krishna to Arjuna, when the Divine spoke to the human, saying, "Be thou the efficient cause."

Out of the vision, the experience, the moment that we call mystical, arises a new being, a transformed being, whose very life is love and compassion. In the poetic words of *The Voice of the Silence*, that gem of transcendental wisdom given to the world by H. P. Blavatsky, dedicated by her to the "few real mystics" among us, we find the summation of that transformation:

> Know that the stream of superhuman knowledge and the Deva-wisdom thou hast won, must, from thyself, the channel of Alaya, be poured forth into another bed.

> Know . . . thou of the Secret Path, its pure fresh waters must be used to sweeter make the Ocean's bitter waves—that mighty sea of sorrow formed of the tears of men.

> . . . when once thou hast become like the fix'd star in highest heaven, that bright celestial orb must shine from out the

spatial depths for all—save itself, give light to all, but take from none.

Now bend thy head and listen well . . . Compassion speaks and saith: "Can there be bliss when all that lives must suffer? Shalt thou be saved and hear the whole world cry?

Harmonizing the Divine and the Human in Ourselves

Published in *The Quest,* Volume 86, October 1998

In 1888, when she was in London and *The Secret Doctrine* was about to be published, H. P. Blavatsky wrote a message to the Convention of the American Section in which she described what she termed "the essence of Theosophy" as

> the perfect harmonizing of the divine with the human in man, the adjustment of his god-like qualities and aspirations, and their sway over the terrestrial or animal passions in him. Kindness, absence of every ill feeling or selfishness, charity, goodwill to all beings, and perfect justice to others as to oneself, are its chief features.

Eleven years earlier, she had written in *Isis Unveiled*:

> Is it enough for man to know that he exists? Is it enough to be formed a human being to enable him to deserve the appellation of man? It is our decided impression and conviction that to

become a genuine spiritual entity, which that designation implies, man must first create himself anew, so to speak—i.e., thoroughly eliminate from his mind and spirit not only the dominating influence of selfishness and other impurity, but also the infection of superstition and prejudice. (1972a, 1:39)

Based on those two statements by HPB, we may explore the question of how we can create ourselves anew in order to bring about that essential harmonizing of the divine and the human within ourselves, which, according to Mme. Blavatsky, is the "essence of Theosophy."

It is appropriate to ask, at the very outset of our inquiry, what is the nature of the human in us and what is meant by the divine or, as HPB suggested, our "god-like qualities and aspirations"? A clear comprehension of the human constitution is necessary if we are to understand these two aspects of ourselves.

All students of the Theosophical philosophy are familiar with the sevenfold enumeration of the human principles and their division into what has been called the lower quaternary or personality and the immortal triad or individuality. This was put very clearly in a letter to A. P. Sinnett from the Mahatma M. in response to a question that Sinnett had asked of his Adept Teacher:

The whole individuality is centered in the three middle or 3rd, 4th and 5th principles. During earthly life it is all in the fourth, the center of energy, volition—will. Mr. Hume has perfectly defined the difference between personality and individuality. The former hardly survives—the latter, to run successfully its seven-fold downward and upward course, has to assimilate to itself the eternal life-power residing but in the seventh and then blend the three (fourth, fifth and seventh) into one—the sixth . . . The chief object of our struggles and *initiations* is to achieve this union while yet on this earth. (1993, Letter 44)

That paragraph has enough to occupy our attention for a life-time. However, note the significance of the statement that the "union" of the personality and the individuality, as the Mahatma terms the process which HPB has described as "the perfect harmonizing of the divine with the human," must take place "while yet on this earth." That can only mean while in human incarnation. This fact is emphasized again and again in *The Secret Doctrine*. It is here that the work is to be achieved, and it is here that we must win conscious immortality. Just one citation will suffice to underline this teaching:

> To become a Self-Conscious Spirit, the latter [that is, the "mortal man"] must pass through every cycle of being, culminating in its highest point on earth in Man . . . it is necessary for each Ego to attain to full self-consciousness as a human, *i.e.*, conscious being, which is synthesized for us in Man. (Blavatsky 1979, 1:192–93)

Nowhere has this truth been more succinctly or beautifully expressed than in the Bhagavad Gita (5:23), when Sri Krishna informs Arjuna: "He who is able to endure here on earth, ere he be liberated from the body, the force born from desire and passion, he is harmonized, he is a happy man."

So we live between two worlds: the world of the human and the realm of the divine, called upon to harmonize the diverse elements in ourselves that represent those spheres. The process of harmonization is, as HPB pointed out in *Isis Unveiled*, that of metempsychosis or a "purifying process," as she defined the term. Metempsychosis is, in fact, the complete transformation of what are known in Theosophical literature as the third, fourth and fifth principles, to which the Mahatma referred in his reply to Sinnett quoted earlier.

The focus is on the fourth principle, *kama* or desire, as the Mahatma emphasized, describing its nature as "energy, volition, will." Only through the one-pointed concentration of our energies,

302

of our will or volition, can we create ourselves anew, as HPB stated was necessary in order to bring about the required "adjustment of [our] god-like qualities and aspirations, and their sway over the terrestrial or animal passions" in us.

Metempsychosis was known in the Theosophical school of Ammonius Saccas, the last of the great Neoplatonists, as "theurgy," to which HPB referred in *The Key to Theosophy*. Simply defined, theurgy means to produce the work of the gods by so purifying one's nature as to align the personality or outer human nature with the inner or divine being. It involves, in other words, that "perfect harmonizing of the divine with the human" in ourselves. The goal, expressed by HPB in *Isis Unveiled* (1972a, 1:296), was that "the human race must, in accordance with the law of evolution, be finally physically spiritualized," a statement that again points to the necessity for incarnation here on earth.

One of the leading Buddhist scholars of our time, Prof. Robert Thurman of Columbia University, has described the Buddhist view of the nature of a human being as having "unlimited potential," adding that "the primary evolutionary mandate of human life is for all human beings to cultivate their powers of wisdom, justice, gentleness, loving, and creativity to the maximum degree." In an article entitled "How the Tibetans Could Save Civilization" (*Noetic Sciences Review*, Autumn 1997), Thurman stated that the Buddha saw the evolutionary essence of the human life form in terms of maximal openness and flexibility, wherein the human individual is poised to consummate the development of intelligence, one-pointed concentration, all-understanding genius, and irrepressible altruistic energy. He saw the human life form as the evolutionary gateway through which the egocentric individual self-preoccupied life process can enter the realm of selfless energetic love and compassion, artfully surrounding all interconnecting beings in an endlessly benevolent web of beauty and opportunity.

From such a point of view, the harmonization of the divine with the human in ourselves requires, as just proposed, that we undertake in earnest the difficult and arduous theurgical task of transforming the passional nature of the personality into the compassional nature of the true individuality.

To reiterate what has already been said and to use the traditional terminology of Theosophy, the task is to purify kama or the emotional nature (given to egocentrism and selfishness) by illuminating it with the light of buddhi (the light of wisdom and compassion). At our stage of evolution, the linchpin is in the fifth principle, manas, whose unique character may best be described as the power of choice.

The very core of our humanity lies in the choice we have either to walk through that evolutionary gateway of which Thurman spoke or to turn our backs upon it and revert to the pre-human state. The essence of our divine nature, then, lies in the choiceless condition—a state of consciousness beyond choice—in which, like the gods, we are one with the law. The journey from choice to choicelessness involves essentially the harmonization process. For as HPB said repeatedly in nearly every book she wrote, "Harmony is the great law of nature."

What then is harmony? In a quite remarkable book, *The World Is Sound: Nada Brahma*, the filmmaker and jazz critic Joachim-Ernst Berendt has explored the concept that the world "vibrates in harmonic proportions." Harmony, then, is in the right relationship of the parts with the whole. As Berendt has demonstrated by references to both music and contemporary science, harmonic correspondences exist everywhere throughout the universe. He writes: "If planetary orbits, leaves and bodies, churches and cloisters obey the laws of harmonics, then these laws must also apply to the earth itself. It too is a harmonic entity." And, he adds:

Entering into harmonic relationships is the goal not only of music. It is the goal of atoms and molecules, of planetary orbits, of cells and hearts, of brain waves and movements, of flocks of birds and schools of fish and in principle—of human beings.

Disease, in such a context, as the musicologist Rudolf Haase quoted by Berendt has put it, is nothing other than "rhythmic chaos." The poet Novalis is quoted as writing, "Every disease is a musical problem," which again is to say that illness of any kind is disharmony at some level. In fact, we may go further and suggest that whenever things go wrong in our daily affairs, we need to look to our harmonic relationships—with ourselves, with others, with the world about us, with all that exists. Right relationships are harmonic relationships, ever sounding the melodious songs of compassion, selflessness, kindness, gentleness, wisdom, and understanding.

Plato taught us this many centuries ago. In his dialogue, the *Timaeus*, he wrote:

> The motions which are naturally akin to the divine principle within us are the thoughts and the revolutions of the universe. . . . By learning the harmonies and revolutions of the universe [each one of us is] renewing his original nature, and should attain to that perfect life which the gods have set before mankind, both for the present and the future.

One writer has proposed that four main qualities characterize the truly civilized person, qualities which, we may suggest, mark individuals who have undertaken the task of creating themselves anew, of engaging in the theurgical process of transforming their entire nature, harmonizing the human with the divine. These qualities may be defined as (1) the person's ability to be a unique individual in interaction with others; (2) a flexibility of character which includes sensitivity to others and to all of life, all beings; (3) a gentleness; and (4) a serene contentment, the ability to enjoy life and find satisfaction in imaginative and original ways, which is true creativity. Quite obviously, the opposite of these qualities include racism and fanaticism, selfishness and rigidity of views, anger and violent reactions, greed and obsession with status, power, or wealth.

As we learn to create ourselves anew, to harmonize the divine potentialities with the human actualities within ourselves, to transform the personality into a beautiful instrument for the individuality, we discover that to be truly human is to walk the path of compassion, to breathe with the rhythms of nature, and to recognize our kinship with all forms of life. With the divine and the human harmonized in us, we open our eyes to the simple and extraordinary beauty that is all about us, and we plant the seeds of peace because we ourselves are peaceful.

In the mystical tradition of Judaism known as Hasidism, as expounded by the great theologian Martin Buber, the mystical experience is founded on the view that the world of our daily mundane existence and the world of spiritual reality are essentially one. It is only our limited perception that has separated them. It is our duty, writes Buber, to reunite the two worlds, adding that we contribute "towards this unity by holy living, in relationship to the world in which [we have] been set, at the place on which [we] stand." Then, concludes Buber,

> If we maintain holy intercourse with the little world entrusted to us, if we help the holy spiritual substance to accomplish itself in that section of Creation in which we are living, then we are establishing, in this our place, a dwelling for the Divine Presence. (1966, 176).

SEEK OUT THE WAY

Published in *The Quest,* Volume 88, July 2000

L ife is a journey. Yes, we've heard that before, and yet the metaphor is still a good one. A journey from here to there, from birth to death, from this room to that. Sometimes we have traveled as tourists, excited over the sights and sounds to be seen and heard, or bored by the long stretches of apparent wastelands.

Many years ago I made a trip, driving from Seattle to Wheaton for the summer sessions at Olcott. Two friends accompanied me on the journey. One sat in front with me as I drove, studying the map but never tiring of pointing out the beauty of the varied landscapes through which we were traveling. The other friend was content to sit in the back seat reading a book, lost in a fantasy world, and glancing up only occasionally when the first friend would excitedly demand that she look out at some unusual scene. My backseat friend reread the same book on the journey back to Seattle.

As tourists we often collect souvenirs of our travels, trinkets and oddments along with descriptive brochures and photographs. We burden ourselves and our suitcases with all kinds of mementos, so that we can regale each other with stories of our adventures. Tourists really love the excitement of going, and they often take pride in the number of places they have visited: twenty countries in ten days.

Then, of course, there have been times when we have traveled our journey as pilgrims. As pilgrims, we have experienced sacred times and sacred places or perhaps not so much places as spaces— sacred spaces in our lives. As pilgrims, we have been content with little, perhaps as small an icon as a stone picked up from the path or a flower to be pressed between the pages of our diary. Helena P. Blavatsky spoke of our entire existence as a pilgrimage, the pilgrimage of the monad, the essential Self. Pilgrims are not so much quantifiers as qualifiers. The importance of a pilgrimage is not the number of places visited but the quality of the experience, its deeper meaning, its significance, a new way of looking at everything, a new way of being in the world.

Pilgrims are also questers. Poet Diane Ackerman said, "We are a life form that quests." We are a restless species. Our innate restlessness has led us to the outermost reaches of space, to the depths of the oceans, to the peaks of the highest mountains, to subterranean caves, and into the core of the earth. From the Arctic to Antarctica we have explored our planet, and its few remaining unexplored regions call temptingly to the adventurer who is determined to go where no one has gone before. We are fascinated with the probes of Mars and Jupiter, and the question of whether the universe is infinite or finite continues to engage the finest minds of science and intrigues us all.

To be a quester means to have questions, though the questions may be different for each of us, and different at different times too. The questions I asked when I was twenty were not the questions I asked at forty nor those asked at sixty and seventy; they are not even the questions I ask today. But somehow each question seems to unfold into another question, and perhaps, if we are really pilgrims, we learn to live with the questions, realizing that the pilgrimage itself is the answer. Questions just set us on the way.

And so we come to the title of these remarks: "Seek Out the Way." That phrase comes from the book *Light on the Path*, the first of the three main Theosophical texts that offer guidance for the pilgrimage. The other two, in order of publication, are *The Voice of the Silence* and *At the Feet of the Master*. Countless members of the Theosophical Society, as well as numerous other seekers, have read those three little classics of the spiritual life and derived inspiration from them.

The phrase "Seek Out the Way," from the first of these spiritual classics to be published, raises the question of what it means to be questers or pilgrims on this journey we are all taking. N. Sri Ram, in his book *The Nature of Our Seeking*, has pointed out that "the nature of our seeking would depend on what it is that prompts it." And he states further, "We often use the words *seeking* and *search*, but without enquiring deeply into their implications, the psychological process in relation to a Truth which is not of the same nature as the facts of the external world, but is a truth to be realized within oneself." He cites Annie Besant and Prince Siddhartha as genuine seekers. We might well add Arjuna, as well as Socrates, to the list, and of course there are many others who are authentic questers.

The first "rule" on the Path is to seek out the way, to discover the path that is one's own. The title for these remarks might well have been "Finding Shoes That Fit," for no one can walk properly in another's shoes. The first "rule" is found in that one word "seek." Unless we seek, unless we realize we are questers on this journey of existence, pilgrims not tourists, there is no way, no path, no road.

Three statements come to the heart of my thesis. The first is the most direct and simplest. It comes from the inaugural address of the president-founder, Henry Steel Olcott, and sets forth beautifully in the most succinct manner possible the work of the Society:

We seek, inquire, reject nothing without cause, accept nothing without proof; we are students, not teachers.

We state in our literature that we are a Society of seekers, a group of inquirers. Yet often it seems that once we have joined the Society, we cease to inquire or to question any of the ideas we have so enthusiastically embraced.

The second statement is from the second mahatmic letter addressed to A. P. Sinnett:

> The adept is the rare efflorescence of a generation of enquirers; and to become one, he must obey the inward impulse of his soul irrespective of the prudential considerations of worldly science or sagacity.

Two ideas confront us in that statement: first, to become an adept requires inquiry; second, we must follow our own "inward impulse" without regard to worldly concerns or the demands imposed by others.

The third statement is from Joseph Campbell's fourth volume of his series *The Masks of God*, devoted to *Creative Mythology*:

> Just as in the past each civilization was the vehicle of its own mythology, developing in character as its myth became progressively interpreted, analyzed, and elucidated by its leading minds, so in this modern world—where the application of science to the fields of practical life has now dissolved all cultural horizons, so that no separate civilization can ever develop again—each individual is the center of a mythology of his own, of which his own intelligible character is the Incarnate God, so to say, whom his empirically questing consciousness is to find.

Campbell adds, "The pathless way is the only way now before us." Implicit in Campbell's words are the two ideas found in the mahatmic communication to Sinnett: inquiry or questing, which Olcott emphasized at the founding of our Society, and the need to find our own way. It is truly a "pathless way," as J. Krishnamurti so often emphasized. There is no way until our feet have trod it. What is all-important to the finding of that way is the seeking. Krishnamurti often said to his audiences as well as in his dialogues with small groups, "Inquire, sirs; you do not inquire."

Just what is it then to inquire, to have what Campbell called a "questing consciousness"? How do we seek? And what is it that we seek? To inquire—genuinely inquire—means that we are in earnest about understanding ourselves and the world in which we are living. It means that we are willing to clear away any and all excess mental and emotional baggage so that the mind is clear, transparent as it were. Only in such a mind, a mind that is without prejudice and preconception, a mind that is not entangled in its own net of favorite and passionately held convictions, a mind that is not shadowed by personal likes and dislikes, only in such a mind can the truth of a way, one's own unique way, arise.

The profound teachings communicated by the Inner Founders of the Society in their letters to A. P. Sinnett and A. O. Hume were the result of inquiries by those two men, their questions, and their earnest seeking for information and understanding concerning inner truths. On many occasions those Adept Teachers nearly despaired of their efforts because, as they pointed out, the minds of the two Englishmen were so cluttered with preconceived ideas, with their own sense of pride in possessing superior knowledge, with their conviction of rightness, that—to paraphrase the Adept Teacher—there was scarcely a niche into which a new idea might be inserted. Again and again, Sinnett and Hume were advised that it was only upon "the serene and placid surface of the unruffled mind," a mind

open and free from the contamination of selfish interests and preoc-
cupations, that the light of truth might shine. The inquiry, in other
words, must be from an authentic openness, not the kind of seeking
that is already convinced of the answer.

We may think that Sinnett and Hume were extremely obstinate
men and wonder how they could have been so stubborn in their
convictions that at times they seemed to argue with their Mahatmic
Teachers! Yet are we not sometimes just as proud of our convictions,
as stubborn in maintaining the correctness of our views? This is the
way reincarnation works, we may say, or this is simply your karma,
or this is how it is after death! Do we feel that the last word has been
given to us on any of these subjects? On Theosophy itself?

We should be grateful to Sinnett and Hume for the questions
they asked and remember that Sinnett produced out of the mass of
material found in the letters those Teachers wrote to him the first
textbook of Theosophical ideas: *Esoteric Buddhism*. Hume also performed services for India, including the founding of the Indian
National Congress, which elicited the gratitude of the mahatmic
adepts. So, whatever one thinks of the faults of these two Englishmen, their persistent questioning, their endless inquiries, called
forth that most magnificent work of our literary heritage, *The
Mahatma Letters*.

But to return to the question posed by the word "seek." Jacob
Needleman in his book, *The Heart of Philosophy*, says, "Philosophy
is no answer to anything." And he continues, "The function of philosophy in human life is to help man remember. *It has no other task.*"
We might substitute "Theosophy" for "philosophy" in those statements. It is often said that Theosophy answers all the questions of
life, but really it does not answer any questions or solve any problems. We ourselves answer the questions; Theosophy just helps us
to remember—it awakens us to right memory. But to be awakened
we must ask the right questions, we must seek, probing deeply into

matters. We have indeed forgotten something. And life calls on us to remember—to remember who we are, because when we remember who we are, we have found the way.

"The magic of real philosophy," Needleman wrote, "is the magic of the specifically human act of self-questioning—of being in front of the question of oneself." This is really to seek. It is what Socrates, the greatest questioner in Western philosophy, demanded. It is the demand of the Upanishadic teachers of ancient India, and the demand of Krishna in awakening Arjuna in the Bhagavad Gita. To stand in front of the question of oneself—that is to remember our authentic Self.

William James wrote, "The deepest question that is ever asked admits of no reply," but demands instead what he termed a resolute "turning of the will." That "turning of the will" may be equated with what the Mahatma K. H. called "the inward impulse of the soul," which then must be obeyed. Out of the seeking, out of the questioning, the inquiring, comes the way—a way that is both a path and pathless. It is a road "steep and thorny," as Blavatsky told us. It is "narrow" and "few there are who find it," as the Master Jesus declared. It is "narrow as a razor's edge," as one of the Upanishads states. But for those who truly seek, as *Light on the Path* reminds us, there opens out before us "the mystery of the new way," when "the star of your soul will show its light."

Genuine seeking, then, involves a question that lies at the core of our being, which is never satisfied with easy answers, but that carries us both outward and inward toward true knowing. Its answer demands that "turning of the will" of which William James wrote and which Plato called "eros," love in its essence. Because of the nature of love, one does not approach the question with the scientific-scholarly mind alone. One stands before the question, as Socrates demanded of his listeners, one gives attention to the question, stripped—as Plato might put it—of all but love itself. In such a condition, one remembers, which is to reassemble a primal knowing. There is no other way, no other path; and because there is no other path, it is essentially and always a pathless way, for until each one of us has done it, no path exists.

In the truest sense, this is what it means to be a Theosophist, not simply a member of the Society, but an authentic Theosophist, a knower and a lover of wisdom, of truth, of beauty. It is to seek, to ask the really big questions, the central questions of human existence, and never be satisfied with answers until we have probed, inquired, ever more deeply.

One of the Upanishads says:

> As a pot with cracks shows light within, so the hidden light of
> Atman shines out through cracks in the mind body complex

Questioning, seeking, inquiring produces cracks. If the seeking makes us "crackpots," so much the better for us. We need ever-widening cracks in our psychological nature, cracks in the "mind-body complex," if ever the light of Atman is to blaze forth in all its splendor. Perhaps the world needs more "crackpots" like us. Certainly we need to shatter the molds of our mental-emotional encasements and let shine forth the light of Atman, the One Self. That is to "seek out the way."

CROSSING THRESHOLDS ON THE INWARD JOURNEY

Published in *The Theosophist*, Volume 122, May 2001

For how many years have we heard talks and read articles in which there appeared the phrase, "the dawn of the new millennium." And now we are here at the beginning of that millennium about which there has been so much talk, a time both anticipated and dreaded, a time about which so many prophecies have been made. Even H. P. Blavatsky in concluding *The Key to Theosophy* indulged in prophecy, when she proposed that should the Theosophical Society survive and live "true to its mission, to its original impulses through the next hundred years"—and it has indeed survived for more than a hundred and twenty-five years—then perhaps "earth will be a heaven in the twenty-first century." Well, perhaps, for we have yet to see what the century and the millennium may hold for humanity.

We know that the date marking such a beginning is a purely fictional one, fabricated out of calculations by a rather obscure monk who lived in Rome in what we now refer to—again by his calculations—as the sixth-century of our era. And we know—if we know anything at all about the diverse cultures and histories of peoples around the globe—that other calendars and other dates and other modes of telling time have been used to mark the passage of years, centuries, and millennia. Yet the calendar that has come to be universally accepted is the one on which that fictional or mythical date has been placed, and so in some way we have all come to accept that we have seen the dawn of a new millennium. And we are now content to speak and write about events that occurred five million and ten million and thirty million years ago, about the likelihood of events that may occur one year or ten years or twenty years from now, all in accordance with that Gregorian calendar by which we agreed that this is the day and time for us to gather here at the Society's ninth World Congress. Consequently, there is a certain tacit agreement that we understand what is meant in terms of the passage of time.

So it is that, as just said, we have all seen the dawn of a new millennium. But there is another metaphor that in so many ways is more appropriate to our lives as Theosophists, as spiritual seekers after truth and understanding and wisdom, a metaphor that marks not so much the passage of time as the growth of the soul. For as HPB told us:

> It is the spiritual evolution of the *inner*, immortal man that forms the fundamental tenet in the Occult Sciences. (Blavatsky 1979, 1:634)

I would suggest, then, that it is less the dawning of a new calendric year or century or millennium which is our concern, but rather that if we are to bring ourselves "in tune with the universe" (which is the theme of our present gathering), we need to give attention to that "spiritual evolution" which is our inward journey, the inward journey of the soul. And for that let me use the metaphor of a threshold, the thresholds to be crossed on that journey. We are all called to live, at times, between two worlds: the objective world of our everyday existence, of calendric time, the world of *kronos*, and the subjective world, the inner world of our thoughts and feelings, our aspirations and knowings, where existence seems far more real, that inner world of *kairos*, as St Paul called it. In that inner world, time is no longer linear. Time in fact becomes irrelevant in the subjective world of consciousness. Thomas Moore, author of *Care of the Soul*, has referred to that world in these words: "There are places in this world that are neither here nor there, neither up nor down, neither real nor imaginary." And these may be called the in-between places, the thresholds we cross on our inward journey.

The very word threshold conjures up so many images, some fearful, some beautiful. And so it is on our inward journey; there are places to be crossed at great risk, as all spiritual texts remind us, and there are places across which we may move with ease and confidence. The word threshold derives from the Latin *terere*, and from the Greek *tornos*, both referring to a turning, a rubbing, and meaning also the process of beating out grain or seed by treading or striking the husks so as to free the grain within. A threshold, used as a metaphor for our inward journey, is the place of the soul's own threshing, and the thresholds to be crossed demand an inner threshing which releases the true Self from its bondage to the personality. I am reminded of a stanza in a beautiful Shaker hymn (the Shakers being a religious group that originated in England in the mid-eighteenth century and who believed, among other things, in leading a simple life under the inspiration of the Holy Spirit):

> When true simplicity is gain'd
> To bow and to bend we shan't be ashamed.
> To turn, turn will be our delight,
> Till by turning, turning, we come round right.

It is that turning, as with a lathe, that removes our rough edges, that threshes off the excrescences that hide the Self. And how many threshold experiences have we had, often without even being aware that we stood at a threshold or crossed one! Consider: have you ever stood on the threshold of a room or of a house afraid to enter? Have you ever been caught between dreaming and waking, suspended on a kind of threshold between knowing and nonknowing? Each of us can remember a moment when a door seemed to open, together with the feeling that it might not remain open for long. Perhaps a decision was required, and we paused, figuratively, on the threshold, unable to go either forward or back. It has been suggested that to view one's life as consisting of a series of thresholds would instill a creative attitude into the process of living, an attitude that can bring a realization of the infinite possibilities of one's existence.

Again to quote Thomas Moore:

> This is the key point about thresholds: they are not the place of life and not the place of death. In their narrow confines you may find fantasy, memory, dream, anxiety, miracle, intuition and magic . . . This is a good place from which to make a decision and get a hunch. It is the true home of creativity.

Certainly it is true that standing in a doorway, on a threshold, you are very often forced into the imagination, wondering what you will find on the other side.

Mircea Eliade, the well-known historian of religions, has written of the threshold as "the limit, the boundary, the frontier, that distinguishes and opposes two worlds—and at the same time the paradoxical place where these worlds communicate, where passage from the profane to the sacred world becomes possible." And the philosopher Martin Heidegger has spoken of the threshold as a space between two worlds, a middle ground that simultaneously holds, joins, and separates the two. He writes:

The threshold sustains the middle point in which the two, the outside and the inside, penetrate each other. The threshold holds the between . . . What goes out and goes in is joined in the between. The joining is the threshold.

In the terminology of *The Secret Doctrine*, the thresholds between the levels of manifested existence as well as between the domains of our human constitution are referred to as the *laya-centers*, those zero points, as it were, or mystical points where a thing disappears from one level or plane and passes onward to reappear in another form or substance at the next level. In fact, HPB resorts to symbol and allegory, as she does so often, to describe these transitional or threshold states in the building of the cosmos. A thorough study of the laya-centers would take us far afield from our present concern, but let me allude to some of the mythological or allegorical and symbolic references to thresholds which may throw light on their importance as we move on the inward journey. And I would remind you that it is precisely because myth and allegory do not refer to historical, chronological time that they depict so well the journey of the soul, a journey never taken *in* time but always *out* of time. They call us, as it were, to the immediacy of the significant moment of inner awakening. So in recounting some of the mythological references to thresholds, I am not concerned with their historicity, but rather—as in the telling of all myths—with what they tell us about our own interior journeys.

The great epic of India, the Ramayana, concludes—at least in some versions—with the story of Sita stepping across the threshold of her husband's home, in violation of the promise she had given to his brother. Sita is then rejected by society, for she has stepped across the boundary of duty, the social order, the threshold which separates the domestic culture of the home from the wilderness, although she did so in obedience to a higher law, the law of compassion. In many traditional Indian households, since women are confined to the home, the men have to cross the threshold repeatedly to bring home food and wealth. Stepping out results in pollution; stepping in necessitates purification. Hence rituals must be performed so that stepping across the threshold, either going out or coming in, may be lawful and in accordance with the nature of things. I know many people who, while perhaps not performing specific rituals, do have certain customs that they perform, almost unconsciously, when crossing the thresholds of their homes. One friend never leaves the house without saying a blessing on the home, and she never returns without a prayer of gratitude to the house for its protection.

In many traditions, there are clear markers to establish boundaries around villages or fields. These define the threshold between the inhospitable wilderness and the orderly social life of the village or the cultivated field. Doorkeepers, sometimes of fanged and armed demonic-looking figures, are often placed at entrances to temples, marking the thresholds between the profane and the sacred. Mara Freeman, who presents workshops on Celtic and British folklore and mythology, has pointed out that the floor, generally earthen, just inside the threshold of old Irish cottages was known as the "welcome of the door." Upon entering, a visitor would stand there and say a blessing for the household, for the threshold was holy ground, an in-between place. It was said to be neither here nor there, but allowed a crack to open between the worlds where power could seep in. Those skilled in walking between the worlds, as it were, knew how to harness the power of the threshold. In the Celtic landscape are many thresholds to the secret country of the gods and fairies, and many Irish legends warn of the dangers of crossing the threshold into the realm of Faerie. Today, in our demythologized and desacralized worldview, the doors of the fairy hills remain sealed simply because we keep the eyes of our mythic consciousness firmly shut. Few, it seems, dare to open what W. B. Yeats called the "flaming door" and explore the power that crackles on the thresholds of our vaunted reality structures, but there are thresholds to be crossed if we would take the inward journey to the One Self, the One Reality.

There is, of course, a danger to be found in threshold places, and leaping over thresholds is not to be taken lightly. So many traditional folk legends speak of worlds into which we are not meant to enter or which we can only enter at the risk of our lives. The cultures of archaic and classical Greece and Egypt treated points of transformation as thresholds to be crossed with respect. The threshold into the mysteries, for example, was of a dual nature, for it was both a barrier and a point of transformation. In those cultures the duality was embodied in the god Hermes, who functioned as a guardian of thresholds and as a guide for those who crossed them. In fact, Hermes became the patron of all those who crossed thresholds, being himself a messenger who crosses the boundary between the world of the gods and the world of humans. Travelers in ancient Greece created piles of stones called *herma* after the god Hermes to signify the crossing of frontiers separating political territories, and each passing traveler would add a stone to signify recognition of the boundary crossed. What would our world be like if we respected all the boundaries we cross as we travel from country to country, from continent to continent?

A study of the rituals and the gods associated with the Greek sanctuaries reveals how an abiding respect for thresholds gave order and stability to life and made transformation meaningful. Many of the thresholds marked the passage from one stage of life to the next, from childhood to adulthood, from adulthood to old age, etc., as well as from life to death and death to rebirth. Some thresholds, as already noted, marked the boundary between the city and the wilderness, symbolic of the boundary between the cultured life of order, the civil life, and the chaotic life of the wild. For example, sanctuaries to the goddess Demeter, whose story was re-enacted in the Eleusinian Mysteries, were usually located at the limits of cultivated land, and Demeter herself sat at the threshold that separated life from death, as the goddess Artemis was at the threshold between childhood and adulthood as well as between the city and the wild.

At each stage of life's way, both outer and inner, there is a door to be opened, a threshold to be crossed. Sometimes the door is obscurely marked or not marked at all, but a door there is if we remain vigilant. Traditional societies, and I have referred to only a very few, took care in respecting boundary conditions, for they knew that the guardians of thresholds are often merciless. They may cut down anyone who attempts to cross without an inner humility of spirit coupled with a bravery that is willing to endure the threshing. Perhaps the best-known guardian of thresholds is the one that was given life by Edward Bulwar-Lytton in his occult novel, *Zanoni*, and referred to on at least two occasions in the Mahatmic correspondence to A. P. Sinnett as well as by H. P. Blavatsky in her writings. In Bulwer-Lytton's novel, the candidate for instruction meets an awesome and demonic figure called the "Dweller on the Threshold." This appears to be a recurrent figure in esoteric lore where confronting the Dweller is inevitably portrayed as a life-shattering event.

The author Richard Smoley, in an article on "Confronting the Sentinel," which appeared in the journal *Parabola* (Spring 2000) writes: "In the Kabbalah, the Dweller on the Threshold—sometimes known as the Sentinel—is connected with the principle *Daat* or Knowledge." The Kabbalistic Tree of Life is comprised of ten principles, or *sefirot*, considered as emanations of the divine that disclose themselves in the worlds of spirit, psyche and matter. In that scheme, *Daat*, the Dweller on the Threshold, is an unmistakable eleventh element, a paradoxical non-*sephirah*, as Smoley suggests, but he proposes that this element gives us a clue to the identity of the Dweller. To quote Smoley:

Daat . . . means knowledge. Clearly this is a knowledge of a much higher kind than mere factual information or technical knowledge . . . One could say that the Dweller on the Threshold is the Tree of Knowledge of Good and Evil. Eating the "fruit" of this tree was not one simple act done by a mythical ancestor thousands of years ago. In fact it could be seen as something each of us is doing all the time. It is an essential part of the human condition.

Consequently, the Dweller on the Threshold may be seen as that core part of ourselves where the decision to know good and evil takes place, and we could say that the entire human condition is the result of that decision to "know" the mixed world of good and evil that we encounter every day. Smoley goes on to say:

One Kabbalist . . . calls *Daat* the "seed of I." It is the point within us where we lose awareness of our unity with the divine and experience ourselves as separate individuals, isolated from each other and from the universe.

In fact, it is that sense of the all-important "I" in the cases of both A. O. Hume and Stainton Moses to which the Mahatma K.H. refers when speaking of the "Dweller on the Threshold" as depicted in Bulwer-Lytton's novel. And in that novel, Bulwer-Lytton indicates that the initiate must encounter that Dweller or Sentinel and face the primal fear that undergirds our experience of ourselves as separate individuals because the inward journey to real knowledge involves a genuine purging of all sense of a personal separated self. This is the threshing that must take place if we would move onwards, the husk of egoism removed that the true Self may be revealed.

So what are the thresholds to be crossed on this inward journey? Every journey contains its own metaphor, for we are all the time being addressed by images. In imagination we conjure up those images that seem most congenial to us, which are most helpful to us, images that we feel depict our own struggles and triumphs on the journey to our goal. I have friends who mark off the days on the calendar, putting a large X through each day as it concludes and then counting the number of days left in a week, a month or a year, feeling that this outer mode of marking the journey somehow relates to steps on an inner path. Other people keep journals, not a diary that records events of each day, although that too can be useful in seeing where one has been and what one has done. Rather a note-book in which no dates may even appear, but in which are written thoughts, and feelings, descriptions of significant moments. Such a journal may record the progress of inner illuminations, understand-ings, and even the darker moments of despair and discouragement, the soul suffering that has been undergone. Such journals are often filled with images that in themselves tell the story of the inward journey. They tell of doors that have opened on new understandings and doors that remain firmly closed. At times these journals, if we record our thoughts and feelings honestly, reveal an inner or spiri-tual poverty which it may be necessary for us to acknowledge if we would open those closed doors and move across new thresholds to further awakenings.

We all have our own favorite images to depict this inward jour-ney. One of the most beautiful series of images involving the pro-found metaphor of thresholds to be crossed, certainly one of my own favorites as I consider the journey to be undertaken, is the one to be found in the work of the sixteenth-century mystic Teresa of Avila. In her major work, *The Interior Castle*, we have the imagery of the pilgrim soul moving from room to room, rooms or chambers arranged in seven concentric rings, each an abode or dwelling place holding unique experiences for the courageous traveler. I realize that castles are not much in favor today, but what appeals to me most in the imagery of St. Teresa is the concentric nature of the journey through the seven rooms, giving the journey a kind of spiral ascent rather than a ladder-like arrangement which is too often used in our classification of the human constitution as well as the domains of manifested existence. Be that as it may, Teresa warns of the dangers involved in crossing thresholds from one room to the next, for at each entry way stands a guardian who must be acknowledged. We have already spoken of these guardians of the thresholds, sentinels who must be respected. We may even have our own names for these guardians if we are alert to their presence within us.

A similar system to Teresa's may be found in the Gnostic tradition, where there is a mystical ascent through seven spheres or planetary systems, each of which is guarded at the threshold by a malevolent being called an Archon. Actually, we find almost the same imagery of a sevenfold concentric series of rooms comprising the abode of the soul in some Sufi writings as well as in the Zoharic mystical tradition. And, of course, we are all familiar with the imagery of rooms or halls in both *Light on the Path* and *The Voice of the Silence*. In *Light on the Path*, we are introduced to only one hall, the Hall of Learning, which I would submit contains all seven chambers in Teresa's schema, while in *The Voice of the Silence*, we have three halls or rooms: Ignorance, Learning, and Wisdom. Again these can be coordinated very easily with Teresa's sevenfold pattern.

A particular reason for choosing Teresa's imagery of the sevenfold concentric rings or rooms is that the movement she envisions is always inward towards the center where abides the Immortal Self, the Divine, the One who is nameless and yet is called by many names. At the same time, it is not a movement away from the world, away from the here and now of existence, but it is a journey that, bringing the pilgrim soul ever closer to the center, ever more in tune with the heart of the universe, with the One, demands selfless action in the world. The world is seen, as it were, through the windows of each of the chambers, but seen always in new perspective, so that—to use a familiar concept—one is in the world but not of it. To anticipate, however, we may recall HPB's words in *The Voice of the Silence*, when, as she puts it, "Thou shalt attain the seventh step and cross the gate of final knowledge," the voice of compassion is heard:

> Can there be bliss when all that lives must suffer? Shalt thou be saved and hear the whole world cry?

We might well say that some echoes of that voice are heard every step of the way or, using Teresa's metaphor, in every room we enter on the inward journey. Perhaps, in itself, it is the threshold voice, if I may call it that, for crossing the threshold into each of the rooms on the journey inwards demands a price, as it were, the price of moving onwards only on condition that we use whatever powers are gained for the service of the world, for the benefit of humanity.

To turn, then, to Teresa's account of that inward journey through crossing the thresholds of the sevenfold concentric rooms, we may keep in mind her advice that the pilgrim soul must be allowed to explore all the rooms, which means simply that we are to know and understand every aspect of ourselves. The whole self must negotiate the entry. Evelyn Underhill, in *The House of the Soul*, has said the same thing:

> We are required to live in the whole of our house, learning to go freely and constantly up and down stairs, backwards and forwards, easily and willingly, from one kind of life to the other; weaving together the higher and lower powers of the soul, and using both for the glory of God. (1947, 74)

And, we would add, as just said, for the service of humanity, indeed for the service of all living beings.

So let us step across the threshold into Teresa's first room. This is that initial step that demands a real heroism, for it is entry into the beginnings of self-knowledge, of becoming attentive to an inner voice, becoming aware of who we really are. Sometimes it takes more courage to begin the inward journey than to continue it, although courage—a bravery of soul—is needed to cross all the thresholds. At this first step, often a real threshing takes hold of us, and we are pulled in two directions at once—the longing to lead a truly meaningful, a genuinely spiritual life and the desire to continue with our old habits, feeling we are not ready for so strenuous an undertaking as walking the spiritual path appears to demand.

Recall, if you will, your initial response when for the first time you read that opening paragraph of *Light on the Path*:

> Before the eyes can see they must be incapable of tears. Before the ear can hear it must have lost its sensitiveness. Before the voice can speak in the presence of the Masters it must have lost the power to wound. Before the soul can stand in the presence of the Masters its feet must be washed in the blood of the heart. (Collins 1944)

Did you feel daunted by such a statement? To be "washed in the blood of the heart"—this is indeed a threshing, a flailing, which seems to remove all we hold most dear, to strip us inwardly naked. So much demanded, and we feel so inadequate. Dante trembled before the words inscribed on the gateway that led him first to hell on his great journey to the supreme: "Abandon every hope, who enter here." But Dante's guide told him: "Here one must leave behind all hesitation; here every cowardice must meet its death." Truly and surely, once we have glimpsed the light beyond, "There is no other way to go."

We have started on our journey and go on we must. Another threshold is to be crossed. This is how Teresa describes it:

> Everyone . . . who wishes to enter the second Mansion, will be well advised, as far as his state of life permits, to try to put aside all unnecessary affairs and business. (1989, 41)

This is a stage familiar to many where we determine our priorities, consider what is important in our lives and what is not important. Here, Teresa advises, one begins to enter into a conscious relationship with the authentic Self. But note what Teresa says further, "hearing His voice is a greater trial than not hearing it." Have you ever wished you had not heard the call to a spiritual life? Have you ever longed for the ease of non-knowing? Teresa puts the matter in very Christian terms, of course:

> Remember that in few of the mansions . . . are we free from struggles with devils. It is true that in some of them, the wardens, who . . . are the faculties, have strength for the fight; but it is most important that we should not cease to be watchful against the devil's wiles, lest he deceive us in the guise of an angel of light. (ibid., 41–42)

Vigilance is indeed called for, a constant attention, as so many spiritual texts tell us. And guardians of thresholds can sometimes be most alluring, promising with their siren calls many rewards for the separate and egoistic self. Psychic powers can even masquerade as spiritual ones, as HPB pointed out so graphically in *The Voice of the Silence* in describing that *mayavic* realm in which "dazzled by illusive radiance thy Soul should linger and be caught in its deceptive light."

Crossing the threshold into Teresa's third room means settling down to business, taking up the work in earnest, for we are now committed to walking on. Yet there are periods of inner aridity or barrenness, along with trying experiences and worries. Let me again quote Teresa, speaking now of the third room:

> If humility is lacking, we will remain here our whole life—and with a thousand afflictions and miseries. For since we will not have abandoned ourselves, this stage will be very laborious and burdensome. We shall be walking weighed down with this mud of our human misery. (1979, 63)

Again and again, Teresa reminds us that we have to be constantly alert for the enemies at our gate, enemies that are not so much those outside ourselves as those within us.

We may be reminded here of that magnificent passage in a letter from the Mahatma K. H. to A. P. Sinnett:

> You were told . . . that the path to Occult Sciences has to be trodden laboriously and crossed at the danger of life; that every new step in it leading to the final goal is surrounded by pitfalls and cruel thorns; that the pilgrim who ventures upon it is made first to confront and *conquer* the thousand and one furies who keep watch over its adamantine gates and entrance—furies called Doubt, Scepticism, Scorn, Ridicule, Envy and finally Temptation—especially the latter; and that he who would see *beyond* had to first destroy this living wall; that he must be possessed of a heart and soul clad in steel, and of an iron, never failing determination and yet be meek and gentle, humble and have shut out from his heart every human passion, that leads to evil. (1993, Letter 126)

Crossing the threshold into the fourth chamber as described by Teresa, a clear transition appears to be made. By now we should be sure of our direction, although we know there is still a great distance to travel. Listen again to what Teresa says:

> One noticeably senses a gentle drawing inward. The senses and exterior things seem to be losing their hold because the soul is recovering what it has lost. (1979, 77–78)

And then she adds further that at this stage in our journey, "without any effort, the soul should strive to cut down the rambling of the intellect, but not suspend either it or the mind." Here we must learn to listen to the voice of intuition, so that we may hear the truths which are beginning to be communicated to us from the depths of our own being.

This fourth stage or room clearly marks the state referred to in the second section of *Light on the Path*. There the aspirant is told to enter the Hall of Learning:

> You who are now a disciple—able to stand, able to hear, able to see, able to speak—who have conquered desire and attained to self-knowledge, who have seen your soul in its bloom and recognized it, and heard the Voice of the Silence—go to the Hall of Learning and read what is written there for you.

We are, as *Light on the Path* further describes it, "on the threshold of becoming more than human." That is the threshold we must some day cross, even though now we may only glimpse what lies in the rooms or stages beyond.

Returning to Teresa's imagery of the journey, there seems little resistance to crossing the thresholds into the fifth, sixth and seventh rooms, for the real threshing has now been accomplished and we are able to walk more freely. Yet there are still interior trials, and all spiritual texts point to these—the crucifixions and resurrections.

For Teresa, the fifth chamber is one in which the essential experience is death/rebirth, the dying to the limited self or personality in order to be reborn into the wider life of the spirit. This stage is portrayed in all the great mystery schools.

Crossing the threshold into the sixth room marks the final renunciation. As *The Voice of the Silence* states:

> And now thy Self is lost in SELF, thyself unto THYSELF, merged
> in that SELF from which thou first didst radiate.

Teresa speaks of great trials and deep sufferings in the sixth chamber, which she perceives as a major threshold reached after the mystical death and rebirth in the fifth. So it is a perilous threshold, entailing spiritual and psychic ordeals, a place where there may also be experienced ecstatic and rapturous states. Across that threshold lie unimaginable beauties, a totally new state of perception, an understanding that defies articulation. And have we not been told that even great ones have fallen back from this initiatory stage?

Again, we may quote *Light on the Path* (Rule 18 of the second section): The knowledge which is now yours is only yours because your soul has become one with all pure souls and with the inmost. It is a trust vested in you by the Most High. Betray it, misuse your knowledge, or neglect it, and it is possible even now for you to fall from the high estate you have attained. Great ones fall back, even from the threshold, unable to sustain the weight of their responsibility, unable to pass on. Teresa finds it hard to distinguish between the sixth and seventh mansions, saying they cannot be rigidly separated. And, indeed, in other traditions such as the Jewish and Sufi the symbolic descriptions of these two chambers seem to mingle into each other. Teresa tells us that we may have a sudden vision of what is in these rooms, a glorious revelation which engraves itself deeply on the memory and yet which is terrible in its intensity and majesty. In her words:

> The soul . . . cannot endure so terrible a sight. I say "terrible" because, though the sight is the loveliest and most delightful imaginable, even by a person who lived and strove to imagine it for a thousand years, because it so far exceeds all that our imagination and understanding can compass, its presence is of such exceeding majesty that it fills the soul with a great terror. (1989, 186)

Those familiar with the final cantos of Dante's circumlocution of the spheres of Paradise in *The Divine Comedy* will recognize that in that work also, there is a similar feeling of awe:

> And so my mind, bedazzled and amazed,
> Stood fixed in wonder, motionless, intent,
>   And still my wonder kindled as I gazed.
> How weak are words, and how unfit to frame
>   My concept . . .
> (33:97, 131)

Then, having crossed the last threshold, entry into Teresa's seventh mansion finds the aspirant at the still, quiet, unmoving center where abides the Self in fullness, the One Self, which remains tranquil and at peace beneath the fluctuations of external action, thought and feeling. Here, as she says, the "shutters of understanding" are opened. We are truly at one with ourselves, balanced and centered. And we have also Dante's immortal description:

> High phantasy lost power and here broke off;
> Yet, as a wheel moves smoothly, free from jars,
> My will and my desire were turned by love,
> The love that moves the sun and the other stars.
> (33:142–45)

It is at the center that we are at one with ourselves and therefore one with all that lives, in tune with the universe. There at the center we know it is only "love that moves the sun and the other stars," love which is infinite compassion as it is infinite wisdom. From that center we must go forth to heal the world, becoming in our turn as so many spiritual texts tell us, the teachers, the saviors, the bodhisattvas, the wise ones, the compassionate ones. HPB spoke of this in *The Secret Doctrine* as well as in *The Voice of the Silence*. And we have it also in the beautiful words that conclude that little manual of the spiritual life, *At the Feet of the Master*:

> The wisdom which enables you to help, the will which directs the wisdom, the love which inspires the will—these are your qualifications. Will, wisdom and love are the three aspects of the Logos; and you, who wish to enroll yourselves to serve God, must show forth these aspects in the world.

We have gone within only that we may go without, acting now in a new way, inwardly illumined and outwardly fully present in all we do and say and think. *The Voice of the Silence* speaks of the responsibility before those who move on the inward journey:

> When thou hast reached that state, the Portals that thou hast to conquer on the Path fling open wide their gates to let thee pass . . . So shalt thou be in full accord with all that lives . . . Give light and comfort to the toiling pilgrim, and seek out him who knows still less than thou . . . If Sun thou can'st not be, then be the humble planet . . . Point out the "Way"—however dimly, and lost among the host—as does the evening star to those who tread their path in darkness.

Every day we cross thresholds, for every day there are doors to be opened, rooms to be entered. If I have a certain fascination with doors and doorways, as I do, it is because they are not only actual thresholds but they serve as powerful images for the transitional passages that may always lead us onwards and inwards. Every moment is a doorway through which we may walk on our way towards deeper understanding, richer illuminations, ever more beautiful realizations. Crossing thresholds is not a matter of linear time. Rather it is a matter of coming awake—as did Teresa of Avila, as did Dante, as did the Buddha, as did countless other lesser seekers and teachers—coming awake to all the possibilities that life holds for us, coming awake to truth and beauty and goodness and love.

Together we—all humanity, all life on this shimmering planet—have crossed the threshold of a new century, a new millennium. Perhaps—just perhaps—we here, you and I, members of the Theosophical Society, striving to "live true"—to use HPB's words—to the "original impulses" that gave the Society birth, crossing thresholds on our own inward journeys, will ensure that HPB's prophecy will indeed come true and "earth will be a heaven in the twenty-first century."

REFERENCES

Anonymous. 1969. *The Quest for the Holy Grail*. Trans. Pauline Matarasso. New York: Penguin Classics.

Arguelles, Jose. 1982. Dharma Art: Universal Law and Human Order. *The American Theosophist* 70, no. 8. Wheaton, IL: Theosophical Society in America.

Arnold, Edwin. 1969. *The Light of Asia*. Adyar, Madras, India: The Theosophical Publishing House.

Berendt, Joachim-Ernst. 1991. *The World Is Sound: Nada Brahma: Music and the Landscape of Consciousness*. Rochester, VT: Destiny Books.

Besant, Annie. 1914. The Meaning and Method of Mysticism. *Mysticism*. London: Theosophical Publishing Society.

———. 1923. On the Watch-Tower. *The Theosophist* 44, no. 9. Adyar, Madras, India: Theosophical Publishing House.

———. 1939. *The Ancient Wisdom*. Adyar, Madras, India: Theosophical Publishing House.

Bhagavad Gita. 1985. Trans. Annie Besant. Adyar, Madras, India: Theosophical Publishing House.

Blavatsky, Helena Petrovna. 1888. Is Theosophy a Religion? *Lucifer* 3, no. 15. London: Theosophical Publishing Company.

———. 1889. Tidal Wave. *Lucifer* 5, no. 27. London: Theosophical Publishing Company.

———. 1897. *The Secret Doctrine: The Synthesis of Science, Religion, and Philosophy.* Vol. 5. Adyar, Madras, India: Theosophical Publishing House.

———. 1968. *The Voice of the Silence.* Adyar, Madras, India: Theosophical Publishing House.

———. 1972a. *Isis Unveiled: A Master-Key to the Mysteries of Ancient and Modern Science and Theology.* Ed. Boris de Zirkoff. 2 vols. Wheaton, IL: Theosophical Publishing House.

———. 1972b. *The Key to Theosophy. An Abridgement.* Ed. Joy Mills. Wheaton, IL: Theosophical Publishing House, Quest Books.

———. 1973. *Theosophical Glossary.* Los Angeles: Theosophy Company.

———. 1979. *The Secret Doctrine: The Synthesis of Science, Religion, and Philosophy.* 3 vols. Adyar, Madras, India: Theosophical Publishing House.

———. 1980. *Collected Writings*, Vol. 12. Comp. Boris de Zirkoff. Wheaton, IL: Theosophical Publishing House.

———. 1981. *Practical Occultism and Occultism versus the Occult Arts.* Adyar, Madras, India: Theosophical Publishing House.

Bowen, Robert. 1960. *Madame Blavatsky on How to Study Theosophy.* Adyar, Madras, India: Theosophical Publishing House.

Buber, Martin. 1966. *Hasidism and Modern Man.* Trans. Maurice Friedman. New York: Harper and Row.

Burnier, Radha. 1990. *Human Regeneration: Lectures and Discussions.* Amsterdam: Uitgeverij der Theosofische Vereniging in Nederland.

Campbell, Joseph. 1968. *The Masks of God: Creative Mythology.* New York: Viking Press.

Collins, Mabel. 1944. *Light on the Path and Karma.* Wheaton, IL: Theosophical Press.

———. 1952. *The Idyll of the White Lotus.* Wheaton, IL: Published by Pyramid Publishing for Theosophical Publishing House.

Dante Alighieri. 1962. *The Divine Comedy, Part 3: Paradise.* Trans. Dorothy L. Sayers. New York: Penguin Classics.

Das, Bhagavan. 1921. *The Metaphysic and Psychology of Theosophy.* Pamphlet. Adyar, Madras, India: Theosophical Publishing House.

———. 1948. *The Science of Peace.* Adyar, Madras, India: Theosophical Publishing House.

Fromm, Erich. 1962. *Beyond the Chains of Illusion.* New York: Simon and Schuster.

Houston, Jean. 1993. *Life Force: The Psycho-Historical Recovery of the Self.* Wheaton, IL: Theosophical Publishing House, Quest Books.

Jinarajadasa, C. J., Comp. 1973. *Letters from the Masters of Wisdom: First Series.* Adyar, Madras, India: Theosophical Publishing House.

———. Comp. 1977. *Letters from the Masters of Wisdom: Second Series.* Adyar, Madras, India: Theosophical Publishing House.

Katz, Steven, ed. 1983. Mysticism and Its Contexts. *Mysticism and Religious Traditions.* New York: Oxford University Press.

Leeuw, J. J. van der. 1968. *The Conquest of Illusion.* Wheaton, IL: Theosophical Publishing House.

Mahatma Letters to A. P. Sinnett from the Mahatmas M. and K.H. Transcribed by A. T. Barker. Ed. Vicente Hao Chin Jr. Manila: Theosophical Publishing House, 1993.

Miller, Jeanine. 1976. *The Vedas: Harmony, Meditation, and Fulfilment.* New Delhi: B. I. Publications.

Moore, Thomas. 1992. *Care of the Soul: A Guide for Cultivating Depth and Sacredness in Everyday Life.* New York: HarperCollins.

Mukerji, Krishna. 1952. *The State.* Adyar, Madras, India: Theosophical Publishing House.

Murphy, Gardner. 1958. *Human Potentialities.* New York: Basic Books, Inc.

Nietzsche, Friedrich. 1969. *Thus Spoke Zarathustra: A Book for Everyone and No One.* London: Penguin Books.

Olcott, Henry Steel. 1972. *Old Diary Leaves.* Vol. 1. Adyar, Madras, India: Theosophical Publishing House.

Prem, Sri Krishna and Mahadava Ashish. 1969. *Man, the Measure of All Things.* Wheaton, IL: Theosophical Publishing House.

Radhakrishnan, Sarvepelli. 1951. *Indian Philosophy,* Vol. 1. London: George Allen Publishing.

Ransom, Josephine. 1934. *Studies in The Secret Doctrine.* Wheaton, IL: Theosophical Press.

Ravindra, Ravi. 2002. *What Calls You Pilgrim?* Video DVD. Wheaton, IL: The Theosophical Publishing House.

Richards, Mary Caroline. 1980. *Toward Wholeness: Rudolph Steiner Education in America.* Middletown, CT: Wesleyan University Press.

Ross, Gillian. 1993. *The Search for the Pearl: A Personal Exploration of Science and Mysticism.* Portland, OR: ABC Books.

Schuon, Fritjof. 1984. *The Transcendent Unity of Religions.* Wheaton, IL: The Theosophical Publishing House, Quest Books.

Sri Ram, N. 1968. *An Approach to Reality.* Adyar, Madras, India: Theosophical Publishing House.

Taimni, I. K. 1973. *Glimpses into the Psychology of Yoga.* Adyar, Madras, India: Theosophical Publishing House.

———. 1976. *The Ultimate Reality and Realization.* Adyar, Madras, India: Theosophical Publishing House.

Teresa, of Avila, Saint. 1979. *The Interior Castle.* Trans. Kieran Kavanaugh. New York: Paulist Press.

———. 1989. *Interior Castle.* Trans. E. Allison Peers. New York: Image Books.

Underhill, Evelyn. 1947. *Concerning the Inner Life, and The House of the Soul.* London: Methuen and Co.

Wachtmeister, Constance. 1976. *Reminiscences of H. P. Blavatsky and The Secret Doctrine.* Wheaton, IL: Theosophical Publishing House, Quest Books.

Whymper, Edward. 1971. *Scrambles Among the Alps.* Berkeley, CA: Ten Speed Press.

INDEX

equilibrium, 78
eros, 313
Esoteric Buddhism (Sinnett), 135, 312
esoteric traditions, 91, 211–17
etheric body, 102–3
ethics, 69, 235
evolution. *See also* Root Races
  Blavatsky on, 29, 30, 144
  Buddha on, 303
  cocreation and, 218
  consciousness and, 187
  holistic view of, 26–27
  love underlying, 78
  Manasaputras and, 118–19
  Masters on, 30
  process of, 253
  responsibility for, 34, 66
  Secret Doctrine on, 154–55
  spiritual, 306, 316
  systems of, 144
examined life, 191–92, 288
existence, goal of, 213
exoteric traditions, 213
experience
  mystical, 291–99
  rebirth and, 330
  wisdom as, 180

F
failure, 95, 270–71
faith, 4, 9, 283
Fates (Greek mythology), 48
Fausset, Hugh l'Anson, 296
Finch, G. B., 135

First Object, 12, 18, 168–69, 225–26
Fisher King, 272
Fohat (cosmic energy), 155
forces in nature, 57
forest, 265–66
form
  planes of, 55, 144
Franklin, Benjamin, 284
freedom
  choices and, 139
  collective and individual, 85–86
  cosmic order and, 239
  dharma and, 8, 137
  factors in establishing, 85–86
  nature of, 86
  release of the Self and, 73
  responsibility and, 66–67
  Saint Paul on, 232, 233
  science and, 5
  stages of achieving, 86–87
  Theosophy and, 5
  thought and, 224
  yoga as path to, 88
Freeman, Mara, 320
Fromm, Erich, 248–49, 257–58
frontiers
  meanings of, 12–13
  of humanness, 18
  of truth, 11
Frost, Robert, 49
future
  Blavatsky on, 35
  consciousness in, 16

freeing, 172, 173

lower and higher, 144

potentialities of, 124

psychological afflictions of, 115

Root Races and, 144

subjectivity of, 115–17

turned inward and outward, 101

universal, 117–19

modern civilization, 59–60, 248, 249

Monad (Atma-Buddhi), 99, 100, 101, 102, 103, 254

humanness and, 64–65, 72

Moore, Thomas, 317, 318

morphogenetic field, 102

Morya (Master M.), 151

Moses, Stainton, 323

motion, 56

motto of Theosophical Society, 126–27

Mukerji, Krishna P., 7, 128–29

Murphy, Gardner, 252–53

mystery schools

ancient wisdom and, 42

experience of death and rebirth in, 330

Lucius Apuleius and, 43–44

thresholds and, 321

mystical experience, 242, 291–99, 306

mysticism, 291, 294, 295–96

Mysticism (Besant), 293

mythology

Campbell on, 268

individual, 310–11

journey in, 280

thresholds in, 320

N

Nagarjuna, 233

Nasr, Hussein

on "cascading of Thatness," 221–22

natural forces, 57

Nature of Our Seeking, The (Sri Ram), 309

Needleman, Jacob, 312, 313

Neoplatonists, 303

Neumann, Erich, 99, 294

new paradigm thinking, 220–21, 275, 276, 277

New World, 35

Nietzsche, Friedrich, 273

nirvana (superspiritual state)

as samsara, 124, 233

Das on, 178

direct beholding and, 202

in cosmic order, 239

study of, 33, 175–76, 243

Noble Eightfold Path of Buddhism, 199–200

non-concern (indifference), 71, 110

noumenon, 114, 201

Novalis, 305

O

objectification, 291

objectivism, 279

worldviews. *See also* Theosophical
   worldview
   current scientific, 220–21
   study of, 185

Y
Yeats, W. B., 320–21

Yin and Yang, 284

yoga, 79, 88, 115

Z
Zanoni (Bulwer-Lytton), 322, 323

Zoharic tradition, 325